John L. Bennett

The Manager's Guide to Coaching for Change

John L. Bennett

The Manager's Guide to Coaching for Change

——

DE GRUYTER

ISBN 978-3-11-100186-9
e-ISBN (PDF) 978-3-11-100241-5
e-ISBN (EPUB) 978-3-11-100322-1

Library of Congress Control Number: 2024933759

Bibliographic information published by the Deutsche Nationalbibliothek
The Deutsche Nationalbibliothek lists this publication in the Deutsche Nationalbibliografie;
detailed bibliographic data are available on the internet at http://dnb.dnb.de.

© 2024 Walter de Gruyter GmbH, Berlin/Boston
Cover image: Warchi/iStock/Getty Images Plus
Typesetting: Integra Software Services Pvt. Ltd.
Printing and binding: CPI books GmbH, Leck

www.degruyter.com

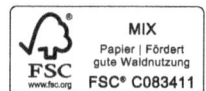

MIX
Papier | Fördert
gute Waldnutzung
FSC
www.fsc.org   FSC® C083411

Advance Praise

Effective coaching is the cornerstone of exceptional leadership. It's the secret sauce that propels teams forward, transforms individuals, and ignites organizational success. In this groundbreaking book, John, a seasoned coach with decades of experience, unveils a treasure trove of insights and practical strategies.

Rene Garza
Senior Vice President
Planetary Health Biosolutions
Novonesis

In *The Manager's Guide to Coaching for Change*, John Bennett makes the case for why coaching is essential in the present moment, how coaching can be a practice within the role of the manager, and further how it can be done effectively. He also reflects on the skills inherent in the coaching process and the complex nuances of contextual differences and continued growth. This is an extraordinary achievement and is itself a map for professional transformation.

Kenneth H. Carter, Jr.
Bishop
The United Methodist Church and
Consulting Faculty, Duke University Divinity School

In the competition to attract and retain the brightest talent, this book will be an indispensable resource. Bennett gives us access to the approaches used by professional coaches, helping leaders feel confident providing targeted, customized coaching support that will enhance effectiveness and drive the highest levels of performance from our teams.

Healthcare teams deserve to have a leader who reads this book and uses it as a guide to support their development.

Jeff Lindsay
President and Chief Operating Officer
UNC Health

Dr. Bennett describes coaching as both a "skillset and a role" in his latest book, *The Manager's Guide to Coaching for Change*. The book explains the urgency for leaders to also be coaches and provides skills for leaders to put into action. I have worked with Dr. Bennett over the years, and he has the uncanny ability to ask questions in a way that forces others to own and solve challenges. This book gives leaders the roadmap to those critical leadership skills.

Dr. Amanda Moran
Assistant Superintendent for Academic Services & Instructional Support
Chatham County Schools, NC

https://doi.org/10.1515/9783111002415-202

In this ever-dynamic world, *The Manager's Guide to Coaching for Change* is a must for any leader seeking to fully unlock the potential of their team. Dr. John Bennett offers powerful insights of the importance of coaching in the manager/employee relationship and offers pragmatic examples for developing as a strong manager-coach.

Denise Hartmann
Senior Vice President
Dispersions, Americas
BASF Corporation

Every great athlete has a coach. And every coach needs the tools to enable them to support others to do and be their best. *The Manager's Guide to Coaching for Change* identifies the skills and tools managers need to be a great coach and to instill greatness in others.

Judith H. Katz, Ed.D.
Executive Vice President, Emeritus
The Kaleel Jamison Consulting Group, Inc.
Co-Author, *The Power of Agency: Cultivating Autonomy, Authority and Leadership in Every Role*

Although there are many books out there on coaching, this one stands out. It is chock full of powerful insights that are well-organized, highly practical, and communicated in clear and cogent way. Bennett has created a terrific resource. New and seasoned leaders will find value for sure.

Steven Rogelberg, Ph.D.
bestselling author of *Glad We Met: The Art and Science of 1:1 Meetings*

Every leader should have this book!

At a time when leaders are dealing with increased organizational complexity and change, this book is a "must read" for anyone who manages people!

A practical, easy-to-use guide for coaching people in any kind of behavioral or organizational change, offering a model for change coaching as well as case examples and coaching questions.

Dr. Mary Wayne Bush
Co-author, *Coaching for Change*

This guidebook can help managers to improve organizational culture and team-development. To be a manager-coaches is a challenging endeavor. For me, the mutual learning is an essential aspect in this book: Manager-coaches are not neutral observers, but active participants, who incorporate their personal experiences, emotions, believes, values and perspectives into their professional practice of coaching and managing. As highlighted: Coaching is about asking questions that help people believe in themselves.

Reinhard Stelter, Ph.D.
Professor of Coaching Psychology
University of Copenhagen, Denmark

This is a brilliant and pragmatic book. It is excellent for any manager who wants to introduce coaching into leadership. However, it is incredibly good even if you are already a professional coach. It is a unique integration of the theory, research, and practice. Using even some of the ideas will lead to better work relationships, engagement, performance, and leadership. I found it helpful myself and will have my leaders buy this book. You should too.

Carol Kauffman, Ph.D.
Assistant Professor, Harvard Medical School
Visiting Professor, Henley Business School
Founder, Institute of Coaching

Dr. Bennett's book is a game changer that every manager should read with a highlighter from cover to cover and then read it again. This is not a book that will collect dust on your shelf but rather one you'll reference time and time again. Dr. Bennett has been my coach for thirty years and I can personally attest that what he teaches works in the real world. I owe a great deal of my business success to Dr. Bennett, and you owe it to yourself and those you manage to read this book and learn from the best!

David Greenberg
Certified Speaking Professional
Founder & CEO
Simply Speaking, Inc.

The Manager's Guide is a practical, comprehensive, navigable resource for equipping and refreshing managers with essential coaching skills. The six coaching skills articulated in Part II of the text provide readers with a clear understanding of the benefit of each skill and how to put them into practice. Managers at all levels, across an organization's value chain will benefit from this terrific guide.

Paul Joyce
Executive Director
The Executive Leadership Institute
Queens University of Charlotte

Professor Bennett has done it again! But this time, he applies his comprehensive coaching model to the needs of managers—managers who value their role in coaching their associates. The focus is on helping managers hone their skills in developing others' effectiveness in accomplishing change objectives. I have always defined a leader as someone who takes responsibility for effecting necessary change. This book provides the tools--reframing, goal-setting, asking effective questions, giving/receiving feedback, cross-cultural navigation--it's all there.

Dr. Pierce J. Howard
Consultant Emeritus
Paradigm Personality Labs

From novice managers to seasoned executives, *The Manager's Guide to Coaching for Change* has something for everyone. John Bennet delivers a comprehensive toolkit, blending theory with practical guidance to help leaders succeed in the face of constant change. Through real-life examples and actionable insights, this book equips managers to successfully drive change and foster growth. A must-read for anyone committed to growth, development, and driving solutions in dynamic environments.

Heather Gordon, Ph.D.
CEO and Founder
HighGround Insights

The Manager's Guide to Coaching for Change provides an actionable tool-kit of coaching skills. Following Bennett's coaching for change model and step-by-step guidance, leaders and managers will be able to leverage coaching to enhance an employee's performance, support team member grow and develop, or help an employee transition to a new level or responsibility or career.

Carson Flowers Tate
Carson Tate Consulting, LLC
Author, *Working Simply*

Join a Master Class in coaching. John's extensive background in coaching, adult learning, and leading for results come together in this theory-based, practical application of essential and effective strategies for manager-coach-team member relationships to find real solutions to real problems mutually. He provides the theories, models, and practice of coaching and suggests opportunities for their application in complex workplaces. A resource for managers, leaders, professional coaches, human resource, and organization development professionals, this book provides a powerful reference for what, why, how, and when to use manager coaching skills and techniques for effective workplace relationships that focus on mutual learning to develop and sustain engaged employees.

Charline S. Russo, Ed.D.
Senior Lecturer, Organizational Dynamics
University of Pennsylvania
Board Chair-President
Graduate School Alliance for Education in Coaching (GSAEC)

In this rapidly evolving tech-driven environment, leaders at all levels are realizing that managing people is about the art and science of human connection. The *Manager's Guide to Coaching for Change* makes the case for applying professional coaching skills to connecting with and managing people. Professor Bennett lays out a practical science-based guide that can truly benefit managers at any level.

> Woody Woodward, Ph.D., PCC
> Director
> Coaching Innovation Lab
> Clinical Assistant Professor of Executive Coaching
> New York University School of Professional Studies

John Bennett has collected recent and classic approaches to coaching and made them accessible for managers. By keeping clear the distinct yet related roles of manager and coach, he supports those in both roles. Practical sample dialogues, actual interviews, process guides, and worksheets accompany theories that give reasons behind the how. Methodical, clear, and useful.

> Heather Berthoud
> Berthoud Consulting

As a CEO, this book has been a revelation, inspiring me to refine my coaching approach in leadership—despite my supposed expertise in the field! Its insights have empowered me to elevate my leadership game, proving that there's always room to grow, even for those well-versed in coaching principles.

> Brian O. Underhill, Ph.D., PCC
> Founder & CEO
> CoachSource, LLC

To the teachers—formal and informal—who have impacted my life and my work.

Contents

Part I: **Foundation for Coaching**

Part II: **Coaching Skills**

Chapter 11
Coaching Skill: Developing Support —— 152

Chapter 12
Integrating Coaching Skills into the Process —— 160

Part III: Special Considerations

Chapter 13
Coaching Across Differences —— 181

Chapter 14
Specialty Coaching —— 193

Chapter 15
Ethical Considerations of Coaching —— 205

Chapter 16
Continuous Development: Managers Leading the Way —— 211

Appendices

List of Figures

https://doi.org/10.1515/9783111002415-204

List of Tables

https://doi.org/10.1515/9783111002415-205

List of Appendices

https://doi.org/10.1515/9783111002415-206

Part I: **Foundation for Coaching**

Chapter 1
Introduction

Caring for people means that we care for them for their own good. We are committed to seeing them succeed for themselves, not just for what they can do for us or our team or organization.
—Heather Younger, 2021, p. 4

According to a 2022 global survey of employees, only 23% indicated that they are thriving at work, 59% are "quiet quitting" or not engaged. The remaining 18% of employees are actively disengaged. This lack of engagement costs the global economy US $8.8 trillion accounts for 9% of global GDP, in lost productivity yearly. We are experiencing "great resignation," economic uncertainty, and labor and talent shortages. There are gaps in talent as the workplace and workforce change rapidly (Gallup, 2023). "90 percent of organizations say they expect at least some managers to coach their direct reports, and 75 percent expect all their managers to do so" (ATD, 2020, p. 4). The speed, complexity, and volume of change are increasing. Leaders, team members, and organizations face huge challenges building the capacity to lead, manage, and respond in this dynamic and challenging environment.

This chapter sets the stage for the book. It provides an overview of what coaching is, why it is essential, and how managers and leaders can use it to support individual and team development, performance, and transformation. This chapter defines coaching, and presents the book's purpose and intended audiences, as well as its structure and format.

Coaching is about change. Leaders and managers at all levels should coach team members to achieve their highest potential. Coaching is intended to change aspects of performance and development, and even transform individuals and groups, which can impact changes in organizations and systems. Effective coaching facilitates an individual's or group's movement from a current state of being and doing, to a new, more desirable state of being and performance. Just as a car, boat, or airplane can get a person from where they are to where they want to go, so can the processes and skills of coaching. Whether coaching a team member to be more strategic, to improve communication, to be accountable for their choices, or to apply knowledge and skills in new or different ways, every coaching conversation promises to move the team member in a better direction or to a more desired state.

Everyone has had a coach. This may be the athletic coach who guided you in a particular way to kick the soccer ball or defend the net in basketball, the teacher who helped you solve a complex math problem, or a manager who guided you to discover your career dreams and ways to achieve them. It might have been a clergy person who provided you with spiritual support as you grieved the loss of a loved one or through the transition to serve as a caregiver for an ill and aging parent. Coaches play a vital role in many aspects of our lives.

https://doi.org/10.1515/9783111002415-001

In the context of organizations, successfully coaching individuals and groups can positively impact change for the individual, teams they participate in or lead, and organizations they belong to and lead. Coaching works best when the individual or team being coached wants to learn, grow, and shift their mindsets and behaviors.

"Individuals who believe their talents can be developed (through hard work, good strategies, and input from others) have a growth mindset," Carol Dweck wrote in her 2007 book *Mindset: The New Psychology of Success*. "They tend to achieve more than those with a more fixed mindset (those who believe their talents are innate gifts)" (p. np).

The bottom line: You need a desire to grow and change. Second, getting feedback related to the desired behavior changes is critical to getting the most from coaching. This may come from a manager, peer, direct report, friend, or family member. Third, you must know what you are doing well and what is off-track concerning your goals. As adults, we can learn a lot from taking on challenging assignments and reflecting on experiences (whether or not they went as well as we hoped). Coaching team members who take advantage of opportunities to stretch outside their comfort zone can use those opportunities to try and perfect new and different behaviors. Fourth, support is essential. This may come in the form of an accountability partner (a person who helps you focus on action plans and goals), a person who will listen with empathy and curiosity to what you are experiencing as you learn and grow, or a book or training program that provides you with additional information.

And finally, making changes to mindsets and behaviors takes time and energy. Coaching team members who make the time (away from distractions and competing priorities) to "do the work" in a coaching relationship get the most out of it. This requires meeting regularly with a manager-coach, following through on action plans, and reflecting on events, circumstances, and actions to gain the most from them.

Individuals and teams need three primary focus areas for change, defined below and illustrated in Table 1.1.

- **Performance.** To improve performance of how things are done—quality and quantity, creating a higher level of excellence or efficiency (or both), and becoming more closely aligned with a strategic target or goal (for example, better, cheaper, or faster). An example of this is increasing sales in a company department.
- **Development.** To learn, build, or grow a skill or capacity, such as developing business acumen or public speaking skills, creating a culture of respect and inclusion, or improving innovation in a group or organization. Development could also support a team member improve strategic thinking or presentation skills.
- **Transformation.** A complete shift from one state to another, such as a corporate acquisition or introduction of a new product line or brand. For example, think of an organization that must completely revamp its product line or an individual who wants to change jobs to a different career path or discipline (Bennett & Bush, 2014).

Table 1.1: Focus of Coaching.

Focus	Examples
Performing	– Applying knowledge and skills to achieve a desired result (e.g., sales, project deadlines, interpersonal relations) – Acting on a plan, making decisions, and following through (accountability)
Developing	– Gaining self-awareness of strengths – Acquiring knowledge about a barrier to performance – Developing a skill – Creating an action plan and building supportive relationships required to implement a course of action – Moving to a new level of human development
Transforming	– Shifting professional and career focus – Transitioning from one level of responsibility to another (e.g., supervisor to manager or senior leader to executive) – Focusing intentionally, creating a legacy and a desired future

What is Coaching?

Coaching as a skill and a process transcends any specific discipline. It is informed and influenced by many disciplines, such as education, human development, leadership, management, psychology, and spirituality. Coaching is an overarching skill set that helps individuals and groups learn how to change and helps them develop the capacity to change. Coaching for change leverages critical inflection points in the change process. It provides just-in-time learning and support to individuals and groups to facilitate successful change while building the capacity for future change.

The International Coaching Federation (2021), a leading global association for people who coach professionally, defines coaching as "partnering with clients in a thought-provoking and creative process that inspires them to maximize their personal and professional potential." The results can be life-changing. Clients often say they've created a new outlook on life—finding within themselves inspiration, courage, confidence, and answers to long-burning questions.

Coaching is a discovery process that focuses on the goals and agenda of the team member being coached. It supports learning, development, and performance. Managerial coaching occurs in the context of the organization in which manager and team member are employed. It is a helping relationship that is centered on the team member, action-oriented, and results-focused. Coaching involves the whole person, with cognitive, emotional, behavioral, physical, and spiritual components. To be effective, it requires curiosity from the manager-coach and the team member, which fosters self-awareness and action. Coaching can be applied at the individual and team levels. It is a mindset and skill set (coaching as a verb) and involves the role of coaching (coach as a noun).

A **manager-coach** is a person who uses coaching-related knowledge, approaches, and skills to coach team members in the organization who report to them or who have sought their coaching. These hierarchical relationships, such as a direct manager-employee reporting relationship or project team leader-member, may be formal. In this context, coaching helps create awareness and support behavioral change that can lead to enhanced performance, development of capabilities, and transformation. Manager-coaches provide relationship-based, on-the-job learning and feedback to develop employees experiencing job transition and displacements due to downsizing; engage and motivate their employees; and retain their top or key organizational talent (Bennett & Bush, 2014).

The difference between a manager-coach and other coach roles—e.g., executive coach, career coach, peer coach—is that the manager also affects the employee's finances and career. This dual role can influence the coaching process both positively and negatively. The manager's awareness of the employee's situation, performance, and function can clarify coaching goals and development but can also promote suspicion, mistrust, and resistance to change. In addition, it can be difficult for the manager to negotiate between roles because managing often requires "telling" or "directing." At the same time, coaching is about discovering, creating possibilities, and taking action to produce desired results. Managers often encourage employees to consider different models or perspectives, envision other possibilities, and reflect and think prospectively. Coaching in any setting can only be truly effective when the team member is willing and open to change. The manager-coach's role is to help create awareness about strengths and areas for development and then support behavioral change (Bennett & Bush, 2014).

Managing involves achieving results through others, communicating information about employee performance upward in the organizational structure, sharing information from higher in the organizational structure down to employees, creating a team from individuals, developing an environment of trust, directing others so that their work meets the expectations of the organization, evaluating individual and team performance against the plan, planning the work of others, and staffing people to specific projects or tasks.

Coaching involves strengthening employees by encouraging them to find their solutions, engaging in candid and collegial open conversations, giving nonjudgmental feedback, guiding reflection on new experiences or skills, helping others reframe challenges, helping others reframe beyond their expectations, helping others accept and learn from failure, providing assignments that stretch employees, providing experience-based insights, reinforcing positive behavior and work strengths to leverage better results, and serving as a trusted sounding board for new ideas.

The roles of manager and coach are complementary, not contradictory. Hamlin et al. (2006) wrote that ". . . truly effective managers and managerial leaders are those who embed effective coaching into the heart of their management practice" and ". . . coaching is an essential core activity of management and leadership" (p. 326–327).

While tracking and managing employee performance is the manager's primary role in the business's success, coaching skills can help address problems and skill deficits that affect performance. Managers can also coach team members on business acumen, political correctness, influential communication, teaming, and other behavioral issues. The difference is that performance management is the manager's responsibility, while coaching is offered at the request and agreement of the team member. Coaching is optional for the employee—management is not.

The employee-manager coaching relationship has been described as a working partnership between a team member and their direct supervisor that is focused on addressing that team member's performance and development needs (Gregory & Levy, 2011). The prominence of managers as coaches has increased and will continue to thrive as organizations recognize the benefits of coaching and begin to integrate methodologies into their management and leadership-development structures. The function of managers as coaches can pose specific unique challenges, but the benefits to the individual, group, and overall organization are entirely worthwhile endeavors. Effective coaching will lead to your ultimate goal of achieving results through and with others (Ellis, 2004; Gentry, 2016). While there are many benefits and advantages to managers providing coaching, there are also challenges. Table 1.2 includes some of the challenges that managers who coach may encounter, and some possible solutions.

Table 1.2: Manager-Coach Challenges and Possible Solutions.

Challenge	Possible Solutions
Managing multiple roles: The manager serving as coach continues to hold the manager role.	– Clarify roles and expectations with the team member by making a clear distinction between being a manager versus a coach during discussions. – Focus on goals and behaviors. – Ask, "Is this a performance issue or a coaching topic?" – Identify any competing agendas between manager, team member, and organization priorities.
Building trust: The manager or team members lack trust in each other; team members may lack trust in the organization or senior leaders.	– Consider the quality of the current manager-team relationship when introducing manager-coaching (not all are ready to be coaches or to be coached). – Offer some guidelines on building trust, and have ground rules about what to expect and how to give feedback if there is a problem. – Ensure that there are regular "process checks" built into the coaching process, and opportunities for both partners to discuss what is going well and what needs to be improved about the interaction.

Table 1.2 (continued)

Challenge	Possible Solutions
Developing knowledge, skills, and abilities: Managers may lack coaching competence.	– Define the scope and role of manager-coaches. – Assess managers to identify appropriate manager-coaches and offer development and ongoing support for them. – Offer orientation to prepare employees to engage effectively in coaching with their managers.
Differentiating between coaching and performance-management issues: Manager-coaches may not distinguish between their roles, or may not select appropriate approaches for addressing performance-related issues vs. addressing developmental or behavioral issues.	– Discuss the difference (in role and approach) with team members. – Clarify which issues are which. – Adopt and communicat standard performance-management systems and processes. – Ask team members to request coaching when it is wanted. – Encourage an environment of safety and openness. – Practice giving respectful feedback.

(Bennett & Bush, 2014; Murphy, 2005)

Why This Book Is Important

Organizational change is increasing, driven by globalization, new technologies, mergers and acquisitions, rapid expansion of knowledge, social and political forces, and the proliferation of complex multinational companies. According to a report from Paycor (2023), in 2022, 40% of employees were considering quitting their jobs. The top three reasons they gave were toxic work culture (62%), low salary (55%), and poor management (56%). Paycor also reported that 60% of human resource leaders indicate "leader and manager effectiveness" will be their top priority in 2023.

This book is meant to acquaint managers with the basics of coaching in the ever-changing workplace and workforce. It is not meant to be an exhaustive reference. Manager-coaches will be introduced to many topics about coaching and change, and are urged to explore other resources to further their understanding.

Coaching is both a skill set and a role. It is also an emerging profession. In 2022, the estimated number of coach practitioners reached 109,200, representing a 54% increase from the 2019 global estimate (International Coaching Federation, 2023). This book provides academically sound and practical approaches to coaching that can be applied in formal and informal contexts. Coaching is about effecting change at the individual, team, and organization levels. This point provides a practical framework supporting change at all levels. Managers often lack the skills to effectively develop the critical asset of organizations—people. This book provides a framework and essential skills for managers to give feedback and coach for development, performance, and transformation.

Many corporations, government agencies, and not-for-profit organizations provide individual or group coaching for leaders at all levels. Examples of companies and other organizations that use coaches for strategy, change management, and leadership development include Bank of America, BASF, BMW, Boeing, Daimler, Deloitte, Lockheed Martin, Lowes, Raytheon, tesa tape, Trane, UBS, U.S. government, United Way Worldwide, and Wells Fargo. In addition to providing external coaches for leaders, many organizations seek to develop the coaching capabilities of leaders at all levels.

A 2023 search of Amazon.com for books about executive coaching indicates more than 2,000 have been published. Searches for "managerial coaching" books show more than 275 have been published. And more than 100 scholarly articles have been published about executive coaching in the past 10 years.

Effective coaching can be applied across all industries and at all organizational levels. In the healthcare industry, practical coaching that emphasizes developing support for behavior changes is crucial for enhancing patient care and satisfaction. Managers and healthcare leaders can use coaching to help healthcare professionals manage stress, improve patient communication, and develop resilience in a demanding work environment. In the rapidly evolving field of information technology, coaching focused on developing support can help IT managers and leaders guide their teams through complex projects. It can also assist in addressing the challenges of constant change and innovation by fostering adaptability and problem-solving skills (Lambert et al., 2012). Coaching in education is not limited to teachers and students; school administrators and leaders benefit as well. Developing support is vital in creating a positive school culture, where teachers feel supported in their professional growth and students receive the guidance they need to excel (Cavanagh et al., 2018). Sales and marketing teams often benefit from coaching. Managers can use coaching to help sales representatives build stronger client relationships, improve negotiation skills, and enhance overall performance (Gentry et al., 2012).

Managers who coach can support change in many ways, including the following. (See Appendix A for 100-plus scenarios for coaching.)

- Helping a direct report develop a career plan or get additional training to improve.
- Helping a direct report understand the importance of an organizational change initiative and act as a change agent.
- Coaching a group to identify key stakeholders for a change and develop an action plan to influence them in supporting the change.
- Coaching an employee to identify and work toward additional goals or projects that would gain extra visibility or lead to promotion in the organization.
- Supporting an individual or group in taking on a new level of responsibility or a developmental experience that is not required, but that will benefit the organization and offer recognition.
- Coaching a leader about envisioning a positive future for the organization can lead to a transformation in the culture or even the company's brand.

– Coaching a manager to consider the results of a stakeholder analysis can make the difference between mere compliance and eager collaboration as employees adopt a change.

Who Will Benefit from This Book

This book is intended for leaders and managers of people and those who want to develop the essential mindset and skills to coach others in a manager-team member relationship. In addition, professional coaches, human resource professionals, and organization development professionals will find it helpful. The person being coached is referred to as a "team member," and the person coaching is referred to as a "manager-coach."

At the risk of limiting who might find this book useful, this book was written for specific audiences. These audiences include managers and leaders who want to develop their capacities to support the development and performance of team members and to support individual, team, and organizational change. It is also intended for professional coaches who want to develop their knowledge and skills related to coaching, and human resource professionals working in organizations who wish to develop their coaching capabilities and support the development of others. It is intended for educators and trainers seeking resources to support their efforts to develop coaching skills in others. It is designed for graduate students who desire to learn about coaching and how to use it in their role as managers.

Building on *Coaching for Change* (Bennett & Bush, 2014), this book is for managers and leaders at all levels who want to help their employees improve performance, develop capabilities, and transition in their lives and careers. Grounded in theory and research, this book provides a practical guide for managers to coach individuals and teams. This book offers a practical guide for managers and leaders to learn and apply a coaching mindset and skill set in various contexts.

How This Book Is Organized

This book is intended to be used as an ongoing resource and reference guide for leaders and managers who seek to learn coaching and then apply that understanding to support team members. Chapters include rich content and examples/cases that will equip and enable managers to apply a coaching approach.

It may be helpful to look at this book in three parts. The first part (Chapters 1–4) provides the foundation for coaching. Chapter 1 introduces coaching and the role of managers as coaches. Chapter 2 provides an overview of the coaching process with examples. Chapter 3 presents six theoretical foundations or approaches to coaching and explains how they might be applied in the manager-coach role. Chapter 4 focuses on using self in the context of coaching. It addresses how manager-coaches can gain awareness, make intentional choices about when and how to engage with team members, and find ways to develop as leaders and human beings. It incorporates various models and theories related to adult development and the use of self.

The book's second part (Chapters 5–12) introduces six coaching skills and concludes with a chapter about how those skills can be applied to the coaching process presented in Chapter 3. Chapter 5 offers an overview of six coaching skills. Chapters 6 through 11 provide detailed explanations and illustrations of the six coaching skills— Providing Feedback, Listening for Understanding, Asking Powerful Questions, Reframing, Providing Insights, and Developing Support—as well as illustrations of each skill, why the skills are essential, and challenges and solutions. Chapter 12 integrates the coaching skills and process.

The third part of the book (Chapters 13–16) addresses special considerations for manager-coaches, such as coaching across differences, other applications of coaching, ethical considerations, and continued development of coaching skills. Chapter 13 explores some of the challenges of coaching people whose social identities are different from the manager-coach's identities, and provides strategies for coaching across those differences. Chapter 14 introduces ways to apply the coaching process and skills in the context of coaching groups and teams. Internal and external professional executive coaches may be used to provide coaching to peers and teams. Chapter 15 recognizes the complexities of manager-employee relationships and those of manager-coach and employee relations. It presents ethical challenges and guidance based on professional coaching standards. Chapter 16 recognizes the importance of applying knowledge and skills to build competence, and it focuses on other applications for coaching and ways for manager-coaches to develop and improve skills continuously.

Each chapter follows a similar structure, including a brief introduction, a description of the content and a summary. Interviews with five leaders who use coaching with team members appear in selected chapters and provide rich examples of how the frameworks and skills of coaching can be applied.

Resources at the end of the book include a bibliography of reference materials, an extensive and accessible glossary of key terms and concepts, and appendices with examples of topics for coaching and sample questions that might be used when coaching.

Case examples help illustrate the coaching process and skills and their integration into coaching conversations. These cases are built on real scenarios, though the names and dialogue have been fictionalized to protect the identities of individuals and organizations and to help illustrate key points.

The format of the book, with extensive use of bulleted and numbered items, bolded words or phrases, and tables and figures, is intended to enhance the accessibility of the material for the busy reader and to make the content more accessible to use as a resource after reading the book.

Helping Relationships

Coaching can be identified as one of a range of "helping relationships." These helping relationships include coaching, consulting, counseling, teaching, training, and mentoring (Schein, 2009). Psychologist Carl Rogers (1989) wrote the following about helping relationships.

> If I can create a relationship characterized on my part:
> . . . by a genuineness and transparency, in which I am my real feelings;
> . . . by a warm acceptance of and prizing of the other person as a separate individual;
> . . . by a sensitive ability to see his world and himself as he sees them;
> Then the other individual in the relationship:
> . . . will experience and understand aspects of himself which previously he has repressed;
> . . . will find himself becoming better integrated, more able to function effectively;
> . . . will become more similar to the person he would like to be;
> . . . will be more self-directing and self-confident;
> . . . will be more of a person, more unique and more self-expressive;
> . . . will be more understanding, more acceptant of others;
> . . . will be able to cope with the problems of life more adequately and more comfortably.
> (pp. 37–38)

In the context of coaching, helping requires a "helper" (the manager-coach) and a "receiver" (the team member or team). It is essential to keep in mind that when helping occurs, there is an imbalance in the relationship. Edgar Schein (2009) describes this imbalance as a "one up-ness" for the manager-coach and a "one down-ness" for the team member or team being coached. In other words, for helping to occur, there must be a giver and receiver of help, and the person or group seeking help is subordinated to the helper. This imbalance places the manager-coach in a dominant role, which leads to potential traps for both parties.

For the helper/manager-coach, traps may include:
–   Dispensing wisdom prematurely
–   Meeting defensiveness with more pressure
–   Accepting the problem and overreacting to the dependence
–   Giving support and reassurance
–   Resisting taking on the helper role
–   Attempting to rescue the person being helped
–   Trying to fix the person or the person's problem

For the person being helped/team member, traps may include:
–   Initial mistrust
–   Relief
–   Looking for attention, reassurance, and/or validation instead of help
–   Resentment and defensiveness
–   Stereotyping, unrealistic expectations, and transference of perceptions.

The helper may assume one or more of the following roles, move back and forth between these roles, and in and out of them. The manager-coach may
- be an expert, having knowledge or wisdom that can guide the team member toward achieving the team member's goals.
- play the role of a physician serving to diagnose the person's situation or needs and provide a prescriptive intervention to "heal" or fix the challenge or situation for the team member.
- serve as a process consultant, offering guidance without imposing the coach's point of view or solution. A process consultant works with and not for the client and is generally contrasted with the role of an expert consultant.

It is important to note that the process consultant is the most preferred and effective of these roles. The process consultant and manager-coach each work with clients to effect change, the relationship is often formalized using a contract, and the process orientation expertise of the manager-coach or consultant guides the team member in developing solutions and implementing actions to achieve desired results (Bennett & Bush, 2014; Schein, 2009).

Being a practical helper requires specific traits. Building on the work of Small (1981), such traits applied to coaching include being concrete; being willing and able to confront the person being coached; empathy for the situation and person; genuineness in care and concern; immediacy of availability, presence, and action; potency of the help provided; respect by the person being coached; a well-developed sense of oneself and ability to use oneself as an instrument in the coaching relationship; appropriate levels of self-disclosure in service of the person being coached; and general sense of warmth.

Summary

Coaching is a helping relationship intended to help others learn, develop, and perform in an ever-changing world of business and society. It is a necessary mindset and skill set that managers can apply to support individuals and teams in achieving desired goals. Leaders at all levels can use coaching to help individuals, groups, and organizations prepare for, excel through, and improve from change. While there are varied approaches to managerial coaching, all coaching is team member-centered, action-oriented, results focused, and supportive of behavioral change. Self-awareness on the part of the client and the coach is required to achieve mastery.

Chapter 2
Coaching for Change Process

Effective managers know that performance comes from enabling and improving what is there rather than controlling it.

—Evered & Selman, 1989, p. 17

Coaching involves engaging in conversations focused on another person's goals. Coaching is most effective when a formal coaching engagement process includes several distinct phases. While accidental success is always possible, it is the exception. Coaching for change requires a planned and methodical approach—the kind of approach at the core of this book.

This chapter provides a foundation for understanding why it is important to follow a process and establish trust and safety in a coaching relationship. In effect, it is a brief literature review. It looks not only at why trust and safety are important, but how to foster them. It also describes the Coaching Mastery Model, and the six-step Coaching for Change Model/Process.

Coaching is a practice and process that can occur in different contexts to enhance well-being and performance in both personal and professional domains. Coaching is also a practice and process that aims, over time to bring about change in organizations. Coaching is not the only intervention that should be considered for change efforts. Training, mentoring, and stretch assignments are just a few approaches that also support improved performance, development, and transition for team members. Coaching can effectively achieve these outcomes when applied as a formal process.

Outcome-oriented dynamic models can describe the coaching process, focus on the team member's agenda/goals, and guide the conversation. Coaching follows the principles of experiential learning, reflection in learning, and problem-solving. A coaching relationship is bidirectional; the coach and team member must be engaged and committed to creating the desired changes (Ratiu & Baban, 2012). One benefit of coaching is that the team member and the manager-coach can learn and develop through the process. During the initial and contracting phases of the coaching process, the manager-coach establishes credibility and models the behaviors of listening and asking questions that are cornerstones of the coaching engagement.

Generally, coaching follows a team member's performance. The team member takes an action, which results in feedback from self-reflection or observation of responses and results. It could also result in direct feedback from others, such as manager, peers, customers, partners, and people who report to the team member. This feedback potentially offers the agenda for coaching—the area(s) of focus.

As with other positive and productive working relationships, there should be an agreement—a "contract"—that assesses whether the team member wants coaching and how the manager-coach and team member will work together. The manager-

https://doi.org/10.1515/9783111002415-002

coach should not assume the team member wants coaching from them at a particular time. Asking a simple question such as, "based on the feedback you received and your self-awareness, would you like me to coach you?" empowers the team member and helps define the working relationship.

Next, coaching occurs. This may be a single, brief (15 minutes or less) conversation, a more extended conversation that might cover various topics, or an ongoing coaching relationship that includes several conversations. Coaching results should consist of additional self-awareness, plans for action, and accountability. Then, the team member acts and continues their work with new insights, mindsets, and skills. This allows for additional feedback, which may result in further coaching conversations on this or other topics.

Three factors are relevant when managers coach their team members:

- The specific coaching behaviors performed.
- The nature of the coaching relationship developed between the manager and the team member being coached.
- The feedback environment.

Hunt & Weintraub (2011) suggest that being an effective coach involves giving feedback, enabling reflection, gaining self-awareness, establishing a constructive relationship with the person being coached, and creating a coaching-friendly context. Effective managerial coaching includes listening, analysis, interviewing, observation, communication, giving feedback, guidance, facilitation, and inspiration (Joo et al., 2012; Heslin et al., 2006).

Coaching Readiness

Team members have varying degrees of receptivity to coaching. While some are highly receptive, others are not, and the rest reside somewhere in between. Team members who are less receptive to coaching limit their development, performance, and transformation. In addition, they fail to own problems by following a single way of action. "Coachability" and "coaching readiness" describe a person's or group's openness to develop, improve performance and transform through engagement with a coach, whether informal or formal. Coachable individuals are committed to change, are motivated to improve their knowledge, skills, and abilities, and are willing to take responsibility for their outcomes. From a learning perspective, the coach should understand developmental readiness and learning goal orientation, including preparedness for change and commitment. Readiness for coaching refers to team members' readiness for change and their needs for change and development (Ratiu & Baban, 2012). In other words, the person being coached must be mentally, emotionally, and developmentally ready to change (Laske, 1999, 2003).

A person's readiness depends on four factors: 1) openness, 2) partnership, 3) engagement, and 4) agenda setting. These four factors are supported by research into the critical client characteristics required for a successful change (Boyatzis, et al., 2006).

1. **Openness.** The mindset of a client is critical to success. Success hinges on a team member accepting that change is needed; having an accurate insight into the fundamental nature, cause, and maintenance of their difficulties; being receptive to the change process; trying and testing new behaviors and perspectives; and willingness to learn from prior mistakes. Highly coachable team members proactively seek feedback instead of waiting to receive it or becoming defensive or devaluing it; and they proactively implement the feedback they receive to drive development and improved performance (Evered & Selman, 1989; Franklin, 2005; Weiss & Merrigan, 2021).
2. **Partnership.** Trust between the manager and team member allows the team member to be open and honest, which is vital to their development. This type of trusted partnership can provide the right amounts of challenge and support throughout the coaching process.
3. **Engagement.** Engagement requires accountability. When the level of trust increases between the manager and team member, the level of engagement increases. A critical factor in the success of a coaching engagement is that the team member must be committed to investing the time and energy needed for the change process. In addition, the team member must possess the knowledge and skills necessary to implement the targeted behavior.
4. **Agenda setting.** It is vital that everyone engaged in the coaching process remember that the team member's agenda is the primary focus during coaching. The team member should be able to set the goals for the work with you in a coaching relationship.

To perform a preliminary screening of coaching readiness, the manager can ask or observe the team member's responses and behaviors related to the following questions:
- What is your understanding of the focus and process of coaching?
- What, if any, experiences have you had working with a coach?
- What change prompts you to seek coaching? What is the nature of the change for which you are seeking coaching?
- What goals do you have for our potential work together?
- How important is it to you to achieve your goals through our potential work together? What happens if you do not achieve these goals?
- What do you consider to be your strengths and area(s) for improvement?
- What would others (boss, peers, direct reports) say are your strengths and areas for improvement in relation to the change?
- What are your expectations of me as your coach?
- How will I know when I have challenged you too much or too strongly?
- What is essential to you in your life (personally and professionally)?
- How do you learn?
- What support do you have for the development work you set out to do?

When Coaching Works Best

Five distinct factors indicate a person is likely to benefit from coaching—whether from a professional coach, manager-coach, or peer.

1. **Embrace a Growth Mindset.** This is a desire to learn, grow and shift their mindsets and behaviors. According to Carol Dweck (2016), "Individuals who believe their talents can be developed (through hard work, good strategies, and input from others) have a growth mindset. They tend to achieve more than those with a more fixed mindset (those who believe their talents are innate gifts)" (p. np). The bottom line: **The team member needs a desire to grow and change**.

2. **Request and Accept Feedback.** While a coach can provide feedback during a coaching session, getting feedback on the desired behavior changes is critical to getting the most from coaching. This feedback may come from a manager, peer, direct report, friend, or family member. **The team member must know what they are doing well and what is off-track** about their goals.

3. **Welcome a Challenge.** As adults, we can learn a lot from taking on challenging assignments and reflecting on experiences (whether or not they went as well as we hoped). Team members who take advantage of **opportunities to stretch outside their comfort zone** can use those opportunities to try out and perfect new and different behaviors.

4. **Seek Support. Support is essential.** This may come in the form of an accountability partner (a person who helps focus on action plans and goals), a person who will listen with empathy and curiosity to experiences of learning and growth, a book or training program that provides additional information.

5. **Invest Time and Energy.** Making changes to mindsets and behaviors takes time and energy. Team members who make the time (away from distractions and competing priorities) to **"do the work"** in a coaching relationship get the most out of it. This requires **meeting regularly with a coach, following through on action plans, and reflecting on events, circumstances, and actions** to gain the most from them.

Manager-Coach and Team Member Relationship

Trust is the foundation for relationships. Managers and team members work together to optimize performance by developing the team member's professional, personal, and social capacities. Their relationship is central to coaching because this relationship can become the principal vehicle through which team members' needs are expressed and goals fulfilled (Jowett, et al., 2010).

In their research on performance feedback, Mayer and Davis (1999) identified trust as a critical component in whether feedback was well received and whether the relationship between the giver and receiver evolved productively. Since feedback is often the entry point for a coaching conversation involving a manager and team member, it makes sense that trust in the performance context also serves the coaching relationship.

Personality research tells us that about 50% of the general population are less trusting of others until there is a reason for them to trust the other person. That means about 50% are more trusting until there is a reason not to trust others (Howard and Howard, 2018). Trust is the faith we put in other individuals, teams, and organizations. Patrick Lencioni (2002), in his popular book about teams, notes that trust is the foundation for working relationships, which in turn are the foundations for effective teams. Manager-coaches must be sensitive to the trust disposition of team members, recognize their perspectives on trust, and work to foster trust.

Mayer and Davis (1999) found that three key components build and foster trust. You might imagine them as three legs of a stool that need to be balanced for trust to flourish. The first component is "ability," which is the group of skills, competencies, and characteristics that allow a person to influence within some domain. In the context of the manager-team member relationship, this might include the team member's perception of the manager's ability to lead, think strategically, communicate for positive impact, negotiate, and assess performance. By the same token, it might also include the manager's perception of the team member's skills, behaviors, and results. Next is "benevolence," which is the extent to which a person is believed to want to do good to others. This includes compassion, empathy, and commitment to others. In the context of the coaching relationship, if the team member believes that a manager cares about the team member's interests, they will see the manager as benevolent toward the team member. "Integrity" is the third component of trust. It is defined as the team member's perception that the manager adheres to a set of principles that the team member finds acceptable. This means that the manager fulfills promises and commitments in the manner agreed upon. This could also be applied in reverse—the manager's perception of the team member. Integrity includes connection with others, results, doing what is right, and consistency.

There are many ways to establish rapport or establish trust. Here are a few examples that manager-coaches can use:

- Show **selective vulnerability** by sharing a personal anecdote about your experience related to the agenda of the person being coached. Acknowledge the challenge the team member is facing. Apologize when you make an error.
- Develop a sense of **familiarity** by relating to something the team member has shared about themselves. This might include referring to a spouse, partner, or child by name or asking about recent personal experiences (e.g., a vacation or child's sporting event).
- Share **common interests**. This might include likes and dislikes or hobbies.
- Demonstrate **concern** for issues and events important to the team member. Examples include births, illnesses, and anniversaries.

– **Acknowledge** strengths, progress, and growth. This might include work preparing for a meeting, taking a risk, or successfully implementing something that has been a goal.

The working alliance between the manager-coach and team member should emphasize the quality and strength of their purposeful collaboration. Edward Bordin (1979, 1994) identified three core features of purposeful collaborative work:
– **Goals** (a clear, shared understanding about the goals of the work and the desired outcome).
– **Tasks** (mutual understanding of how the coaching will take place along with agreement on those tasks or roles that coach, client, and key stakeholders will undertake).
– **Bonds** (mutual empathy and respect).

The coaching alliance is an interpersonal, interactive, dynamic, collaborative relationship (Jowett, et al., 2010). It reflects the quality of the client's and coach's engagement in intentional collaboration within the coaching relationship and is jointly negotiated and renegotiated throughout the coaching process (O'Broin & Palmer, 2010).

Five broad aspects are essential in establishing, developing, and maintaining a coaching alliance. These are:
1. Active negotiation (and, where necessary, renegotiation) of the alliance.
2. The use of alliance-fostering strategies.
3. The recognition that there are different conceptual approaches to the relationship and that therefore implications for the interventions and activities of coaching also differ.
4. Awareness and management of interpersonal dynamics of both coach and client.
5. Renegotiation of any disruptions in the alliance.

The coaching intervention maximizes its efficiency by adjusting to the developmental needs of the team member. Coaching needs represent a unique combination of individual and organizational needs. Coaching follows the principles of experiential learning, reflection in learning, and problem-solving. A coaching relationship is bidirectional; both manager-coach and team member must be engaged and committed to creating the desired change (Jowett, et al., 2010).

Another critical element in the manager-coach and team member relationship is psychological safety. Managers must foster an environment of trust and safety for the team member to express themselves clearly and as thoroughly as necessary for you to provide coaching. Psychological safety involves being able to show oneself without fear of negative consequences of self-image, status, or career. It is a shared belief that a person or team is safe for interpersonal risk-taking. Team members feel accepted and respected. In his book, *Think Again*, Adam Grant (2021), wrote that when psychological safety is present, team members see mistakes as opportunities to learn, are willing to take risks, share their perspectives in meetings, openly share challenges or struggles, and trust others (teammates and managers). In the context of coaching, managers should foster a work environment and professional relationships with team members that enable safety. This will help build working relationships and allow you to work with team members as whole people, not simply as cogs in a wheel of productivity.

You can enhance the working relationship in the context of coaching by being warm and engaging, showing strength and confidence, being consistent and dependable, and modeling honesty and integrity. In addition, as the manager-coach, you can restrain your personal needs and stay focused on the needs of the person being coached in the context of the business. Be careful with self-disclosure: Coaching is about the person being coached—not the coach. You can find ways to resonate with what you sense going on for the team member and demonstrate agility and flexibility without making it about you.

Coaching In the Context of Performance, Development and Transformation

Chapter 1 discussed the focal areas of coaching: enhancing performance, developing capabilities, and supporting transformation. Team members may be categorized as needing to develop and grow, having the skills to perform well, or needing to develop and grow or leave. Theoretically, most team members are in the middle category, as shown in Figure 2.1.

Team members who are new to the organization or their role probably need to be developed so they can grow their knowledge and skills and exhibit higher levels of performance. For team members in the far-left section of the distribution curve, coaching will probably be developmental and transformative. The overall goal for team members in this group should be to become seasoned, skilled, and high-performing contributors. The manager-coach needs to provide feedback about their performance and growth, as well as direction or guidance. And the manager-coach needs to provide coaching.

Team members in the middle category are seasoned, skilled performers. Ideally, most team members are in this category. They probably need continued development as they face new and more complex challenges and opportunities. The manager-coach needs to provide feedback, support, and coaching.

Team members in the far-right category are underperformers. The overall goal is to help them develop and grow into skilled performers—or change responsibilities, leave the team or leave the organization. These team members need coaching focused on development, performance, and transformation. The manager-coach needs to provide direction, management, and coaching.

Notice that the manager-coach provides both feedback and coaching to employees in all three categories.

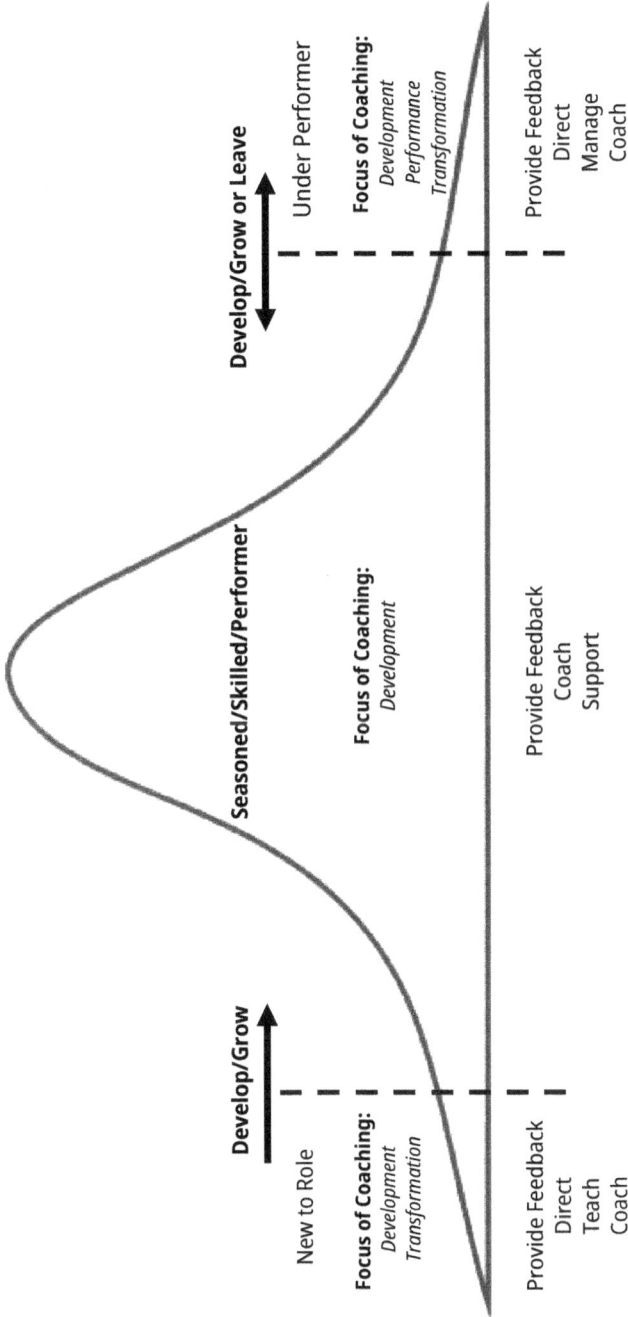

Figure 2.1: Coaching in the Context of Performance, Development and Transformation.

Coaching Processes

Having a process or model for coaching guides the coaching conversation, offers a proven approach that enhances credibility, is predictable for the person being coached, provides a sense of direction and comfort, and increases the likelihood that positive and productive outcomes will emerge.

There are a variety of coaching models and processes. For example, the GROW model is an acronym for the five steps in the process: Goal setting, Reality, Obstacles, Options, and Way forward. While no one person can be identified as the originator of this model, Graham Alexander, Alan Fine, and Sir John Whitmore (2009) are recognized for making significant contributions to it. GROW is well known in the business context and has applications in everyday life.

The development pipeline model was developed from research conducted by Peterson (1993, 1996, 2006; Peterson & Hicks, 1996). Peterson suggests that there are five necessary and sufficient conditions for behavioral change.

Each stage in the pipeline responds to a fundamental question:
1. **Insight.** Does the team member know what they want to improve and where improvement will make a difference?
2. **Motivation.** Is the team member willing to invest time and energy to accomplish those results? Is the team member aware of the personal payoff?
3. **Capabilities.** Does the team member have the skills and knowledge to make the change?
4. **Real-world practice.** Does the team member experiment with what they know in an authentic setting to break down old habits and build new habits?
5. **Accountability.** Does the team member stick with the change, and are there meaningful consequences for making the change? (Kauffman & Bachkirova, 2008).

One of the main tools that a manager-coach uses to help team members move through change is conversation. All coaching involves conversation, although other skills, including observation and assessment, are often leveraged to support the process. A coaching conversation's predictable and purposeful structure makes it distinct from, say, a chat with a friend. The coaching conversation aims to provide a vehicle for forward movement while the chat can ramble and have little purpose other than creating or sustaining rapport. The purpose of a chat with a friend is not necessarily or predictably action oriented.

The Change Coaching Model illustrated in Figure 2.2 enables the manager as coach to guide the coaching conversations within this context (Bennett & Bush, 2014). The steps are:
1. **Current Situation and Context.** This explores what is present for the team member, what has occurred since your last coaching conversation, and what progress they made toward previously established action plans.

2. **Needs and Desired Goals.** This step involves helping the team member identify their goals for the current coaching conversation. This step often requires a great deal of discernment and clarification. There is a saying in management consulting that applies to coaching: The presenting issue is rarely the real issue.

3. **Information Gathering.** This includes helping the team member discover things like what is known and unknown, what has been tried, lessons learned from previous experiences that may relate to the current agenda for coaching, resources available, impacts of actions and desired impacts, as well as identification of possible criteria for evaluating possible actions.

4. **Possible Actions.** In this step, the manager-coach helps the team member identify possible actions they could take to address their goals/agenda. Then, you help the team member consider those actions and select the one(s) to act upon. You may offer ideas to help stimulate creativity by the team member, but it is crucial that the person being coached develop the possible action. Avoid telling the team member what to do.

5. **Action Planning.** The team member should develop a specific action plan for each action they chose to implement. This should include what will be done, when, for what desired outcome, and with what support.

6. **Summary and Agreement.** The final step in the change coaching process is to have the person being coached identify what they have gained from the coaching conversation and summarize the action plans they are committed to taking before the next coaching conversation or other mutually agreed-upon deadline.

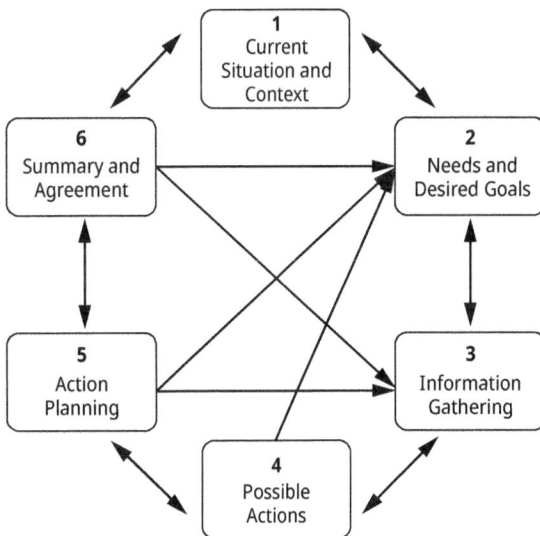

Figure 2.2: Change Coaching Model.
Source: Adapted from Bennett & Bush, 2014.

Effective coaching conversations begin with Step 1 and end with Step 6. However, they are dynamic, and conversations are likely to flow back and forth through the intermediate steps as the manager-coach seeks to define, explore, and advance understanding of the team member's issues. Here is an example of a hypothetical coaching conversation and the potential flow through the steps of the coaching model. (See Table 2.1)

Table 2.1: Example of a Coaching Conversation.

Manager-Coach and Team Member Dialogue (excerpts)	Essential Coaching Process Steps
Manager-Coach: *How has your work on the XYZ project been going since our last conversation?* **Team Member:** The big project is going well	Step 1: Current Situation and Context
Manager-Coach: *As we focus our time together, what would you like us to focus on today?* **Team Member:** My challenge is getting everything completed on time. **Manager-Coach:** *Tell me more about the challenge.* **Team Member:** I have so many deadlines . . . . I never seem to have suitable material with me at meetings . . . . And I don't think we have the right priorities for the change project . . . **Manager-Coach:** *So, you would like to focus on time management.* **Team Member:** Yes.	Step 2: Needs and Desired Goals
Manager-Coach: *Tell me more about the time management challenges you are having.* **Team Member:** I have not met some critical deadlines, putting others and the project behind schedule. Recently, I've noticed that some other work is taking longer than expected and is reducing the time I have to work on the XYZ project. In addition, it has caused some key team members to work on other priorities and not work on the ABC project.	Step 3: Information Gathering
Manager-Coach: *As we focus on what is essential for you today, I hear at least three potential coaching topics: managing deadlines, having material for meetings, and project priorities. Which would you like to focus on first?* **Team Member:** Well, now that I hear those three played back to me, I think managing deadlines is essential for me today. That is the one that I have the most control over. The priorities for the change project, however, are critical. I have some influence, but not control, over those priorities.	Step 2: Needs and Desired Goals

Table 2.1 (continued)

Manager-Coach and Team Member Dialogue (excerpts)	Essential Coaching Process Steps
Manager-Coach: *I want to make sure we meet your needs today. So, which do y you want to focus on first?* **Team Member:** Deadlines.	
Manager-Coach: *OK . . . deadlines . . . tell me more about the deadline challenge.* **Team Member:** I have so much to do. I always seem to have competing deadlines. Sometimes I don't know what to do first. And, since we lost a member of my team last month, I have been unable to reassign that work, so I've been trying to do it as well as my job. **Manager-Coach:** *Let's start with the last item—the team member. Is there anything keeping you from reassigning that work?* **Team Member:** No. . . . just time to do it. **Manager-Coach:** *OK. I wasn't sure if there was something else going on.* **Team Member:** If I took time to reassign that work, I would probably reduce my stress, increase my productivity, and be able to do the things that are most important for me to do.	Step 3: Information Gathering
Manager-Coach: *It sounds like you believe taking time to reassign that work would be a wise step.* **Team Member:** Yes. **Manager-Coach:** *Is there anything else you can think of to do?* **Team Member:** Yes . . . block out the time on my calendar and do it.	Step 4: Possible Actions
Manager-Coach: *OK. So, you are already planning some action.* **Team Member:** I need to schedule two hours to review the work I picked up when the team member left the team and to set priorities. Then, two hours more to consider who is best suited to do it.	Step 5: Action Planning
Manager-Coach: *When you review the work that needs reassignment, what criteria will you use to decide priority and reassignment?* **Team Member:** For priority, I will consider whether or not the work is "mission critical," impacts another project, or can wait until I hire a new team member. For reassignment, I will consider who has the knowledge and skills to do the work and who has time, and, you know, I will also use this as an opportunity to give some other team members "stretch assignments" to build their capacity.	Step 3: Information Gathering

Table 2.1 (continued)

Manager-Coach and Team Member Dialogue (excerpts)	Essential Coaching Process Steps
Manager-Coach: *I'd like to recap. . . . You have a focus, a plan of action, and your criteria for decision-making.* **Team Member:** What's next?	Step 4: Possible Actions
Manager-Coach: *When will you get this started?* **Team Member:** I will find the time on my calendar today. I intend to find time by the end of this week to review the work and by the middle of next week to determine who might receive the new assignments. One more step I'd like to add . . . after I draft the reassignments, I'd like to meet with each team member impacted and discuss it with them. They must know why I'm asking them to do more work and assure them I will support them. What do you think? **Manager-Coach:** *I think you have a terrific plan. How soon do you expect you can meet with each of your team members?* **Team Member:** I think completing this will take me two weeks from today. In the meantime, I'll keep the priorities and deadlines in order.	Step 5: Action Planning
Manager-Coach: *Great. As we wrap up today, please summarize what you received from the coaching session and your next steps.* **Team Member:** I gained clarity about my challenges and the need to delegate. I developed a plan of action to reassign the work of the team member who left. And I feel terrific. Knowing that I have a plan of action gives me a sense of relief. Thank you! **Manager-Coach:** *Good. . . . And I believe we are scheduled to meet again in 1 week.* **Team Member:** Yes. And at that point, I will be able to report on my work to manage the deadlines, delegate work, and support the development of my team members.	Step 6: Summary and Agreements

These are descriptions of each step in the change coaching model and sample questions or statements to support each step. Manager-coaches will want to find language that is natural and comfortable for them.

Step 1: Current Situation and Context

The focus of this step is to establish or reestablish the relationship between manager and team member, and obtain an update from the team member on recent occurrences in the context of the coaching goals. In addition, this step is to assess progress on previous action items, and acknowledge success and breakthroughs that may have occurred.

Suppose this is the first coaching session in a multi-session coaching engagement. The primary focus should be establishing the relationship and defining the engagement's purpose, scope, and operating agreements. If this is a single-session coaching engagement, the relationship development and contracting, as well as the coaching process described here, will all occur in the single session.

Sample questions that might be used with this step in the coaching process:
– How are you today?
– What has happened since we last met?
– What's the most significant thing that happened to you today?
– What have you accomplished related to your action plans from the last time we met?
– What progress have you made since we spoke?
– What accomplishments (or setbacks) have you experienced since our last coaching session?

Step 2: Needs and Desired Goals

The focus of this step is for the coach to gain an understanding of the team member's current reality, and to understand and agree upon the goals for the coaching session. You and the team member will also align those goals with the overall goals of the coaching engagement, and adjust the goals of the engagement if necessary. You and the team member will also adjust the goals of the overall engagement as the focus becomes clearer. This determination will be based on whether clarity and mutual understanding exist between the manager-coach and team members. You can align with the team member's goals via conversation with the team member.

Sample questions that might be used with this step in the coaching process:
– What are we going to focus on in this coaching session today?
– Of the _ things you mentioned that we might focus on today, which do you want to start with?
– What is essential for you to accomplish in our coaching work today?
– What will you have accomplished if this coaching session is a massive success?
– How would you rate this goal on a scale of 1–10 (10 being most important)?
– What would that look like if we were to "hit a home run" in this coaching session?
– For this coaching session, what will success look like for you?

Step 3: Information Gathering

The focus of this step is to gather information that serves the team member's agenda, gain a mutual understanding of that information, and identify the need for additional data (which may become an action item for later consideration). As the process manager, the coach must determine whether the conversation has developed enough information and shared understanding to progress to Step 4 (Possible Actions). If not, it must go back to Step 2 to refine Needs and Desired Goals.

Sample questions that might be used with this step in the coaching process:
- How important is that to you?
- How is your behavior impacting others?
- What does that feedback mean to you?
- In what, if any, ways are you rushing to judgment?
- What are you missing?
- What matters most?
- What are you inclined to believe about __?
- What is the opposing view?
- Which of the conflicting views has more evidence behind it?
- What are you afraid of and why?

Step 4: Possible Actions

This step focuses on exploring possibilities for action that will serve the team member's needs and desired goals for the coaching session. The team member generates ideas for possible action, establishes criteria to evaluate those options, considers barriers to implementing them, and establishes priorities for action.

Sample questions that might be used with this step in the coaching process:
- How might you improve the situation?
- What possible actions have you not explored?
- What have you seen others do that might work here?
- If none of the current options were available, what would you do?
- What is the counterintuitive choice?
- What would an outsider do?
- What ideas do you have for addressing this?
- How will you decide which step to take next?
- What has worked for you in the past?
- Offer (sparingly) ideas or questions to "prime the pump."

The manager-coach will need to determine whether to progress to Step 5 (Action Planning), go back to a previous step (Information Gathering, Needs and Desired Goals), or continue developing possible actions. This determination will be based on whether there is a clear understanding of the information available, possible actions to support achieving the desired goals, and a commitment to consider action steps for implementation.

Step 5: Action Planning

The focus of this step is to develop action steps (what the team member will do, by when, with what outcome, and with what support), ensure accountability and commitment for implementation, and determine resource and support needs as well as how to acquire those resources.

Sample questions that could be used with this step in the coaching process:
- What action will you take?
- What support do you need?
- What are you committed to doing? By when?
- What support do you have that you will call on to accomplish your action plan?
- What challenges or barriers do you anticipate, and how will you address them?
- What support will you access to achieve your action plans?
- What support do you have in place to help you?
- What support do you need? What will you do to secure it?

The manager-coach will need to determine whether to progress to Step 6 (Summary and Agreement), go back to a previous step (Information Gathering, Needs and Desired Goals, Possible Actions), or continue developing possible actions. This determination will be based on whether the team member is clear about and committed to the action steps designed, and whether there is agreement about what the team member will do next—by when, and with what support (if appropriate).

Step 6: Summary and Agreement
The focus of this step is to review insights and commitments gained from this coaching session, identify possible agenda items for future coaching sessions, and reinforce that the team member owns the coaching agenda and actions.
Sample questions that might be used with this step in the coaching process:
- What have you gained from this conversation?
- What are your key takeaways from our work today?
- What are your next steps?
- What are you committed to doing?
- What will you do as a result of this coaching session?
- What did you gain from this coaching session?
- Please remind me. What will you do as a result of this coaching session?

The manager-coach will need to determine whether to end the coaching session or return to a previous step in the coaching process (Information Gathering, Needs and Desired Goals, Possible Actions, Action Planning). This determination will be based on whether there is shared agreement about the next steps, whether the designated length of the coaching session has ended, and whether a new area of focus has emerged.

Suggestions for More Successful Coaching

Manager-coaches can take specific steps to coach individuals and groups more effectively. Here are some of the most significant:

- Build trust, respect, and credibility with team members.
- Let the team member set the agenda.
- Help the team member stay focused on the team member's agenda for coaching.
- Help the team member stay focused while helping the team member continually refine and redefine the focus.
- Master the art of asking high-impact questions. (See Chapter 8)
- Help the team member identify options and possibilities.
- Help the team member determine the action to be taken.
- Define action steps: Do what? By when? What outcomes/results?
- Help the team member discover barriers to successful implementation and develop strategies to overcome the obstacles.
- Speak less than 20% of the time. Don't be afraid of periods of silence. Ask simple, focused questions and then wait at least seven seconds for a response.
- Actively listen for content, context, meaning, what is being said, what is not being said, congruence, and incongruence.
- Be willing to maintain silence while the team member processes.
- Celebrate breakthroughs and achievements.
- Ask the team member for feedback on the coaching: What is working well? What is not working well? What should be done differently?
- Allow team members to take full responsibility for their own discoveries, growth, ideas, and achievements. Avoid imposing solutions on team members.
- Help team members be responsible for their actions.
- Coaching is about helping team members discover their own answers, not about the coach's being a sage. A person does not need to be a content expert to be an excellent coach.
- Challenge any incongruence between what the team member has said previously and what she says in the current coaching conversation.
- Challenge any discrepancies between the team member's commitment to action and their lack of action.
- Respect the communication and thinking styles of the team member, while keeping the conversation moving through the coaching process.

Summary

Coaching can be introduced into an organization in a variety of ways. The most effective technique is based on a formal coaching engagement process, applying a planned and methodical approach. Each coaching session encompasses six essential steps:
1. Current Situation and Context
2. Needs and Desired Goals
3. Information Gathering
4. Possible Actions

5. Action Planning
6. Summary and Agreement.

The coachability—or coaching readiness—of individuals is an important consideration for coaches. Coachable individuals are committed to change, have a solid motivation to improve their knowledge, skills, and abilities, and are willing to take responsibility for their outcomes.

Managers can improve the effectiveness of their efforts in many ways, including building trust, respect, and credibility with team members, letting them set the agenda, helping them stay focused, mastering the art of asking high-impact questions, defining action steps, and helping them identify and overcome barriers.

A Conversation with Ben Wilhelm, DBA
President and Chief Operating Officer
McFarland Construction

This conversation was recorded and transcribed, then edited for clarity and conciseness.
John Bennett (JB): *Tell me about your work.*

Ben Wilhelm (BW): McFarland is a mid-sized general contractor. We're growing quickly and expect to double or triple this year. So, there are big shifts going on. That growth put a lot of pressure on our entire work structure to help elevate roles and positions both internally and recruiting externally. There's a lot of people in new roles. I've spent the last two years trying to get functional leadership roles populated in the organization so that we could build the infrastructure to grow. As you can imagine, that creates a lot of room for conflict. Coaching conversations enable me to tamp down some of the natural conflicts and have higher quality dialogue rather than people digging in on their positions on topics. This allows us to focus on the interests versus positions. Aside from all the task-oriented decision-making that accompanies my role; human dynamics is an important part of my role.

JB: *I'm interested in how you use coaching in your role. You mentioned specifically using it to address conflict. Say more about that, and any other ways you see coaching showing up.*

BW: As a leader manager, I've become very comfortable with having coaching conversations on an individual level, either where I have a conflict with one of my direct reports or they have a conflict with one of their direct reports. I incorporate coaching as a conversation, not telling someone what to do, instead having an open-ended dialogue about what they might do, bringing awareness by asking open-ended questions, being curious, and holding up a mirror to the person. I look for what resonates with them and how their actions may contribute to their challenge. Sometimes, I use role play to determine how they may address one of their direct reports. That's where I've been able to separate myself and be a buffer between one of our functional leaders and their employees or their direct reports versus me having an immediate issue with a colleague under my direct supervision. I also use coaching as a leader manager in group contexts.

JB: *You've talked about using coaching with individuals and groups, especially in conflict situations. Are there other contexts?*

BW: Yes. I'm using coaching to develop people's thinking and help them see things from a broader lens or a broader perspective. This allows them to recognize that they have something to offer and that I have something to offer. I encourage people to be more open to what they have to offer and treat people how they want to be treated. So, I feel some emotional intelligence is derived by having conversations that way and using coaching skills to manifest that kind of behavior. I would say it's a fair comment that I find myself using coaching in conflict more so than I see it as a developmental tool.

As I shared, our business is moving fast. When you're moving fast, you don't often step back and think strategically about what things you could do that would help develop people, and that's where strategy fails, when you're spread (too thin).

JB: *I know you've had formal education related to coaching. Beyond that, how do you develop your mindset and the skill set as a manager-coach?*

BW: I've challenged myself to approach leading people by coaching rather than telling and being directive. If, for example, I am trying to bring awareness to people by solving their problems, then I know I'm still being an authoritative leader versus trying to have the conversation where they arrive at their own decision, which wouldn't have necessarily been mine. That means that I've done something to make it about their agenda for how they want to engage in a challenge versus my agenda and how they want to engage in a challenge. The more quality, the more conversations begin and end with others saying, "Here's what I'm going to do." When I can help others figure out how they want to do something, and I facilitate the conversation, then the more ownership they have taken for it. They are responsible for making it happen, and that shift in perspective is powerful.

JB: *How is your approach to leading and managing through coaching being received?*

BW: Every industry has nuances, and it's sort of the DNA for how it shows up. And in my 30 years of construction, it's very much a reactive business, full of what we would call "cowboys." Traditionally, everybody has their way of doing things. So, buildings are all very different; there's no building that's ever built the same, and no person that shows up in our business the same. It's very dictatorial. There's a strong command and control, authoritative approach: "Do it my way because I said so." When you have a coaching conversation in my industry, it's a much more sophisticated way to go about things. I don't think it's for everybody, but when you find the people that resonate with it, it engenders loyalty and respect in a way that I don't see very common in our business.

It's a different approach for folks. For some who are much more accustomed to having a rigid, very straightforward linear solution to everything, it's uncomfortable. For many people, they are surprised to be empowered. They say, "Wow, you want my opinion and are open to how I would solve this challenge. I'm not sure exactly how to do that, but there's a much better way."

There's a much higher level of receptivity for people who don't like the top-down philosophy. I find it a mixed bag with folks who have been in the industry for a long time and are used to certain command-and-control philosophies. I have really struggled with the way to engage them. A few people have left the organization because there's not enough structure to feel like they can be successful.

JB: *What challenges do you face using a coaching approach as a manager and leader? And how have you overcome them?*

BW: I have a point of view, and I'm not objective in all of my coaching conversations because I have opinions. There are times when the business must come first, which may conflict with my being open to their way of doing something. Examples include personal preferences for working at home and working hybrid, avoiding a challenging conversation with someone who needs to be held accountable, and how we're investing our resources.

When these conflicts arise, I recognize that I have a conflict and try to appreciate where you're coming from. I realize that something may not align with the other person's values and where you are today, so we need to talk to you about it. So, I use coaching to help people become aware. And then help them be informed about their choices instead of making choices for them. I would much rather they have the autonomy to select for themselves rather than me to choose for them.

JB: *Tell me about a story where you used your role as a manager but also used coaching skills. Is there a specific example?*

BW: I'm trying to take on the philosophy that I shouldn't always be working the hardest to solve everybody's problems. As we've continued to promote people within the organization, we recently had this example. One colleague was promoted to an executive position. They inherited some challenging personalities that were much more Type A, dominant, reactive leaders who were very proud. I'm trying to remove myself from that management layer so this leader can ascend and take ownership of those teammates. We had a coaching conversation. I knew the conflict was related to the roles and responsibilities of this manager. One team member was very frustrated about not having better clarity. We knew that this needed to be addressed. So, the leader role-played with me how the conversation might go with the team member. It helped the leader think through how they wanted this meeting to go. I offered to be a "fly on the wall." The leader said, "You need to not be involved and I think it'll empower me to be on the front line of this conversation." They had the conversation, and it went well. The team member is showing up much better.

JB: *What do you see as the value of using a coaching approach as a leader?*

BW: It's like learning a foreign language. We have a lot of Hispanic Latino employees in our industry. Many speak a limited amount of English. I don't speak Spanish. When I go to construction sites, I need someone to translate for me. Otherwise, I am not able to communicate with half the people. And when they are talking, I am relatively useless in that conversation because I don't add value. Learning the language of coaching opened a whole new world of possibilities about how to engage people. And that has been transformational. For me, it was having the ability to engage people. As a leader, it has enhanced my effectiveness.

JB: *What advice would you give a leader manager considering using a coaching approach in their work?*

BW: I would say a couple of things. Find people in their universe or sphere of influence that they can connect with who use coaching approaches and learn from them. And if you don't want to learn from them or have a different type of learning style, read about it. And if you're really all engaged, find a program that can help you develop the skills and focus on it for professional development. I don't think it's for everybody. I think you have to be open to reframing how you engage people. That doesn't necessarily lend itself to everyone. Some of the fundamentals of coaching—such as asking open-ended questions, being an active listener, attending to the relationship, and making the coaching conversation about somebody else's agenda—when you say them out loud, they sound pretty intuitive. Often, we are too focused on expediency in our business because we're so task oriented. As a result, we take a shortcut and tell others what to do because that's how we know the job will get done. But as a leader manager, how are you going to scale yourself if you are always working in this dependent culture that requires you to always tell everybody what to do? It's just not very productive.

JB: *Is there anything that we didn't talk about or anything you wanted to share that you didn't have an opportunity to share?*

BW: Not everyone engaging in this leader-manager approach of having coaching conversations is aware of the available models and processes. I like the Bennett and Bush (2014) model because it helps you focus on a process, especially when learning how to have coaching conversations. I think having a model enables you to facilitate the conversations, no matter the issue. If you have a process you can fall back on, you can effectively have higher-quality dialogue. Also, listen for your agenda and the questions you ask people. If you're asking open-ended questions and suspending your assumptions, you will help people articulate the situation. What are they feeling? How are they thinking about possible solutions? That would be an outstanding achievement. Don't ask leading questions. Ask questions that help people believe in themselves.

JB: *Is there something you've seen that indicates that somebody is more likely to be receptive to coaching?*

BW: I'm always excited about the folks leaning into those conversations and seeking the opportunity to have those coaching approaches. They come in and ask questions. They're trying to figure it out, and don't presume they have all the answers.

When I do find that dominant personality with a fair amount of bravado in my industry where they're pretty confident, behind the curtain they may have their fears of looking vulnerable to the idea of the coaching. For those who have a fixed mindset, I struggle with having a coaching conversation. After a couple of attempts to have a coaching conversation, I will give them hard feedback about why their actions resulted in us being in our situation. I have a metaphor in my business that says if you can solve a problem in the field, it costs $10. If it makes it into the job site trailer, it costs $100 because now you have twice as many people involved, and you have more resources involved. If it makes it into the office, it is a $1,000 problem because now you've got legal, COO, finance, and HR involved. And so, how can you solve $10 issues as much as possible?

JB: *Right, and when you find somebody with that fixed mindset, how do you bring that awareness?*

BW: I don't know if I always put a fine point on it because I don't want to confront it so that it turns the person off, and they walk out being entirely defensive. You're in a leadership role, and it's crucial for the success to be tied to your ability to get things done and for people to buy into your leadership. If three or four people don't want to work with you, it limits your potential in the organization or with our stakeholders. So yeah, I would deliver feedback very much like that to hopefully make a connection that their behavior or way of addressing situations has some detrimental effects or outcomes.

Chapter 3
Theoretical Foundations of Coaching Applied

There is nothing so practical as a good theory.

—Kurt Lewin

Coaching is a trans-disciplinary field of practice influenced by various professional techniques and delivered in the context of providing help to a range of clients (Wilkins, 2000, 2003). Coaching draws on many disciplines and practices, a rich cross-disciplinary heritage that also makes it trans-disciplinary. How are these terms different? Cross-disciplinary means to involve two or more academic disciplines, whereas trans-disciplinary adds the element of systematic coordination among fields to study and develop theory and practice.

This chapter explores the trans-disciplinary nature of coaching and provides a theoretical framework for coaching for change at the individual, group, and organizational levels. The focus is on establishing a framework for considering the disciplines and practices that inform coaching and the work of coaches who focus on change—i.e., the change coach. For a thorough understanding of these topics, you will need to study them in depth.

This chapter explores the disciplines that coaches may draw as sources of wisdom. Then it examines the practices in which coaches may have been trained or educated, and the sources of those coaching practices. It presents applications to managerial coaching, and then illustrates specific approaches to personal change—the foundation for coaching. The chapter concludes with a framework for mutual learning to guide coaching and support development, performance, and transformation.

Frameworks for Coaching

Coaching uses various frameworks of skill sets and professional practices, for example:
- Cognitive behavioral
- Solution-focused
- Gestalt
- Existential
- Positive psychology
- Transactional analysis

These are approaches to coaching, not theoretical or academic disciplines. Most of these approaches are rooted in psychology and the practice of therapy or counseling.

There are many genres or contexts of coaching. For example:
- Career coaching
- Executive and leadership coaching

https://doi.org/10.1515/9783111002415-003

- Life coaching
- Managerial coaching
- Peer coaching
- Team coaching

All coaching is oriented toward the agenda of the person being coached. Executive, leadership, team, and peer coaching, for example, are also oriented toward the relationship between the coach and client in an organization or system. As noted earlier (Chapter 2), coaching is a process that supports change at the individual, group, and organizational levels.

Drawing on an analogy developed by Stein (2004), imagine a large tree as the foundation and manifestation of change coaching. The tree's roots symbolize the academic disciplines that nurture and support the growth of coaching. These disciplines include communication, health, human development, leadership, learning, philosophy, psychology, and spirituality. Coaching is informed by many fields—no single domain owns it. The trunk of the tree provides strength to coaching. The professional practices that emerge from the roots and inform coaching include consulting, management, mentoring, pastoral care, teaching, and therapy/counseling. Finally, the branches and leaves on the tree are the foliage, the new growth, which provides the seeds for further development. This portion of the tree symbolizes how coaching is applied. Examples include peer coaching, managerial coaching, teachers coaching students, internal and external coaches coaching leaders in organizational settings, and parents coaching children.

Approaches to Coaching

Many of the approaches to coaching come from psychology, human development, and learning. Table 3.1 summarizes six approaches to coaching, selected to provide a foundation for coaching by managers. Each approach to coaching includes the focus of the coaching agenda, which provides for developmental, performance, and transformational orientations.

Managers may employ several approaches when coaching a team member. These choices may be based on several factors, including personal comfort, familiarity, and appropriateness for the coaching situation. Managers are encouraged to become familiar with various approaches, develop expertise, and select the most fitting approach for the coaching situation. Table 3.1 presents six approaches that are most closely aligned with managerial coaching: cognitive behavioral, solution-focused, gestalt, existential, positive psychology, and transactional analysis with some of their techniques, applications, benefits, and limitations of each. This table also shows how the three area of focus for coaching (development, performance, or transformation) may best be applied to each of the six approaches to coaching.

Table 3.1: Coaching: Types, Frameworks/Approaches, and Focus.

Type of Coaching/ Theoretical Framework or Approach	Cognitive Behavioral (CBC) Focuses on helping the team member address disturbing or limiting thoughts and beliefs to change self-defeating behaviors that undermine performance.	Solution-Focused Focuses on helping the team member articulate and define a desired future state, then develop thinking and an active approach to achieve the desired goals.	Gestalt Focuses on helping the team member experience the present moment, environmental context in which this takes place, and self-regulating adjustments resulting from the overall situation.	Existential Focuses is on helping the team member clarify the dilemma when they experience personal, professional, and interpersonal challenges to their way of being.	Positive Psychology Focuses on the positive aspects of human nature and inspires growth and change.	Transactional Analytic Focuses on identifying how behavioral patterns of communication reveal something of the psychodynamic and intra-psychic; transactional structures of ego states (parent, adult, child)
Executive Coaching	X	X	X	X	X	X
Peer Coaching	X	X		X		
Managerial Coaching	X	X	X	X		X
Group or Team Coaching	X	X	X	X	X	X
Internal Coaching	X	X		X	X	X
Personal/ Life Coaching	X	X		X	X	X
Health & Wellness Coaching	X	X		X		

(continued)

Table 3.1 (continued)

Type of Coaching/ Theoretical Framework or Approach	Cognitive Behavioral (CBC)	Solution-Focused	Gestalt	Existential	Positive Psychology	Transactional Analytic
	Focuses on helping the team member address disturbing or limiting thoughts and beliefs to change self-defeating behaviors that undermine performance.	Focuses on helping the team member articulate and define a desired future state, then develop thinking and an active approach to achieve the desired goals.	Focuses on helping the team member experience the present moment, environmental context in which this takes place, and self-regulating adjustments resulting from the overall situation.	Focuses is on helping the team member clarify the dilemma when they experience personal, professional, and interpersonal challenges to their way of being.	Focuses on the positive aspects of human nature and inspires growth and change.	Focuses on identifying how behavioral patterns of communication reveal something of the psychodynamic and intra-psychic; transactional structures of ego states (parent, adult, child)
Focus of the Coaching						
Development	X	X	X			X
Performance	X	X			X	
Transformation	X			X		X

Cognitive Behavioral Approach

The cognitive behavioral approach is based on a therapeutic approach that effectively treats various psychological disorders. In recent years, cognitive behavioral therapy (CBT) has extended beyond traditional therapy settings to other areas, such as coaching. The theory behind CBT is rooted in cognitive psychology and behavioral psychology. CBT and cognitive behavioral coaching (CBC) are based on the premise that our thoughts, feelings, and behaviors are interconnected and that our thoughts influence our emotions and behaviors. Therefore, we can change our feelings and behaviors if we change our thoughts.

The approach was developed by Aaron Beck (1976), who was working with patients with depression. Beck noticed that many of his patients had negative thoughts and beliefs about themselves and their abilities, and that this contributed to their depression. He developed a therapeutic approach to help patients identify and challenge their negative thoughts and replace them with more realistic and positive beliefs. Cognitive psychology emphasizes the role of thoughts in shaping our emotions and behaviors. According to this perspective, people's mental representations of the world (i.e., schemas) influence how they perceive and interpret events. These interpretations, in turn, affect their emotional reactions and behaviors (Beck, 1976).

On the other hand, behavioral psychology emphasizes the role of environmental factors in shaping behavior. Behavioral theories propose that behavior is learned through the process of conditioning. Positive reinforcement (reward) increases the likelihood of a behavior, while negative reinforcement (punishment) decreases the probability of a behavior (Skinner, 1953).

Empirical Evidence

There is growing evidence to support the effectiveness of CBT in coaching. One study found that coaching interventions incorporating CBT principles improved executives' emotional intelligence and leadership skills (Grant, et al., 2009). A meta-analysis of 29 studies on executive coaching found that CBT was the most commonly used approach in coaching interventions and that it improved various outcomes, including leadership skills, job satisfaction, and well-being (Jones, et al, 2016).

Cognitive behavioral therapy is an evidence-based approach successfully applied to executive coaching. CBT can help team members identify and challenge unhelpful thinking patterns, develop coping strategies for dealing with stress and pressure, and improve their emotional intelligence and leadership skills.

Benefits and Limitations

Cognitive behavioral coaching has several benefits and limitations. First, the benefits include:

- **Empowerment and Self-Efficacy.** One of the primary benefits of CBC is that it empowers individuals to take control of their lives by providing them with the tools and strategies to manage their thoughts, feelings, and behaviors. By teaching individuals how to identify and challenge negative thought patterns, CBC can improve their self-efficacy, the belief in one's ability to accomplish tasks and achieve goals (Bandura, 1997).
- **Goal-Oriented.** CBC helps individuals define and achieve their objectives. CBC focuses on the present and future rather than dwelling on past events, allowing individuals to move forward and progress. The coach works with the team member to establish specific, measurable, achievable, relevant, and time-bound (SMART) goals tailored to their needs and preferences.
- **Evidence-Based.** CBC has been extensively researched and found to be effective in treating a wide range of psychological disorders and emotional issues. Research has shown that CBC is as effective as medication in treating depression and anxiety and more effective than other psychological interventions, such as psychoanalysis and psychodynamic therapy (Butler et al., 2006).
- **Customizable.** CBC can be tailored to the specific needs and preferences of the individual. The manager-coach works with the team member to identify their unique challenges and develop strategies to overcome them. This personalized approach ensures the coaching process is relevant, engaging, and effective.
- **Measurable Outcomes.** The CBC focuses on quantifiable results. The manager-coach works with the team member to establish specific goals and regularly monitors progress toward achieving them. This approach ensures that the coaching process is transparent, accountable, and effective.

The cognitive behavioral approach to coaching has several limitations, including:
- **Limited Focus on Emotions.** CBC acknowledges the role of emotions in behavior, but it tends to prioritize the cognitive aspects of behavior over the emotional ones. This prioritization can be problematic, especially for individuals with deep-seated emotional issues that require more attention and support than CBC can provide (Greenberger & Padesky, 1995).
- **Overemphasis on Rational Thinking.** CBC can emphasize analytical thinking at the expense of other modes of thought, such as intuition and creativity. While the CBC effectively addresses cognitive distortions, it can also stifle creativity and spontaneity, essential aspects of personal growth and development.
- **Short-term Approach.** CBC focuses on the immediate problem rather than exploring the underlying causes of behavior. While this can effectively address specific issues, it may not be sufficient for individuals with complex and long-standing emotional problems that require more in-depth exploration (Wampold et al., 1997).

Practical Applications

CBT is applied to various mental health issues, including anxiety, phobias, post-traumatic stress disorder, and eating disorders. The approach is practical in numerous studies and is considered one of the most widely used and researched forms of psychotherapy (Hofmann et al., 2012). CBC combines these two theoretical perspectives by focusing on the interplay between thoughts, emotions, and behaviors. CBC aims to identify and modify maladaptive thoughts and behaviors contributing to psychological distress.

CBT can be applied to coaching in several ways. First, CBT techniques can help team members identify and modify maladaptive thoughts and behaviors that may interfere with their leadership effectiveness. For example, a team member prone to catastrophic thinking may benefit from cognitive restructuring to challenge negative thoughts and develop more realistic and adaptive thinking patterns. Second, CBT techniques can help team members develop coping strategies for managing stress and other emotional challenges. For example, an executive who struggles with anxiety may benefit from relaxation techniques or exposure therapy to manage their symptoms. Third, CBT techniques can help team members enhance their self-awareness and emotional intelligence. Mindfulness techniques can help team members become more aware.

Key Techniques and Interventions

CBC involves various techniques to help people being coached identify and modify maladaptive thoughts and behaviors. Some of the methods used in CBC include:

- **Cognitive Restructuring.** CBC involves identifying and challenging negative or irrational thoughts contributing to psychological distress. Team members are taught to recognize their negative thoughts, evaluate their validity, and replace them with more adaptive thoughts.
- **Behavioral Activation.** CBC involves increasing engagement in positive activities to improve mood and decrease negative thoughts and behaviors. Team members learn to identify enjoyable and meaningful activities and schedule them into their daily routines.
- **Exposure Therapy.** CBC involves gradually exposing team members to anxiety-provoking stimuli in a safe and controlled environment to reduce anxiety and sensitivity to fears.
- **Relaxation Techniques.** CBC involves teaching team members to use relaxation exercises such as deep breathing, progressive muscle relaxation, or meditation to reduce stress and anxiety.
- **Mindfulness.** CBC teaches team members to focus on the present moment and observe their thoughts and feelings without judgment. The goal is to increase awareness and acceptance of one's internal experiences.

- **Identifying Negative Thought Patterns.** The coach and team member work together to identify negative and self-defeating thoughts that are hindering progress. These thoughts may include beliefs such as "I'm not good enough" or "I'll never succeed."
- **Challenging Negative Thoughts.** Once negative thoughts are identified, the manager-coach helps team members challenge them by questioning their validity and evidence. For example, the manager-coach may ask the team member, "Is it true that you're not good enough? Can you provide evidence to support this belief?"
- **Developing New Thought Patterns.** The manager-coach helps team members develop new, positive thought patterns that align with their goals. For example, instead of believing that they're not good enough, the team members may create the belief that they're capable of achieving their goals with hard work and dedication.
- **Creating New Behaviors.** The manager-coach helps the team member develop new behaviors consistent with their new thought patterns. For example, if the team member wants to improve public speaking skills, the manager-coach may help them develop a plan to practice speaking and provide feedback on their progress (Williams et al., 2018).

Solution-focused Approach

The solution-focused approach to coaching (SFC) is a relatively new technique rapidly gaining popularity. This approach is based on the belief that team members can solve their problems and that the manager-coach's role is to help team members identify their strengths, resources, and solutions to achieve their desired goals.

SFC emerged in the 1980s from the work of Steve de Shazer and Insoo Kim Berg, founders of the Brief Family Therapy Center in Milwaukee, Wisconsin. They developed a solution-focused therapy model based on the idea that people's problems are not necessarily caused by their past experiences or underlying psychological issues but rather by their current patterns of behavior and thinking. They believed that change is possible when clients maintain focus on strengths, resources, and solutions rather than problems. The solution-focused approach was adapted for coaching to help clients achieve their goals. SFC is an effective method used in various settings, including executive, sports, and life coaching.

Empirical Evidence

Research supports the benefits of solution-focused coaching. For example, a study conducted by Green et al. (2007) found that SFC effectively improved goal attainment, job satisfaction, and well-being. Grant and O'Connor (2014) found that SFC significantly enhanced employee job satisfaction and work-related well-being. Furthermore, a meta-analysis by Kim et al. (2018) revealed that solution-focused interventions were more effective than traditional problem-focused interventions in enhancing psychological well-being and decreasing symptoms of anxiety and depression. In personal development, a study by Macaskill and Macaskill (2017) demonstrated the positive impact of solution-focused coaching on self-esteem and goal attainment. Similarly, in education, a research study by Franklin and Kimber (2015) showcased the effectiveness of SFC in promoting academic engagement and success among students.

Benefits and Limitations

The solution-focused approach to coaching has several benefits and limitations. First, the benefits include:

- **Focus on Strengths.** SFC helps team members identify their strengths and resources, which can help them build confidence and self-esteem.
- **Focus on Solutions.** SFC's focus on solutions rather than problems is a critical benefit. The manager-coach helps team members identify their strengths and resources and uses them to solve their challenges. This approach enables the team members to feel empowered and motivated to act toward achieving their goals.
- **Time-Efficient.** SFC focuses on the present and the future rather than the past. The manager-coach helps the team member identify what they want to achieve, allows them to create solutions to achieve their goals, and identify steps they need to take to get there. This approach can help team members achieve their goals quickly and efficiently.
- **Positive and Motivational.** In SFC, the manager-coach helps the team member identify their strengths and resources, which can help them feel more confident and motivated to act toward achieving their goals.
- **Client-Centered.** SFC helps team members feel more in control of their lives and more empowered to act toward their goals.
- **Flexible.** SFC is a flexible approach. The manager-coach works with team members to identify what works for them and what does not. This approach can help the team members feel more comfortable and confident in the coaching process, leading to better results.

While solution-focused coaching has many benefits, it also has limitations that must be considered. These limitations are:

- **Limited Focus on the Past.** SFC focuses on the present and the future, and does not dwell on the past. While this can be an advantage, it can also be a limitation. Team members who have experienced trauma or have deep-rooted issues may benefit from exploring their past to better understand themselves and their current situation.
- **Overlooking Underlying Issues.** SFC may ignore underlying issues contributing to team members' challenges. For example, a team member struggling with time

management may benefit from exploring why they are struggling rather than just focusing on creating a schedule.

– **Lack of Structure.** SFC may lack structure, which can disadvantage some team members. Team members who prefer a more structured approach may find SFC too open-ended and may struggle to make progress.

– **Limited Applicability.** SFC may not apply to everyone or to all situations. Some team members may require a more directive approach, while others may require a more exploratory approach.

Practical Applications

Solution-focused coaching is based on the idea that people can find solutions to their problems and that the manager-coach's role is to help team members identify and use their strengths to create positive change in their lives.

Solution-focused coaching is increasingly used in business settings to help individuals and organizations achieve their goals. You can help individuals identify common goals and develop strategies to work together to achieve them. For example, you can work with a business owner to develop a plan to grow their business or improve their profitability. SFC can also help employees improve their performance or develop new skills. It can be beneficial in situations where there is conflict or disagreement, and it can help individuals build stronger relationships and improve communication.

Solution-focused coaching has many practical applications in education. Teachers and educators can use this approach to help students set goals and develop strategies to achieve them. For example, a teacher can use solution-focused coaching to help a student struggling with a particular subject. The teacher can help students identify their strengths and weaknesses, set specific goals, and develop a plan to achieve them. This approach can benefit students with low self-esteem and a lack of confidence in their abilities. In addition to helping students, SFC can benefit educators themselves. Many teachers face burnout and other challenges that can affect their performance in the classroom. Solution-focused coaching can help educators identify the root causes of their challenges and develop strategies to overcome them. It can also help educators improve communication skills and build stronger relationships with their students.

Solution-focused coaching is increasingly used in healthcare settings to help patients make positive life changes. For example, a coach can work with a patient struggling with a chronic illness to develop a plan to manage their symptoms and improve their quality of life. SFC can help patients quit smoking, lose weight, or manage stress. SFC can be particularly effective in helping patients with mental health issues. Many mental health disorders, such as depression and anxiety, can be improved through goal setting and behavior change. SFC can help patients identify their strengths and develop strategies to overcome challenges. This approach can also help patients build resilience and develop coping skills to manage their symptoms.

Key Techniques and Interventions

The solution-focused approach to coaching is based on principles that guide the manager-coach's interactions with team members. These principles include:

– **Focus on Solutions.** The manager-coach focuses on finding solutions rather than dwelling on problems. The manager-coach helps the team member identify their goals and focus on how they can achieve them.

– **Team Member-Centered.** The manager-coach believes the team member is the expert in their life and can find solutions. The manager-coach supports them in discovering their strengths and resources.

– **Positive Language.** The manager-coach uses positive and empowering language to help the team members create a positive self-image and view of their future.

– **Small Steps.** The manager-coach helps the team member break their goals down into small, achievable steps they can take to move forward.

– **Focus on Success.** The manager-coach encourages the team members to focus on their successes and build on them to create more success.

– **Use of Questions.** The manager-coach uses a range of questions to help the team member explore their strengths and resources, identify their goals, and find solutions.

Solution-focused coaching uses various techniques to help team members achieve their goals. These techniques include:

– **Scaling.** The manager-coach uses a scaling question to help the team members evaluate where they are on a scale of 1 to 10 concerning their goal. The manager-coach then helps the team members explore what they need to do to increase their ranking.

– **Miracle Question.** The manager-coach asks the team member a question that allows them to imagine their life after their problem has been solved. The manager-coach then helps the team members identify what they must do to make that vision a reality.

– **Exception Question.** The manager-coach asks the team member about times when the problem has not been present to help the team member identify their strengths and resources.

– **Coping Question.** The manager-coach asks the team members about how they have managed similar situations in the past to help the team member identify their strengths and resources.

– **Future Pacing.** The manager-coach helps the team members imagine themselves achieving their goals in the future using visualization techniques.

Gestalt Approach

The Gestalt approach to coaching emphasizes the person's entire experience, in the coaching process, including their physical sensations, emotions, and behaviors. Gestalt coaching is based on the principles of Gestalt psychology, which emphasizes the importance of holistic and experiential learning. Gestalt psychology emerged in the early 20th century as a response to the reductionist and mechanistic approaches of behaviorism and psychoanalysis. According to Gestalt psychology, human experience is not a sum of isolated parts but an integrated whole. The meaning of an experience is derived from the whole, not its parts (Perls et al., 1951).

The Gestalt approach to coaching applies these principles by emphasizing the importance of the coach-client relationship, the team member's awareness of their experience, and the team member's responsibility for their actions. Gestalt therapy is a holistic approach that emphasizes the importance of the individual's experience in the present moment. The focus is on the individual's awareness of their current experience and how they can take responsibility for their actions and choices.

Gestalt's approach to coaching involves the individual's understanding of how their choices affect their role as a leader or team member. The Gestalt approach to coaching is a humanistic and team member-centered approach that focuses on helping clients become aware of their thoughts, feelings, and behaviors in the present moment (Bluckert, 2018).

Several fundamental principles, including the following, characterize the Gestalt approach to coaching:

– **Holism.** The Gestalt approach to coaching emphasizes viewing the client's experience rather than breaking it down into isolated parts. The manager-coach helps the team members become aware of their thoughts, feelings, and physical sensations and integrate them into a coherent whole.
– **Awareness.** The Gestalt approach to coaching emphasizes the importance of the team member's understanding of their experience. The manager-coach encourages the team members to be present now, pay attention to their internal experience, and notice their thinking, feeling, and behavior patterns.
– **Responsibility.** The Gestalt approach to coaching emphasizes the team member's responsibility for their actions. The manager-coach helps the team members take ownership of their experience, acknowledge their role in creating their reality, and take action to change it.
– **Relationship.** The Gestalt approach to coaching emphasizes the importance of the coach-team member relationship. The manager-coach creates a safe and supportive environment where the team member can explore their experience, and the team member and manager-coach work collaboratively to achieve the team member's goals.

The Gestalt approach to coaching is based on several key concepts essential to understanding the approach's philosophy and practice. These concepts include the following:

– **The Here-and-Now.** The Gestalt approach to coaching emphasizes the importance of the team member's awareness of their experience in the present moment. The manager-coach helps the team members be present, focus on their immediate experience, and notice their thinking, feeling, and behavior patterns.

– **The Figure-Ground Relationship.** The figure-ground relationship is between the foreground and the background of an experience. The Gestalt approach to coaching emphasizes the importance of the client's awareness of the figure-ground relationship, helping the team members to identify the foreground and background elements of their experience and to integrate them into a coherent whole.

– **Contact.** Contact refers to the relationship between the individual and their environment. The Gestalt approach to coaching emphasizes the importance of the team members' awareness of their connection with their environment, helping them identify the obstacles that prevent them from making contact and take action to overcome them.

– **Resistance.** Resistance is often "a way of protecting oneself from an actual or perceived threat or lack of support . . ." (Mann, 2021, p. 77). The Gestalt approach identifies the polarities related to the resistance, for example, deflection and being mesmerized, or projecting and owning everything, or self-monitoring and lack of field constraints. Within each of these is an ability to flexibly move along the continuum congruent with the team member's situation. Using the Gestalt approach, the coach affirms and works with the contact-resistance continuum, assuming the resistance holds the key to a future state.

Empirical Evidence

While a limited amount of empirical research specifically focused on the Gestalt approach to coaching, the principles of Gestalt therapy, upon which this approach is built, have shown promising results. A study by Brownell et al. (2016) demonstrated that gestalt therapy interventions significantly improved psychological well-being, self-esteem, and interpersonal relationships. Moreover, a review by Clarkson (2014) highlighted the effectiveness of gestalt therapy in fostering personal growth and self-awareness.

Benefits and Limitations

The Gestalt approach to coaching has several benefits and limitations. First, the benefits include:

– **Focus on the Present Moment.** The Gestalt approach to coaching emphasizes the present moment. This means that the manager-coach and team members work together to explore the team member's experiences, thoughts, and feelings in real time. This focus on the present moment can benefit team members experiencing difficulties with anxiety or depression. The Gestalt approach to coaching can help team members develop new ways of coping with difficult emotions.

- **Holistic Perspective.** The Gestalt approach to coaching takes a holistic view, which considers the team members' environment, relationships, and individual experiences. This perspective can help team members better understand how their environment influences their experiences and how they can change their settings to support their personal growth. For example, a team member struggling with work-related stress may benefit from exploring their relationship with their boss or colleagues.
- **Focus on the Client's Resources.** The Gestalt approach to coaching strongly emphasizes the team member's resources. This means the manager-coach works with the team members to identify their strengths, values, and abilities, which can help team members develop a greater sense of self-efficacy and confidence. This approach can help clients identify and build on their resources.
- **Use of Experiential Techniques.** The Gestalt approach to coaching uses experiential practices, such as role-play, imagery, and visualization. These techniques can help clients explore their experiences in a safe and supportive environment. For example, a team member struggling with assertiveness may benefit from practicing assertive communication techniques in a role-play scenario. Using experiential techniques in the Gestalt approach to coaching can be particularly helpful for clients who have difficulty expressing their emotions.

The Gestalt approach to coaching has several limitations, including:
- **Lack of Structure.** The Gestalt approach to coaching can lack structure, which means the coaching process may be less predictable than other coaching approaches. Some team members may find this lack of structure challenging, mainly if they prefer a more directive coaching style.
- **Limited Focus on Goal Setting.** The Gestalt approach to coaching does not strongly emphasize goal setting. As a result, the coaching process may focus less on achieving specific outcomes. While this can benefit team members looking for a more exploratory coaching experience, it may not suit those looking for a more goal-focused approach. The lack of focus on goal setting can be a barrier to team member satisfaction.
- **Emphasis on the Team Member's Experience.** The Gestalt approach can be challenging to apply to team members uncomfortable with introspection. The gestalt approach relies heavily on the team member's ability to explore their inner experience and reflect on their thoughts and emotions. However, some team members may find this problematic because they are uncomfortable with introspection or lack the necessary self-awareness to engage in this work. In these cases, you may need to adjust the approach to better meet the team member's needs. While exploring the team member's experiences can help gain a deeper understanding of their thoughts, feelings, and behaviors, it can also be limiting.

The focus on the present moment and the team member's experience may make it difficult for the manager-coach to explore their past experiences, which may influence their current behavior. While the Gestalt approach can help explore the team member's present experience, it may not be as effective in addressing deep-seated issues.

- **Potential for Resistance to Change.** The approach encourages team members to become more aware of their patterns of behavior and thought, which can be challenging and uncomfortable. This may lead to resistance to change, as team members may be reluctant to confront difficult emotions or change longstanding behavior patterns. The Gestalt approach can effectively promote personal growth, but it requires team members to be willing to engage in difficult or unfamiliar emotions that they might be ill-equipped to confront.

- **Measuring Effectiveness.** It can be challenging to measure the effectiveness of the Gestalt approach, a holistic and intuitive process tailored to team members' needs. This can make it difficult to measure the approach's effectiveness in a standardized way. While self-report measures of well-being and satisfaction with coaching can be used to measure effectiveness, these measures may not capture the full complexity of the coaching process.

- **Suitability.** The Gestalt approach to coaching may not be suitable for team members dealing with severe mental health issues. While it can be practical for team members dealing with issues such as stress, anxiety, and relationship difficulties, it may not be appropriate for team members dealing with severe mental health issues, such as depression or bipolar disorder. In these cases, team members may require a more specialized form of therapy and manager-coaches who are not trained in mental health counseling may not be equipped to provide the necessary support.

- **Balancing Supporting and Challenging.** It can be challenging for manager-coaches to balance supporting the team member's self-exploration and challenging them to make changes. The Gestalt approach emphasizes the importance of self-exploration and encourages team members to explore their inner experiences. However, this can sometimes lead to team members getting stuck in their thinking and behavior patterns. Manager-coaches using the Gestalt approach must balance this need for self-exploration with the need to challenge team members to make changes and act.

- **Time-Consuming and Resource-Intensive.** The approach requires a significant amount of time and energy from both you and the team member. Manager-coaches using the Gestalt approach must be prepared to invest time and energy in the coaching process. Team members need to be willing to commit significant time to the coaching process.

Practical Applications

The Gestalt approach to coaching has many applications and can be used in various coaching contexts. The approach is particularly effective in the following areas:

- **Leadership Coaching.** The Gestalt approach to coaching is particularly effective in leadership coaching. The approach emphasizes the importance of awareness and personal responsibility, critical traits of influential leaders. The Gestalt approach also encourages experimentation and feedback, which can help leaders at all levels develop new skills and behaviors.
- **Career Coaching.** The Gestalt approach to coaching is also effective in career coaching. The approach encourages team members to explore their values, strengths, and passions, which can help them identify career paths aligned with their interests and goals. The Gestalt approach also emphasizes the importance of personal responsibility, which can help team members take ownership of their career development.
- **Relationship Coaching.** The Gestalt approach to coaching encourages team members to explore their thoughts, feelings, and behaviors in the context of their relationships, which can help them identify patterns of behavior affecting their relationships. The Gestalt approach also emphasizes personal responsibility, which can help people take ownership of their relationships and work to improve them.

Key Techniques and Interventions

- **Empty Chair.** The Empty Chair technique is one of the most well-known techniques used in the Gestalt approach to coaching. This technique involves placing an empty chair in front of the team members and asking them to imagine a person or situation they must confront or resolve. The team member then speaks to the empty chair as if the person or situation is present. The manager-coach may encourage the team members to express their feelings and explore the case in a safe and supportive environment. The Empty Chair technique can benefit team members struggling with difficult emotions, such as anger or resentment. It can help team members become more self-aware and develop new ways to cope with difficult emotions.
- **Two-Chair.** The Two-Chair Technique is another commonly used technique in the Gestalt approach to coaching. This technique involves placing two chairs facing each other and asking the team member to sit in one of the chairs. The team member is asked to imagine a conflicting part of themselves or a relationship they must work on. The team member then moves to the other chair and speaks to their conflicting interest or the person they are struggling with. This technique can help team members explore their internal conflicts and develop greater self-awareness. The Two-Chair technique can benefit team members working with self-doubt or indecisiveness.

- **Body Awareness.** Body awareness is a critical component of the Gestalt approach to coaching. This technique involves helping team members become more aware of their physical sensations, such as tension or discomfort, and their emotional experiences. The manager-coach may ask the team members to focus on their breathing or to pay attention to physical sensations in their bodies during a coaching session. Body awareness can be beneficial for clients who are experiencing stress or anxiety. Body awareness techniques can help team members become more self-aware and develop greater resilience.
- **Exaggeration.** Exaggeration is another technique used in the Gestalt approach to coaching. This technique involves encouraging the team member to exaggerate a behavior or emotion they are struggling with. The manager-coach may ask the team member to act out the behavior or emotion exaggeratedly, such as speaking louder or making a more significant gesture. Exaggeration can help team members to become more self-aware and gain new insights into their behavior or emotions. Exaggeration can be particularly helpful for team members struggling with self-expression or assertiveness.
- **Awareness Dialogue.** The Awareness Dialogue is a technique used in the Gestalt approach to coaching that involves a conversation between the team member and their coach. The manager-coach asks the team member to describe their experiences, thoughts, and feelings in the present moment. The manager-coach then reflects on the team member's experience and invites them to explore their understandings further. The Awareness Dialogue can be particularly helpful for team members seeking a more exploratory coaching experience. Awareness Dialogue can help team members become more self-aware and develop greater insight into their experiences.

Existential Approach

The existential approach to coaching is based on the principles of existential philosophy, which emphasizes the importance of human freedom, choice, and responsibility. According to this approach, individuals are responsible for creating meaning and must confront their mortality.

Existential coaching focuses on the individual's personal experience of their situation and encourages them to take responsibility for their choices and actions. The manager-coach works with the team members to explore their values, beliefs, and assumptions and identify any existential challenges they may face. The manager-coach helps the team members develop strategies for addressing these challenges and creating a more meaningful and fulfilling life.

The existential approach to coaching is a powerful and effective tool for executives seeking more profound insights into themselves and their leadership styles. Focusing on their subjective experiences with their situation can help team members develop greater self-awareness, resilience, and authenticity.

One of the critical features of the existential approach to coaching is its focus on the present moment. The manager-coach helps the team member become more aware of their thoughts, feelings, and behaviors and recognize how they influence their leadership style. By developing this awareness, the executive can become more intentional and mindful in their actions and decision-making. Another critical aspect of the existential approach to coaching is its emphasis on authenticity. The manager-coach helps the team member explore their true selves and identify how they may present a false or inauthentic self to others. By developing greater self-awareness and authenticity, the team members can build more trusting and meaningful relationships with their colleagues and employees.

The existential approach to coaching is rooted in existentialism, which emphasizes the importance of individual freedom, responsibility, and the search for meaning and purpose in life. At its core, this approach recognizes that individuals have unique experiences, values, and beliefs that shape their worldview and their relationship to their work. To be effective, the manager-coach must understand and respect the team member's individuality and work with them to explore their purpose and meaning.

One of the fundamental principles of the existential approach is the idea that individuals have the power to create their reality. This means individuals can make choices and take actions that shape their lives and work. However, with this freedom comes responsibility. Individuals must take responsibility for the choices they make and the impact those choices have on their work and their relationships with others.

Another core principle of the existential approach is the belief that individuals are constantly in the process of becoming. This means that individuals continually evolve and change, and their sense of purpose and meaning in life is not fixed or predetermined. Instead, individuals must continuously re-examine their values and beliefs and work to align their actions with their evolving sense of purpose (Spinelli, 2018a).

Empirical Evidence

The existential approach to coaching is a powerful and effective tool for executives seeking more profound insights into themselves and their leadership styles. Growing evidence suggests that the existential approach to coaching can be highly effective in helping team members develop greater self-awareness, resilience, and authenticity. Focusing on the individual's subjective experience of their situation can help team members develop greater self-awareness, resilience, and authenticity.

Studies have indicated that engaging in existential coaching is associated with increased well-being and life satisfaction. Research by van Nieuwerburgh and Golsworthy (2016) explored the effects of existential coaching on participants' psychological well-being. The findings revealed that participants reported higher levels of life satisfaction and a greater sense of purpose after undergoing existential coaching interventions. A study by Yalom and Josselson (2010) demonstrated that participants who engaged in existential group coaching experienced a significant reduction in their levels of existential anxiety. This suggests that coaching interventions that target existential concerns can positively impact individuals' emotional well-being.

Existential coaching helps individuals clarify their values and goals, leading to improved decision-making and goal attainment. A study by Egan and Reynolds (2017) examined the effects of existential coaching on career decision-making. The results indicated that participants who underwent coaching reported a greater alignment between their career choices and personal values, resulting in increased job satisfaction and commitment. Empirical evidence suggests that existential coaching can positively impact work-related outcomes. In a study by van Nieuwerburgh (2012), employees who received existential coaching demonstrated improved job performance, increased motivation, and greater engagement in their work. This indicates that addressing existential concerns can create a more fulfilling and productive work environment. According to Krum (2012), existential coaching can reduce stress by helping clients understand that openness to experience is a way of gaining insight into their need for control.

One reason the existential approach to coaching may be practical is that it focuses on the individual's subjective experience of their situation. By helping the leaders explore their values, beliefs, and assumptions, the manager-coach can help them identify the underlying causes of any challenges they may face. This deeper self-awareness can help leaders make more meaningful and purposeful choices in their personal and professional lives.

The existential approach to coaching's emphasis on the present moment increases the team members' mindfulness and awareness, helping them become more intentional and purposeful in their actions and decisions. This can help them build more trusting and meaningful relationships with their colleagues and employees, positively impacting the organization's overall performance.

Benefits and Limitations

The existential approach to coaching has several benefits and limitations. First, the benefits include:

- **Improved Self-Awareness.** Team members can better understand their thoughts, feelings, and behaviors by engaging in reflective dialogue and mindfulness practices.
- **Increased Motivation.** By aligning their actions with their sense of purpose and meaning, team members are more likely to be motivated and engaged in their work.
- **Greater Authenticity.** By exploring existential themes such as authenticity, team members can develop a greater sense of authenticity and integrity in their work.
- **Improved Communication.** By creating a deeper understanding of their values and beliefs, team members can better communicate their ideas and perspectives to others.

- **Focus on the Present Moment.** The approach encourages clients to become more aware of their everyday experiences, which can help them gain a deeper understanding of their thoughts, feelings, and behaviors. Focusing on the present moment can help can identify patterns in behavior and thought processes that may limit personal growth. By working in the here and now, you can help team members become more aware of their habitual patterns of behavior and recognize the impact of these patterns on their lives and relationships.
- **Emphasis on the Team Member's Experience.** The approach recognizes that individuals have unique understandings of the world and that this experience shapes their thoughts, feelings, and behaviors. By exploring team members' experiences, the manager-coach can help them better understand their values, beliefs, and goals. This can help the team members make more informed decisions and take actions that align with their values and goals.

The existential approach to coaching has several limitations, including:
- **Limited Applicability.** The existential approach may not be suitable for all team members because it focuses on philosophical inquiry and abstract concepts. Research by George Yancy (2018) highlights that team members from diverse cultural backgrounds or those who prefer concrete, pragmatic problem-solving might find the existential approach bewildering or unproductive. The emphasis on introspection and philosophical reflection may alienate team members who require more practical guidance or have urgent, tangible issues to address.
- **Lack of Practical Framework.** One of the critical limitations of the existential approach is its relative lack of concrete techniques or structured methodologies. Unlike other coaching approaches that provide step-by-step processes or tools, the existential approach relies heavily on open-ended conversations and self-exploration. While this can foster creativity and self-discovery, it can lead to ambiguity and uncertainty in sessions. Gyllensten and Palmer (2017) argue that without a clear framework, manager-coaches might struggle to guide team members effectively through the coaching process, potentially leaving them feeling lost or frustrated.
- **Ethical Considerations.** Existential coaching often delves into deeply personal and existential questions, which can raise ethical concerns. As manager-coaches explore team members' values, beliefs, and fears, they may inadvertently trigger strong emotional reactions. Without proper training in managing these dynamics, manager-coaches might inadvertently cause distress or psychological harm to clients (Spinelli, 2018b). Respecting team members' emotional boundaries while encouraging self-exploration requires a delicate balance that necessitates advanced training and sensitivity.
- **Limited Evidence Base.** Compared to some other coaching approaches that have accumulated empirical support, the existential approach has a relatively narrow body of research demonstrating its effectiveness. While anecdotal evidence and

case studies abound, a dearth of rigorous empirical studies hinders the establishment of the approach's reliability and efficacy (Evers et al., 2006). This lack of empirical grounding might deter team members from seeking evidence-based practices and hinder the approach's credibility in professional coaching settings.

–   **Potential for Stagnation.** Existential coaching, focusing on exploring fundamental questions, might inadvertently lead team members into a spiral of rumination or analysis paralysis. While encouraging team members to confront existential concerns can be transformative, it also carries the risk of perpetuating negative thought patterns. Team members might become overly absorbed in their internal struggles without making tangible progress in their personal or professional lives (van Deurzen, 2016). This potential for stagnation requires manager-coaches to delicately balance exploration with action-oriented interventions.

Key Techniques and Interventions

The existential approach to coaching involves several techniques designed to help individuals explore their sense of purpose and meaning in life. These techniques include:

–   **Reflective Dialogue.** This involves deep, thoughtful conversations with team members to explore their values, beliefs, and experiences.

–   **Mindfulness.** This involves helping team members understand their thoughts, feelings, and behaviors better.

–   **Exploration of Existential Themes.** This involves exploring themes such as freedom, responsibility, authenticity, and mortality to help the team members understand their values and beliefs better.

–   **Goal Setting.** This involves working with the team members to set goals aligned with their sense of purpose and meaning.

Positive Psychology Approach

Positive psychology is the scientific study of human flourishing, focusing on the positive aspects of life, such as happiness, well-being, and personal growth (Seligman & Csikszentmihalyi, 2000). Seligman argued that psychology had traditionally focused on the negative aspects of human experiences, such as mental illness and pathology, and had neglected the positive elements, such as happiness, well-being, and human flourishing. He proposed that psychology shift its focus to positive attributes and experiences and explore ways to promote them. Positive psychology emphasizes the importance of positive emotions, positive relationships, and positive experiences in human life. It seeks to promote well-being and resilience rather than just treating pathology. The principles of positive psychology have been applied to various domains, such as education, healthcare, and business.

Positive psychology is a field of psychology that focuses on the strengths and positive attributes of individuals and aims to promote their well-being and flourishing. Coaching, on the other hand, is a process of helping individuals, particularly leaders and executives, improve their performance and achieve their goals. In coaching, positive psychology can help individuals identify and use their strengths, increase their resilience and optimism, and enhance their overall well-being and happiness. The positive psychology approach to coaching emphasizes using positive interventions and techniques to help individuals enhance their strengths, develop their potential, and overcome their limitations (Boniwell & Kauffman, 2018).

The positive psychology approach to coaching is based on the theoretical foundations of positive psychology, which emphasize the following key concepts:

- **Strengths and Virtues.** Positive psychology emphasizes identifying and developing an individual's strengths and virtues, such as courage, creativity, kindness, and wisdom. These attributes are key determinants of well-being and success, and manager-coaches using the positive psychology approach seek to help individuals identify and enhance their strengths. Strengths refer to the natural talents, abilities, and character traits individuals possess and can develop to improve their well-being and performance. The strengths-based approach to coaching focuses on identifying and building on an individual's strengths rather than fixing their weaknesses. Research has shown that strengths-based interventions can enhance subjective well-being, engagement, and performance (Seligman et al., 2005).

- **Positive Emotions.** Positive psychology recognizes the importance of positive emotions, such as joy, gratitude, and love, in promoting well-being and success. Positive emotions are important because they broaden one's thinking and attention, build social bonds, and increase resilience (Fredrickson, 2001). Manager-coaches using the positive psychology approach seek to help individuals cultivate positive emotions and use them to enhance their performance and achieve their goals.

- **Goal Setting and Achievement.** The positive psychology approach to coaching emphasizes the importance of setting goals aligned with an individual's values and strengths. Manager-coaches using this approach help individuals set challenging yet achievable goals and develop strategies. The focus is on promoting a sense of accomplishment and fulfillment.

- **Meaning and Purpose.** Positive psychology emphasizes the importance of having a sense of meaning and purpose in life and the role of these factors in promoting well-being and success. "Meaning" refers to understanding the purpose, significance, and coherence individuals derive from their lives. Manager-coaches using the positive psychology approach seek to help individuals identify their values and goals and develop a sense of purpose that will guide their actions and decisions. The meaning-based approach to coaching aims to help individuals identify their core values and goals and align their actions with their sense of purpose. Research has shown that individuals who perceive their lives as meaningful experience higher levels of well-being and lower levels of stress and depression (Steger et al., 2006).

- **Resilience.** Resilience refers to adapting and thriving in adversity, challenge, or trauma. Research has shown that resilience can be developed through various interventions, such as cognitive behavioral therapy, mindfulness, and positive emotion regulation (Southwick & Charney, 2012). Resilience-based coaching aims to help individuals develop the skills, attitudes, and resources necessary to overcome obstacles, manage stress, and maintain well-being.

Empirical Evidence

Numerous studies have examined the effectiveness of positive psychology coaching in enhancing individual well-being and performance. Several studies have found positive psychology coaching can improve well-being, including positive emotions, life satisfaction, and happiness. For example, research by Gander et al. (2013) found that positive psychology coaching significantly increased positive emotions, life satisfaction, and overall well-being compared to a control group.

Positive psychology coaching can help enhance resilience and coping skills. A study by Sin and Lyubomirsky (2009) found that positive psychology interventions significantly increased resilience and coping abilities compared to a control group. These findings suggest positive psychology coaching can help individuals develop the skills and resources to cope with stress and adversity.

In addition to these findings, positive psychology coaching has enhanced academic achievement. A study by Suldo et al. (2014) found that positive psychology coaching effectively improved academic achievement among middle school students. These findings suggest that positive psychology coaching can help individuals achieve their goals and aspirations by enhancing their performance.

Benefits and Limitations

The positive psychology approach to coaching has several benefits and limitations. First, the benefits include:

- **Strength-Based Approach.** The positive psychology approach to coaching focuses on an individual's strengths rather than weaknesses. This helps team members build on their strengths, resulting in greater self-awareness, self-confidence, and self-esteem.
- **Goal-Oriented.** Positive psychology coaching's goal orientation helps team members set specific, measurable, attainable, relevant, and time-bound goals. This approach enables team members to achieve their goals in a structured and focused way, which leads to increased motivation, productivity, and overall success.
- **Positive Emotions.** The science of positive emotions grounds the positive psychology approach to coaching. This approach helps team members cultivate positive emotions such as gratitude, joy, and hope, essential for overall well-being and happiness.

- **Resilience.** Positive psychology coaching helps team members develop resilience, the ability to bounce back from setbacks and adversity. This approach enables team members to develop coping strategies and skills that help them to navigate challenging situations.
- **Self-Awareness.** Understanding their emotions, thoughts, and behaviors helps team members develop self-awareness and the ability to identify their strengths and weaknesses—essential for personal growth and development.

The limitations of the positive psychology approach to coaching include the following:
- **Overemphasis on Positivity.** A positive psychology approach to coaching can sometimes overemphasize positivity and ignore negative emotions. This approach can be harmful as it can lead team members to suppress or deny negative emotions, leading to increased stress and anxiety.
- **Not suitable for Everyone.** A positive psychology approach to coaching may not be ideal for everyone, especially those with severe mental health issues. For these individuals, a more traditional approach to coaching that focuses on problem-solving may be more appropriate.
- **Limited Evidence-Based.** The positive psychology approach to coaching is relatively new, and there is limited research on its effectiveness. While some studies support the benefits of positive psychology coaching, more research is needed to validate its effectiveness.
- **Overemphasis on Individualism.** A positive psychology approach to coaching can sometimes overemphasize individualism and ignore the impact of social and cultural factors on an individual's well-being. This approach can be limiting, especially for individuals who come from collectivistic cultures.
- **Lack of Focus on Underlying Issues.** The positive psychology approach to coaching may not address the underlying issues causing a team member's problems. For example, if a team member is experiencing stress due to work-related matters, positive psychology coaching may not address the root cause of the stress.

Practical Applications

Manager-coaches can incorporate positive psychology into their practice in several ways. These approaches include:
- **Strength-Based Coaching.** This approach focuses on identifying and using an individual's strengths to achieve goals. The manager-coach works with team members to identify their strengths and find ways to use them to achieve their objectives.
- **Positive Emotion Coaching.** This approach focuses on increasing positive emotions such as gratitude, joy, and happiness. The manager-coach works with team members to identify the positive feelings they experience and find ways to increase these emotions in their daily lives.

- **Mindfulness Coaching.** This approach focuses on increasing mindfulness, which involves being present and aware of one's thoughts and feelings. The manager-coach works with team members to develop mindfulness practices such as meditation and deep breathing exercises.
- **Goal-setting Coaching.** This approach focuses on helping individuals set and achieve goals that are meaningful and aligned with their values. The manager-coach works with team members to identify their goals, develop a plan to achieve them, and monitor their progress.

Key Techniques and Interventions

The positive psychology approach to coaching incorporates various techniques and practices to enhance the individual's well-being and performance. Some of the standard procedures and methods include:

- **Gratitude.** Gratitude is a technique used in positive psychology coaching to help individuals focus on the positive aspects of their lives. It involves expressing gratitude for the things that one has and the people in one's life. The manager-coach helps the individual practice gratitude through various exercises, such as a gratitude journal. This technique involves writing down three things one is grateful for each day. Gratitude journaling has increased positive emotions, life satisfaction, and resilience (Emmons & McCullough, 2003).
- **Strengths Assessment.** This practice involves identifying and assessing one's natural talents and character strengths using standardized tools such as the Values in Action (VIA) Character Strengths Survey. Strengths are the positive qualities and characteristics that an individual possesses. Individuals can achieve their goals and well-being by identifying and using their strengths. The manager-coach helps individuals identify their strengths using various assessments and exercises, such as the VIA Character Strengths assessment (Peterson & Seligman, 2004). Once the individual has identified their strengths, the manager-coach helps them develop strategies to use these strengths to achieve their goals. Research has shown that focusing on strengths can lead to increased happiness, satisfaction with life, and improved performance (Seligman et al., 2005). Individuals can overcome challenges and achieve their goals more effectively by identifying and using their strengths. Strengths assessments have been found to enhance self-awareness, self-efficacy, and goal attainment (Biswas-Diener, et al., 2011).
- **Positive Imagery.** This technique involves creating mental images of positive experiences, such as success, achievement, and joy. Positive imagery has been found to increase positive emotions, self-confidence, and motivation.
- **Values Clarification.** This practice involves identifying and prioritizing core values and goals. Values clarification has increased well-being, life satisfaction, and meaning in life (Deci & Ryan, 2000, 2008).

– **Mindfulness.** Mindfulness is a technique used in positive psychology coaching to help individuals focus on the present moment and become more aware of their thoughts, feelings, and sensations. It involves paying attention to the present moment without judgment. The manager-coach helps the individual practice mindfulness through various exercises, such as meditation, deep breathing, and body scanning. By practicing mindfulness, individuals can reduce stress, improve their mood, increase emotional regulation, improve cognitive functioning, and increase their overall well-being. Research has shown that mindfulness can decrease stress levels (Baer, 2003).

– **Goal Setting.** Goal setting is a critical technique used in positive psychology coaching. It involves setting specific, measurable, achievable, relevant, and time-bound (SMART) goals that align with an individual's strengths, values, and purpose. The manager-coach helps individuals identify goals and break them down into actionable steps. The manager-coach also encourages the individual to visualize themselves achieving their goals and create a plan of action to help them get there. Research has shown that goal setting improves self-esteem, self-efficacy, and well-being (Gollwitzer & Sheeran, 2006). By establishing and achieving goals, individuals gain a sense of accomplishment and purpose, which can increase their motivation and self-confidence.

– **Positive Reframing.** Positive reframing is used in positive psychology coaching to help individuals change their perspective on adverse events or situations. It involves looking at a situation from a different angle and finding the positive aspects of it. The manager-coach helps the individual to reframe their negative thoughts by asking questions such as "What is the best possible outcome of this situation?" or "What can you learn from this experience?" By reframing negative thoughts, individuals can reduce stress, improve their mood, and increase their resilience. Research has shown positive reframing can improve coping skills, decrease stress levels, and increase overall well-being (Tugade & Fredrickson, 2004). By learning to reframe negative thoughts, individuals can overcome challenges and achieve their goals more effectively.

– **Resilience and Optimism.** Resilience is the ability to bounce back from adversity, while optimism is the belief that positive outcomes are possible. In executive coaching, resilience and optimism are essential for helping the executive overcome challenges and setbacks, and maintain a positive outlook. One way to promote resilience and optimism in executive coaching is through positive reframing. Positive reframing involves helping the executive to reframe negative situations in a positive light. For example, suppose the executive is facing a challenging project. In that case, the coach can help them see it as an opportunity for growth and development rather than a source of stress and anxiety.

Transactional Analysis Approach

The transactional analysis (TA) approach to coaching has gained attention recently due to its focus on helping individuals improve their communication skills and relationships. Eric Berne (1964; 1976) first introduced transactional analysis in the 1950s as a theory of personality and a system for understanding human behavior.

TA is based on the idea that individuals have three ego states—parent, adult, and child—and that these states interact in transactions with others. Each ego state has its thoughts, feelings, and behaviors, and individuals can move between these states depending on their situation. According to Berne, individuals develop their ego states through their early experiences with their caregivers. The parent ego state is based on the attitudes and behaviors of a person's parents or other authority figures. In contrast, the child-ego state is based on the feelings and behaviors of the individual as a child. The adult ego state is based on rational, objective thinking and is not influenced by past experiences.

Berne also proposed that people communicate through transactions that involve the exchange of messages between ego states. A transaction can either be complementary or crossed. A complementary transaction occurs when the response from one ego state is directed at the same ego state of the other person. A crossed transaction occurs when the answer is required at a different ego state of the other person.

TA also includes the concept of psychological games, which are patterns of behavior that people use to interact with others to get their needs met. Games are often based on unconscious beliefs or assumptions and can harm individuals and their relationships if not recognized and addressed (Berne, 1964).

Benefits and Limitations

The transactional analysis approach to coaching has several benefits and limitations. First, the benefits include:

1. **Improved Communication Skills.** Transactional analysis provides manager-coaches with a robust framework for understanding and improving communication. The concept of ego states (parent, adult, and child) helps individuals recognize their own communication patterns and those of their team members. Through TA, manager-coaches can learn to communicate more effectively by shifting between these ego states as appropriate. This enhanced communication fosters better understanding, reduces conflicts, and promotes a more cohesive work environment (Stewart & Joines, 1987).

2. **Enhanced Self-awareness.** Effective managerial coaching often begins with self-awareness. Transactional analysis encourages manager-coaches to analyze their own behavior, thoughts, and emotions through the lens of ego states. By identifying their own predominant ego states and understanding how these states influence their interactions with others, managers can make conscious efforts to

adopt a more productive and adaptable adult ego state. This heightened self-awareness can lead to improved decision-making, emotional intelligence, and overall leadership effectiveness (Lowe & Lowe, 2018).

3. **Conflict Resolution.** One strength Transactional analysis is its ability to address conflicts constructively. The concept of games in TA refers to repetitive and unproductive patterns of interaction. Manager-coaches can use TA coaching to identify these games in their team members and learn how to break these patterns. This approach fosters a culture of open and honest communication, which is crucial for resolving conflicts efficiently and maintaining a harmonious work environment (Stewart & Joines, 1987).

4. **Goal Setting and Achievement.** TA provides a structured framework for setting and achieving goals. The process of defining objectives, analyzing potential obstacles (such as script beliefs), and creating action plans aligns well with the coaching process. Manager-coaches can help your team members apply these concepts to set clear, achievable goals and monitor progress. TA's focus on understanding how past experiences shape current behaviors also aids in identifying and addressing self-limiting beliefs that may hinder goal attainment (Napper & Newton, 2018).

5. **Relationship Building.** TA emphasizes building positive and healthy relationships by fostering trust and open communication. Manager-coaches can use TA coaching to help their team members understand the impact of their behaviors and communication on relationships. This can lead to stronger, more collaborative teams and improve leaders' ability to create a supportive work environment. By recognizing and addressing issues related to the "script," which represents a person's life plan and decisions, managers can help team members overcome personal barriers to effective relationships (Stewart & Joines, 1987).

The limitations of the positive psychology approach to coaching include the following:

1. **Subjectivity and Interpretation.** Transactional analysis heavily relies on subjective interpretations of individuals' behaviors and communication patterns. What one person perceives as a parent ego state might be interpreted differently by someone else. This subjectivity can lead to misinterpretations and misunderstandings, making it challenging to apply TA consistently in coaching sessions.

2. **Complexity and Depth.** While TA offers a comprehensive framework for understanding human behavior, it can be quite complex and may require significant time and effort to fully grasp. Manager-coaches must invest substantial resources in training and development to effectively use TA in coaching. This complexity may deter some manager-coaches from adopting TA as their primary coaching approach (Stewart & Joines, 1987).

3. **Resistance to Change.** Manager-coaches who use TA may encounter resistance from team members who are not open to self-exploration and change. Some team members may find it uncomfortable or intrusive to delve into their past experien-

ces and question their deeply held beliefs and scripts. This resistance can hinder the effectiveness of TA-based coaching and may require additional strategies to overcome (Lowe & Lowe, 2018).

4. **Limited Applicability.** TA may not be suitable for all coaching scenarios. Its emphasis on self-awareness and communication skills may not address more complex issues such as organizational restructuring, strategic planning, or technical skill development. Manager-coaches must recognize when TA is appropriate and when other coaching approaches may be more effective (Napper & Newton, 2018).

5. **Lack of Scientific Validation.** While TA has gained popularity in coaching and therapy, it lacks the same level of empirical validation as some other psychological frameworks. The subjective nature of TA and the absence of extensive scientific research to support its efficacy can be a limitation for manager-coaches seeking evidence-based coaching methods.

Practical Applications

The TA approach to coaching focuses on helping individuals improve their communication skills and ability to build and maintain effective relationships with others. Manager-coaches using this approach work with team members to identify their ego states and how they interact with others in both positive and negative ways. They also help team members recognize their psychological games and work to develop more constructive and healthy ways of interacting with others.

One of the critical principles of TA coaching is the concept of "strokes," which are verbal or nonverbal expressions of recognition, appreciation, or attention from others (Berne, 1964). Strokes can be positive or negative, and individuals need both types of strokes to feel valued and validated. Manager-coaches using the TA approach help team members identify their stroke needs and work to develop strategies for getting the strokes they need in healthy and constructive ways (Widdowson, 2003).

Another fundamental principle of TA coaching is the concept of "life scripts," which are unconscious beliefs or assumptions individuals have about themselves and their lives. Life scripts are often based on early experiences and can be limiting or self-destructive if not recognized and addressed. Manager-coaches using the TA approach help team members identify their life scripts and work to develop new, more positive scripts that will help them achieve their goals and improve their relationships with others (Widdowson, 2003).

Key Techniques and Interventions

Coaching using the transactional analysis approach involves the coach and the team member exploring the team member's ego states and transactions. The manager-coach helps the team member understand their behavior patterns and how they affect their relationships with others. The manager-coach also helps the team member identify their basic psychological needs and how they can be met. The manager-coach works with the team members to develop strategies for healthily meeting their needs.

Using the transactional analysis approach, the first step in coaching is establishing a trusting relationship between the coach and the team member. The manager-coach creates a safe, nonjudgmental environment that encourages team members to share their experiences and feelings. The manager-coach then helps the team member identify their dominant ego state and how it affects their behavior and interactions with others.

The manager-coach also helps the team member identify their drivers, which are the unconscious beliefs and attitudes that influence their behavior. Drivers can be positive or negative, and they can either help or hinder the team member's personal and organizational growth. The manager-coach helps the team member understand their drivers and how they can be changed to promote personal and corporate growth.

Another aspect of coaching using the transactional analysis approach is helping the team member identify their basic psychological needs and how they can be met. As a manager-coach, you can help team members understand their need for recognition, stimulation, structure, intimacy, and autonomy. You can then work with team members to develop strategies for meeting these needs in healthy ways that promote personal and organizational growth.

The manager-coach also helps team members identify their life positions (basic beliefs that we hold about ourselves and others, which are used to justify our decisions and behaviors) and the unconscious beliefs about themselves and others that influence their behavior. Life positions can be positive or negative, and they can either help or hinder personal and organizational growth. The manager-coach helps the team member understand their life positions and how they can be changed to promote personal and corporate development (Berne, 1962).

The final aspect of coaching using the transactional analysis approach is helping team members develop practical communication skills. The manager-coach helps team members understand the different types of transactions and how they can be used to promote effective communication. The manager-coach also supports the team members to develop assertiveness skills that enable them to express their needs and opinions in a way that promotes personal and organizational growth.

Frameworks for Personal Response to Change

There are many approaches to personal and organizational change. We present three approaches and apply them to coaching individuals and teams. The first is William Bridges' (1991, 2000) model of how individuals experience transitions due to change. The second is Rick Maurer's (1996, 2002) approach to how individuals experience resistance to change. The third adapts a change mastery model developed by Bennett & Bush (2014).

Transitions

Change is an inevitable process in any organization or individual's life. The ability to manage change is crucial to the success of any enterprise. The William Bridges (1991, 2000) model of change has gained significant popularity in recent years, particularly in coaching. This model provides a framework for understanding change's emotional and psychological impact on individuals and organizations.

The Bridges model of change is a three-stage process describing the emotional and psychological transition individuals and organizations experience when facing change. These three stages are:

1. **Ending, Losing, and Letting Go.** This stage involves acknowledging the need for change and letting go of the old ways. This stage is critical because it allows individuals to let go of the old ways and embrace the new. It is essential to recognize what is ending and acknowledge the emotions and feelings associated with the loss.
2. **The Neutral Zone.** In this stage, individuals are in limbo, neither fully in the old nor the new way. This stage can be confusing and disorienting, but it is also a stage of great potential. It is an opportunity to explore new possibilities and ways of doing things.
3. **The New Beginning.** This stage involves embracing the new way fully. It is a time of renewed energy and enthusiasm as individuals and organizations begin to reap the benefits of the change.

This model of change emphasizes the importance of acknowledging and addressing the emotional and psychological impact of change. By recognizing change's emotional and psychological aspects, individuals and organizations can better manage the transition and make the change successful. The Bridges model of change is highly applicable to coaching, which involves helping individuals navigate change and achieve their goals. The model provides a framework for manager-coaches to understand change's emotional and psychological impact on their team members.

You can help your team members navigate the three stages of change and make the transition successful in these ways:

1. **Acknowledge and Address Loss.** Manager-coaches can help their team members acknowledge and address the emotions and feelings associated with loss. This involves helping team members understand what is ending and why letting go of the old ways is essential. By addressing the loss, team members can let go of the old and embrace the new. In coaching, the ending phase involves helping individuals identify and acknowledge what they are losing due to the change. This may include exploring the emotions associated with the loss and supporting the individual to come to terms with it. For example, a manager-coach may help an employee being laid off identify what they are losing, such as job security, routine, and colleagues. By acknowledging these losses, the team member can begin to

work through the emotions associated with them and prepare for the next phase of the transition process.

2. **Embrace the Neutral Zone.** Manager-coaches can help team members explore new possibilities and ways of doing things during the neutral zone. This stage can be disorienting and confusing, but it is also a stage of great potential. Manager-coaches can help their team members see the opportunities and possibilities in this stage and make the most of them. In coaching, the neutral zone involves assisting individuals in exploring new options and opportunities due to the change. For example, a manager-coach may help a promoted individual explore the new responsibilities and challenges of the new role. By exploring these possibilities, the individual can see the change as an opportunity for growth and development.

3. **Embrace the New Beginning.** Manager-coaches can help their team members fully embrace the new way of doing things. This involves helping team members overcome any resistance or fear of the latest change and helping them see the benefits of the change. In coaching, the new beginning consists of helping individuals implement the changes and develop new habits and routines. For example, a manager-coach may help an individual who has moved to a new city develop new social connections and practices. Implementing these changes makes the individual feel more comfortable and settled in the new environment.

Research has shown that the model of change effectively controls change's emotional and psychological impact. By acknowledging and addressing change's emotional and psychological aspects, individuals and organizations can better manage the transition and make the change successful. Bridges' model of change has been widely applied in coaching to guide individuals through transitions by providing a structured and supportive environment for team members to navigate change successfully. The model offers a framework for understanding individuals' emotional and psychological processes during transition and provides a roadmap for navigating these processes well.

Change Resistance

Change is an inevitable aspect of life, and organizations must continually adapt to changing conditions to survive and thrive. However, change can be challenging to implement, and resistance to change is expected. Rick Maurer's (1996; 2002) model of change resistance and coaching offers a helpful framework for understanding and addressing opposition to change. Maurer's Model of Change Resistance is applied to five types of resistance to change. These types of resistance are interdependent and can be present in different combinations and degrees, depending on the context of the change initiative. The five types of resistance are:

1. **Logical/Cognitive Resistance.** Logical resistance is based on a rational analysis of the change initiative and the belief that it will not be successful or beneficial.

This type of resistance is expressed through questions or objections that challenge the rationale behind the change. To address logical resistance, you should engage individuals and teams in a dialogue that focuses on the rational analysis of the change initiative. Manager-coaches should encourage team members and groups to ask questions, voice concerns about the change, and provide evidence supporting the rationale for the difference.

2. **Emotional Resistance.** Emotional resistance is based on feelings of fear, anxiety, or other negative emotions associated with the change. This type of resistance is often expressed through statements or behaviors that indicate a lack of confidence or enthusiasm for the change. To address emotional resistance, coaches should help individuals and teams to acknowledge and manage their emotions. You should encourage individuals and teams to express their feelings and provide a safe space. Manager-coaches should also offer support and encouragement to help individuals and teams manage their emotions.

3. **Behavioral Resistance.** Behavioral resistance is another common barrier to change. People may have developed habits and routines that are difficult to break, or they may resist new ways of doing things. This can be particularly challenging in organizations with a culture of resistance to change. Manager-coaches need to help team members develop new habits and routines to overcome behavioral resistance. This may involve training or coaching to help people learn new skills, or incentives or rewards to encourage people to adopt new behaviors. Manager-coaches must also be prepared to provide ongoing support and feedback to help people stay on track.

4. **Cultural Resistance.** Cultural resistance is based on the values, norms, and beliefs of the organization or team and the perceived threat that the change poses to these cultural elements. This type of resistance is often expressed through resistance to changing established processes, procedures, and working methods. To address cultural resistance manager-coaches should help individuals and teams understand and appreciate the values, norms, and beliefs underpinning the organizational or team's culture.

5. **Systemic Resistance.** Systemic resistance is perhaps the most challenging resistance to change. This refers to the organizational structures and processes that may hinder change efforts. For example, an organization may have rigid hierarchies, siloed departments, or outdated systems that make it challenging to implement new initiatives. Manager-coaches need to work with organizational leaders to identify and address the underlying issues to overcome systemic resistance. This may involve redesigning processes or structures, providing training or coaching to help people adapt to new working methods, or even changing the organization's culture. Manager-coaches must be prepared to work at all levels of the organization, from frontline workers to senior leaders, to ensure that change efforts are successful.

Maurer's model suggests that resistance to change is a natural response to the disruption and uncertainty that change can bring. However, the model also suggests that resistance can be overcome through coaching that addresses each type. Coaching to overcome resistance to change can be a practical approach to overcoming resistance to change, as it enables individuals and teams to identify and address the root causes of resistance. Based on Maurer's model, coaching interventions can be designed to address each type of resistance.

Change Mastery Model

Pursuing successful personal change is a progressive process that predictably follows five stages: awareness, acceptance, adoption, integration, and mastery. The stages are outlined in the Change Mastery Model (See Figure 3.1), an adaptation of the Bennett and Bush (2014) Mastery Model. A goal of all coaching should be to help the person being coached to develop mastery.

The goal of moving through these stages of change is broader than successfully dealing with any change—the goal is developing the individual, team, and organization's capacity to change. This is a more general, visionary, and strategic concept than just "change management," It requires an acceptance of change as the "new normal," employs interventions at multiple levels and requires a longer timeframe. Building change capacity must become an ongoing, multifaceted development focus. Meyer and Stensaker (2006) define change capacity as three interrelated capabilities: to maintain daily operations, to implement a single change, and to implement subsequent changes. They argue that "the capability to effect strategic change is a core dynamic capability" and that building change-capable organizations should be a significant priority (p. 7). Developing this capacity can mean a competitive advantage and differentiation in the market.

Team members going through coaching and change experience a similar process moving through these five stages. An individual will move through the stages of the Change Mastery Model during a successful coaching engagement, and it is possible to see evidence of these stages, explained in further detail below, occurring during group and organizational change. With the focus on coaching individuals and teams, not organizational change, this description of the model will be limited to individuals. A similar approach can be taken when developing a team or organization's capacities for change. This involves moving from being unconsciously incompetent to consciously incompetent to consciously competent to unconsciously competent (Howell, 1982). Figure 3.1 illustrates that mastery requires awareness, acceptance, adoption, and integration.

Awareness: Team members know that a change is imminent, planned, or needed. There is often shock, confusion, and concern at this time, especially if the change is perceived as a threat or mandated without the individuals' choice. Reactions occur on at least three levels:

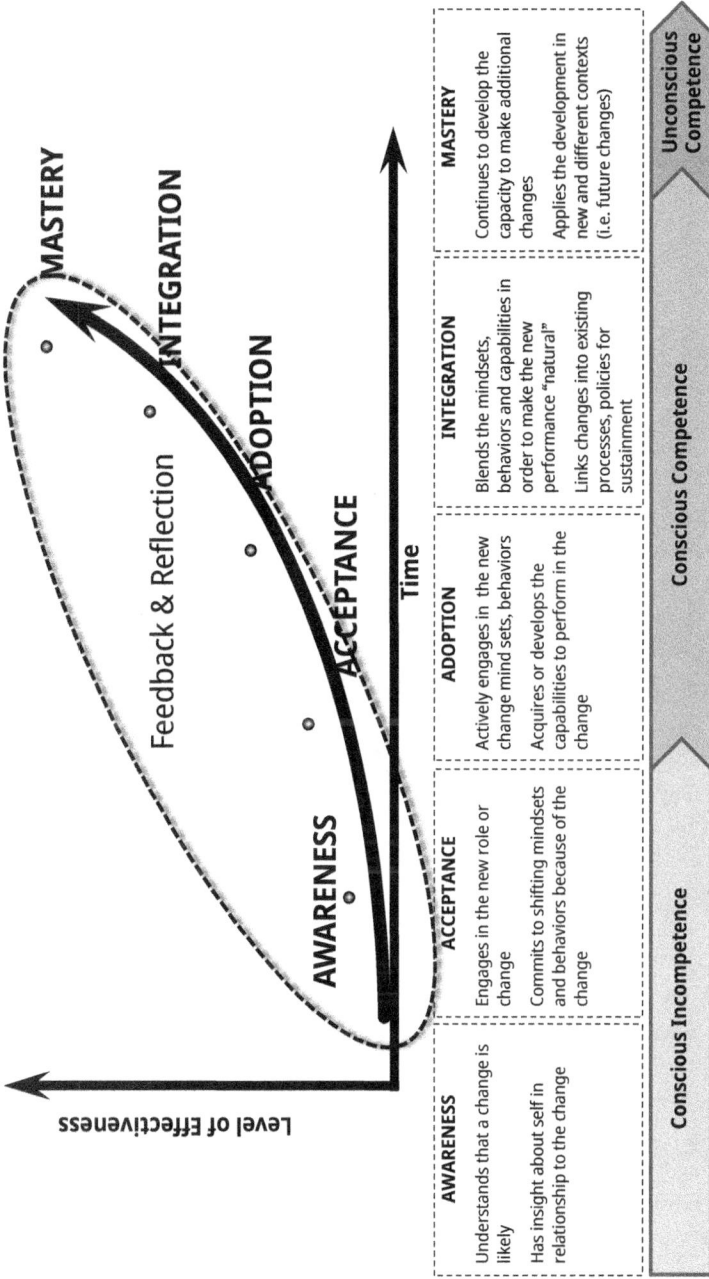

Figure 3.1: Change Mastery Model.

- *Cognitive*, as team members become aware of what the change will mean to them and how they work or live.
- *Practical*, as team members realize the impact the change will make on the structures, relationships, rewards, goals, and processes that have meaning for them.
- *Behavioral*, as team members understand what the change will mean to the way they work and interact in the organization.

In this stage, people may seek information or clarity about the change. They need to understand what it will mean to them and how it will affect how they work and interact with others. Prochaska (2018) posits a prior stage of change for individuals, that of "pre-contemplation," where an individual is not yet aware of the need to change or is in denial.

Acceptance. Team members make peace with the change and explore what the change will mean to them—including how to make the transition successful. There may still be concerns, confusion, and skepticism, but the intention and attitude shift from "Why should we do this?" to "How can we make this successful?" This stage can manifest on three levels:
- *Cognitive*, as team members learn more about what the change is about, what it will mean, and the impact it will have on the organization and themselves.
- *Affective*, as team members commit to shifting their mindsets and behaviors to support the change, perhaps while still having concerns or questions.
- *Behavioral*, as team members engage in the new way of working, try it out, adjust to make the change work, ask questions and voice concerns, and offer feedback and suggestions for improvement.

Adoption. In this stage, team members actively engage in the new mindsets, behaviors, and interactions that support the change. They acquire or develop the capabilities to perform in new ways and often help others understand and make the needed changes. They act as advocates for the change and give feedback to help improve and develop the change, which can be manifest on three levels:
- *Cognitive*, as team members learn more about what the change is about, what it will mean, and how it will impact how they work and interact with others.
- *Affective*, as team members commit to shifting their mindsets and behaviors to support the change, perhaps while they still have concerns or apprehensions.
- *Behavioral*, as individuals engage in new roles, new behaviors, vocabulary, and interactions, ask questions, and offer feedback, concerns, and alternative suggestions for improvement to make the change successful.

Integration: Team members have become used to working and interacting in a new way, and often, there are results or accomplishments to show from the change that has been implemented. What was once the "new" change has been linked to organizational processes and culture to ensure it is not seen as new. The change has been embedded into existing structures, systems, and techniques so that it is part of how the organization operates and does not depend on current leadership to drive it. The organizational culture now sustains the change—it is now "the way we do things around here." This stage exists on three levels:

- *Cognitively*, as team members master the mindsets, behaviors, and capabilities to make the new change "natural," they do not need to think about the transition to perform or interact successfully in a new way.
- *Affectively*, believing that the change is a positive step forward, "part of the culture; the way things are done around here."
- *Behaviorally*, performing in a new way without needing to think about it; finding ways to link changes to existing processes and policies in order to sustain the changes.

Mastery: Team members continue integrating the change into other personal and organizational levels, perhaps with additional teams, external suppliers, or other business units. They also build increased agility and resilience, demonstrating an improved capacity to make further changes. They demonstrate agility, reflective practices, experimentation with innovative approaches, apply seemingly unrelated experiences to resolve new challenges, continue seeking to learn from experiences and demonstrate skills gracefully. This stage exists on three levels:

- *Cognitive*, as team members understand the benefits of being agile, flexible, and resilient, and identify ways to change a personal and organizational differentiator.
- *Affective*, as team members embrace change positively as an ongoing, challenging part of organizational life and demonstrate skills and knowledge to make change a personal and corporate competency.
- *Behavioral*, as team members develop skills in making and integrating changes, demonstrating increased agility, flexibility, and resilience, and applying this development to change in new and different contexts (i.e., future changes).

Feedback and Reflection. In the context of developing toward mastery, feedback and reflection are ways for team members to increase self-awareness and progress through the steps toward mastery. Feedback is data about past behaviors offered in the present. It is intended to reinforce or alter behaviors. There are many sources of feedback, including internal responses, observations of impacts against intentions, and responses from others. In the context of the coaching conversation, manager-coaches can and should provide feedback to team members on an ongoing basis and during coaching sessions. Your feedback can be the entry into a coaching conversation, or you may give it during a coaching conversation. Team members should reflect on experiences and feedback to make meaning and determine what additional actions may be appropriate as they seek to achieve their goals for performance, development, or transformation and develop mastery. Chapter 6 provides specific guidance on when and how to provide feedback.

Mutual Learning

Coaching is a process where a coach guides, motivates, and inspires an individual or a team to achieve their goals by unlocking their full potential. It involves using a structured approach to guide people toward positive changes in their personal or professional lives. Manager-coaches act as facilitators, helping team members identify their goals, develop a plan of action, and overcome obstacles hindering their progress. The coaching process is based on mutual trust, respect, and collaboration between the manager-coach and the team member. The success of coaching depends on the ability of the manager-coach to establish effective communication and build a positive relationship with the team members. One way to achieve this is by applying Roger Schwarz's (2013a, 2013b) mutual learning model. This model provides a framework for effective communication, problem-solving, and decision-making that can be used in coaching to enhance the coaching process.

The mutual learning model emphasizes the importance of mutual learning and communication in coaching. Unfortunately, most leaders use a unilateral control mindset and behaviors under pressure. Unilateral control involves values such as win, don't lose; be right; act rational; and minimize expressions of negative feelings. A person using this approach is likely to state their views without asking for the opinions of others, withhold relevant information, speak in general terms without gaining agreement on what important words mean, keep their reasoning private and not ask others about their reason, focus on positions over interests, act on tested assumptions and inferences, work to control conversations, and work to avoid or ease into complicated issues. These behaviors have many negative results, such as lower-quality decisions, increased costs, a lower commitment by others, reduced learning, unproductive conflict, reduced motivation, limited development opportunities, and increased stress. (Schwarz, 2013a, 2013b)

Model of Mutual Learning

The mutual learning model is based on the principles of systems thinking, emotional intelligence, and the theory of action. According to Schwarz (2013a, 2013b), mutual learning is a collaborative problem-solving process where individuals work together to generate solutions that benefit everyone involved. Mutual learning requires an open mindset, curiosity, and a willingness to listen and learn from others. In coaching, mutual learning involves the manager-coach and team members working together to achieve the desired goals.

The mutual learning model comprises these values:

1. **Transparency.** Individuals openly share their perspectives, beliefs, and assumptions.
2. **Curiosity.** Individuals ask questions to understand each other's perspectives and to seek new information.
3. **Free and Informed Choice.** This involves making decisions based on available data and ensuring that all parties can make decisions that align with their values and goals.
4. **Accountability.** This ensures that all parties are committed to the decisions and take ownership of the outcomes.
5. **Compassionate Interactions Involve.** Showing empathy and understanding toward others and maintaining positive relationships even under challenging situations.

The mutual learning model employs eight behaviors:

1. State views and ask genuine questions.
2. Share all relevant information.
3. Use specific examples and agree on what important words mean.
4. Explain reasoning and intent.
5. Focus on interests, not positions.
6. Test assumptions and inferences.
7. Jointly design next steps.
8. Discuss undiscussable issues.

Benefits of Mutual Learning in Coaching

The mutual learning model has several benefits for coaching. Some of the benefits are:

1. **Improved Problem-Solving.** Mutual learning fosters collaborative problem-solving, which leads to more effective and sustainable solutions. By working together, manager-coaches and team members can generate solutions considering all perspectives and interests.
2. **Enhanced Communication.** Mutual learning promotes open and honest communication, which improves the manager-coach/team member relationship. When team members feel comfortable sharing their thoughts and ideas, they are more likely to be receptive to feedback and guidance from their manager-coach. By being transparent and empathetic, you can create a safe and supportive environment for your team members.
3. **Increased Accountability.** Mutual learning promotes internal commitment to decisions, which leads to greater responsibility. When team members take ownership of their goals and actions, they are more likely to be motivated and committed to achieving them.

4. **Increased Self-awareness.** Mutual learning encourages team members to reflect on their beliefs, assumptions, and values, which enhances their self-awareness. By understanding themselves better, team members can make more informed decisions and take actions that align with their goals and values.

Strategies for Applying Mutual Learning in Coaching

Manager-coaches can use several strategies to apply the mutual learning model to coaching to create an environment that fosters mutual learning. Here are some of them:

1. **Create a Safe Space for Open Communication.** One of the critical principles of the mutual learning model is the importance of creating a safe space for open communication. Manager-coaches can achieve this by actively listening to their team members, acknowledging their feelings, and responding with compassion and understanding. In coaching, this means creating an environment where team members feel comfortable sharing their thoughts and ideas without fear of judgment or retribution.

2. **Focus on Valid Information.** The mutual learning model emphasizes the importance of correct information. Coaching means ensuring team members access accurate and relevant information to help them make informed decisions. Manager-coaches can achieve this by conducting research, gathering data, and providing team members with feedback that is both constructive and actionable.

3. **Encourage Free and Informed Choice.** The mutual learning model emphasizes the importance of promoting free and informed choice. Manager-coaches can achieve this by asking open-ended questions, exploring various options with their team members, and helping them make choices that align with their values and goals. In coaching, this means helping team members develop a plan of action tailored to their individual needs and circumstances.

4. **Foster Internal Commitment.** The mutual learning model also emphasizes fostering internal commitment. Coaching means helping clients develop a sense of ownership and accountability for their goals and actions. Manager-coaches can achieve this by encouraging team members to set goals that are meaningful and achievable and by helping them develop a plan of action that is realistic and sustainable.

5. **Active Listening.** Manger-coaches must listen to their team members to understand their perspectives and experiences. Active listening involves paying attention to verbal and nonverbal cues, asking open-ended questions, and paraphrasing to ensure understanding.

6. **Clarify Assumptions and Beliefs.** Manager-coaches must help team members explain assumptions and ideas that may limit their thinking or decision-making. This involves asking probing questions to uncover underlying assumptions and challenging them when necessary.

7. **Encourage Multiple Perspectives.** Manager-coaches can encourage their team members to consider various perspectives when problem-solving. This involves exploring different viewpoints and brainstorming solutions that benefit all parties.

8. **Promote Transparency.** Manager-coaches must be transparent about team members' intentions, strategies, and limitations. This involves being honest and open about what can and cannot be achieved through coaching.

9. **Provide Feedback.** Manager-coaches must give feedback to their team members to help them improve their performance and achieve their goals. This involves providing specific and actionable feedback based on observation and evidence.

Application of the Mutual Learning Model in Coaching

The model of mutual learning has several implications for coaching. Manager-coaches can apply the four elements of the model to enhance communication, problem-solving, and decision-making in coaching.

1. **Transparency.** Transparency is essential in coaching as it helps build trust and respect between the manager-coach and team members. Transparency promotes honesty, openness, and accountability, which are crucial for a successful coaching relationship. Manager-coaches should encourage team members to be transparent by openly sharing their thoughts, feelings, and concerns. Manager-coaches should also share their perspectives and feedback with the team members.

2. **Curiosity.** Curiosity is another critical element in coaching. Manager-coaches should encourage team members to ask questions to better understand each other's perspectives. Curiosity helps coaches and team members gain new insights and information they might not have considered before. Asking questions also shows a willingness to learn and grow, which is an essential component of coaching.

3. **Informed Advocacy.** Informed advocacy is the presentation of an individual's views and opinions based on their knowledge and expertise. Informed advocacy promotes critical thinking, problem-solving, and decision-making. It also allows team members to take ownership of their learning and development. Manager-coaches should encourage team members to present their views and opinions based on their knowledge and expertise.

4. **Reflection.** Reflection considers feedback and alternative perspectives. Manager-coaches should encourage team members to reflect on their experiences and feedback to gain new insights and learning. Reflection helps team members become more self-aware and develop a growth mindset. It also promotes continuous learning and development.

Summary

Coaching is grounded in many traditions and theoretical frameworks. Cognitive behavioral, solution-focused, gestalt, existential, positive psychology, and transactional analytic are six approaches that may be most useful for manager-coaches. The discussion of techniques, applications, benefits, and limitations of each framework provide perspectives that help manager-coaches understand approaches they could use as they develop their coaching skills.

Frameworks for responding to personal change can also be applied to coaching. Change is inevitable, and helping individuals manage change is essential to the organization's success. The Bridges model of change is a three-stage process:

1. Ending, Losing, and Letting Go.
2. The Neutral Zone.
3. The New Beginning.

The Change Mastery Model's goal is developing the individual, team, and organization's capacity to change. The Model of Mutual Learning describes values that the manager-coach and team member apply to working together.

Chapter 4
Use of Self in Managerial Coaching

Yesterday, I was clever, so I wanted to change the world. Today, I am wise, so I'm changing myself.
— Rumi

The concept of "use of self" has gained prominence in various professional fields that involve helping individuals navigate complex challenges and achieve personal growth. Professionals such as coaches, counselors, social workers, and leaders increasingly recognize the importance of their subjectivity in facilitating meaningful and transformative interactions with team members or employees, peers, and more senior managers. While use of self may be associated with psychotherapy and counseling, it extends to many professional fields. For instance, manager-coaches leverage their personal experiences to empathize with team members and facilitate growth. Social workers incorporate subjectivity to build rapport and understand team members' needs (Miehls & Moffatt, 2000). Leaders and managers use their values and beliefs to inspire and guide their teams. This chapter focuses on the use of self in the context of managerial coaching.

Central to effective managerial coaching is the concept of use of self, where manager-coaches draw upon their personal experiences, values, and behaviors to create a positive and effective coaching relationship with their team members to facilitate meaningful development in their team members. The use of self refers to deliberately and strategically incorporating your personal experiences, emotions, beliefs, values, and perspectives into the professional practice of coaching and managing. The two parts of the use of self are "self" and "use." "Self" is who we are. The self is the "centralizing process" that unifies the consciousness and unconsciousness in a person (Jung, 1974). Self is accumulating and distilling all experiences, lessons, talents, preferences, culture, and more. The available portion of the totality can change as experience and perspective are added, and the subconscious becomes conscious. There is more "self" available to a person than they are now or know themselves to be. Therefore, the use of self suggests an ongoing, expanding development process. "Use" is what we do with self —skills, knowledge, perspective, feelings, etc. Use of self emerges from awareness of self and by taking action (Berthoud & Bennett, 2020).

Manager-coaches are not neutral observers, but active participants whose subjectivity can profoundly influence their interactions with team members and others they serve. The use of self refers to a manager-coach's ability to effectively leverage their own experiences, emotions, and perspectives to facilitate coaching sessions. Coaching, as a process, involves a manager-coach helping team members achieve their goals, improve workplace performance, enhance leadership effectiveness, improve personal growth, and overcome obstacles. In coaching and mentoring, using self is instrumental in building rapport, fostering trust, and facilitating team members' self-discovery (Rostron, 2009). Coaches often share relevant personal experiences, insights, and reflections

https://doi.org/10.1515/9783111002415-004

to connect with team members and illustrate concepts. Authenticity and empathy are critical drivers of effective coaching relationships. In leadership and management roles, influential leaders recognize that their use of self can inspire and motivate their teams. Leaders who openly communicate their values and vision and authentically engage with employees foster a sense of purpose and commitment. The use of self can bridge the gap between leaders and team members, promoting collaboration and shared goals.

This chapter discusses the importance of using self, its impact on coaching relationships, and strategies for enhancing the use of self. It explores the multifaceted dimensions of using self in managerial coaching by examining its significance, challenges, and ethical considerations. It explains how the self can be harnessed to drive positive organizational outcomes. It also explores the importance of the coach's use of self, its associated challenges, and the ethical considerations that must be upheld. Drawing from various coaching models and contemporary research, this chapter explains how effectively using one's self can foster positive managerial outcomes.

The Foundation of Use of Self

Several theoretical frameworks contribute to our understanding of the use of self in coaching, including person-centered, psychodynamic, and constructivist approaches. Carl Rogers' (1980) person-centered approach emphasizes empathetic understanding, unconditional positive regard, and congruence in the manager-coach's interactions with the team member. This approach underlines the importance of the manager-coach's authentic and empathetic presence in fostering an environment that is conducive for coaching. Managers who adopt this approach recognize that their genuine presence and compassionate understanding are powerful tools for building trust and facilitating team members' self-exploration.

The psychodynamic perspective suggests that manager-coaches' unconscious biases, transference, and countertransference dynamics can influence coaching interactions (Gyllensten & Palmer, 2006). Managers are encouraged to examine their emotional responses and prejudices, which may provide valuable insights into team members' dynamics. Acknowledging and managing countertransference contributes to a deeper understanding of team members' experiences. Recognizing and addressing these dynamics is vital for effective use of self in coaching.

Constructivist theories emphasize the co-construction of meaning between manager-coach and team members and inherently incorporate the concept of using self. In constructivist approaches, the manager-coach is viewed as actively participating in the team member's meaning-making process. Manager-coaches adapt their communication and interventions based on their understanding of the team member's unique perspective, highlighting the dynamic nature of the use of self.

Effective use of self can lead to several positive outcomes in coaching, including enhanced self-awareness, improved problem-solving skills, increased motivation, and greater self-efficacy. It can also contribute to establishing a robust relationship between manager-coach and team member that is characterized by trust and authenticity. Conversely, ineffective use of self, such as imposing one's values or judgments, can hinder the team member's progress and damage the coaching relationship (Peltier, 2001).

In Abraham Maslow's (1943, 1954) Theory of Self-Actualization, he conceives becoming who you are as something gained after essential needs are met. It is premature to strive for self-actualization when the needs for self-esteem and belonging are wanting. Likewise, self-esteem and belonging are unimportant when you're unsafe, or your body is not cared for.

Carl Jung, the psychoanalyst, referred to a similar journey of becoming who you are as individuation. Jungian psychology sees the self as many things, including psychic structure, developmental process, transcendental postulate, affective experience, and archetype. The self "has been depicted as the totality of body and mind, the God-image, the experience of overpowering feelings, the union of opposites and a dynamic force which pilots the individual on his/her journey through life" (Schmidt, 2023, n.p.). Individuation describes how this agency works. Jung saw it as the process of self-realization, the discovery and experience of meaning and purpose in life. This is how team members find themselves and become who they are.

Coaching can be seen as an individuation process. It fosters and accelerates individuation, and it creates conditions in the relationship between team members and manager-coach that offer the possibility for experiences and self-transformation, which otherwise may not happen. This is because the coaching allows both the team member and manager-coach to join in a quest for the truth, to express and experience the self in ways often prohibited by the compromises made in the service of social acceptance in other professional contexts and relationships (Society of Analytical Psychology).

Seashore, et al. (2004) suggest that using the self involves self-differentiation of the unconscious to the conscious about behavior styles and patterns, habits, defenses, and needs. This allows for deliberate choices about actions, which is the use of self. Use of self can be effective in many endeavors, including leadership, facilitation, development of others, and leading change, as well as in one's own ongoing growth and development.

From a practical perspective, using self requires self-awareness, trust, authenticity and vulnerability, empathy and emotional intelligence, personal values and beliefs, cultural sensitivity and inclusion, and balancing self-disclosure.

Self-Awareness

Self-awareness is the cornerstone of effective use of self in coaching. Manager-coaches must deeply understand their values, beliefs, biases, emotions, and triggers. This self-awareness allows manager-coaches to recognize when their reactions or judgments may affect the coaching process (Bachkirova, 2011). Self-awareness forms the bedrock of effective use of self. Manager-coaches must engage in ongoing self-reflection to gain insight into their values, beliefs, biases, and emotional responses. This process of self-examination allows manager-coaches to recognize how their subjectivity may impact their interactions with team members.

Once manager-coaches know their emotional responses and biases, they must practice self-regulation. This involves managing emotions and reactions, particularly in situations that conflict with the team member's perspectives or values. Self-regulation ensures that the coaching focuses on the team member's needs and objectives.

Manager-coaches can employ various self-management strategies to enhance their use of self. These strategies may include mindfulness practices, journaling, peer supervision, and seeking feedback from team members or colleagues. By continually monitoring and refining their use of self, manager-coaches can improve their effectiveness and maintain a team-member-centered approach. Self-regulation, an integral component of self-awareness, entails managing one's emotions, reactions, and biases during professional interactions. As conceptualized by Daniel Goleman (1995), emotional intelligence encompasses recognizing, understanding, and managing emotions —both one's own and those of others. Manager-coaches with high emotional intelligence are better equipped to navigate the emotional terrain of use of self, especially in emotionally charged situations.

Appendix B is a questionnaire that can be used to assess your self-awareness. Based on the work of Sutton (2016), this questionnaire can be used as a tool to focus on the ongoing development of the use of self.

Trust

Trust is the linchpin of the relationship between manager-coach and team member and is a critical aspect of the effective use of self (Hawkins & Smith, 2013). Team members must trust that their manager-coach has their best interests at heart and that the coaching relationship is a safe space for exploration and growth. Manager-coaches build trust through authenticity, consistency, and confidentiality. Rapport is an integral part of trust-building. Manager-coaches must establish rapport by actively listening, demonstrating empathy, and showing genuine interest in team members' perspectives. Rapport fosters open communication and encourages team members to share their thoughts and feelings more freely.

Authenticity and Vulnerability

Authenticity is a crucial component of the effective use of self. Manager-coaches who are authentic in their interactions with team members create a sense of genuineness and transparency that encourages team members to be open and vulnerable in return. However, manager-coaches must balance authenticity and professionalism to maintain appropriate boundaries.

Empathy and Emotional Intelligence

Empathy is a central element of the use of self in coaching. Manager-coaches need to develop a deep understanding of their team members' emotions, perspectives, and experiences. Empathy enables coaches to connect with team members emotionally and demonstrate that they genuinely care about the team member's well-being and growth. Empathy in using self involves recognizing the team member's emotions and conveying understanding and support. Manager-coaches can employ active listening, paraphrasing, and nonverbal cues to demonstrate empathy. When team members feel heard and understood, it paves the way for deeper self-reflection and growth. Emotional intelligence, as coined by Daniel Goleman, encompasses the ability to recognize, understand, and manage one's emotions and the emotions of others (Goleman, 1995; Goleman, et al., 2002). Manager-coaches with high emotional intelligence are better equipped to navigate the emotional terrain of coaching conversations and respond empathetically to team member's needs (Schutte et al., 2009).

Personal Values and Beliefs

Manager-coaches must also grapple with their values and beliefs, which can influence their professional practice (Corey et al., 2015). Being mindful of their values allows manager-coaches to avoid imposing their ideas on team members, respecting their autonomy and unique perspectives. Manager-coaches should balance remaining true to their values and being open to the diversity of values they encounter.

Cultural Sensitivity and Inclusivity

In today's diverse workplaces, manager-coaches must be culturally competent to use themselves effectively. Cultural competence involves an awareness of cultural differences and biases and adapting coaching approaches to accommodate team members from various backgrounds (Sue et al., 2009). Not acknowledging and respecting cultural nuances can lead to misunderstandings and hinder coaching effectiveness. Manager-coaches must be vigilant about their biases and stereotypes when working with team members from different cultural backgrounds (Pelled & Xin, 1999). Biases, such as assumptions about communication styles or leadership approaches, can manifest subtly. Manager-coaches should engage in self-reflection and cultural sensitivity training to mitigate these biases. Culturally inclusive coaching involves adapting techniques and communication styles to align with team members' cultural preferences and values. Manager-coaches who embrace cultural inclusivity enhance their use of self and create a more welcoming and practical coaching environment.

Balancing Self-Disclosure

Self-disclosure is a delicate aspect of the use of self. Manager-coaches can share personal experiences or insights to illustrate a point, build rapport, or normalize a team member's experience. However, self-disclosure should be used judiciously and always serve the team member's growth and development rather than the manager-coach's agenda.

Benefits

The benefits of continuously developing self and the use of self for manager-coaches include:

- **Enhancing the Helping Alliance.** Effective use of self-enhances the therapeutic alliance—the collaborative and trusting relationship between manager-coaches and team members (Norcross & Lambert, 2018). When manager-coaches authentically engage and empathize with team members, they foster a robust therapeutic bond that can positively influence team members' outcomes. Team members are more likely to feel understood, supported, and motivated to make meaningful changes.
- **Fostering Empowerment and Autonomy.** Manager-coaches whose use of self is skillful empower team members to take charge of their lives. By sharing relevant personal experiences and insights, manager-coaches validate team members' experiences and promote a sense of self-efficacy. Team members become active participants in their growth and development.
- **Bridging Cultural and Socioeconomic Gaps.** Cultural competence and culturally sensitive use of self can bridge gaps in understanding between manager-coaches and team members from diverse backgrounds (Sue et al., 2009). When manager-coaches acknowledge their own cultural biases and subjectivity, they can better navigate the complexities of cross-cultural interactions. This, in turn, enhances the effectiveness of interventions and promotes inclusivity.

Ethical Considerations

Ethical considerations are paramount when employing the use of self in professional practice (Corey et al., 2015). Manager-coaches must establish clear boundaries and maintain confidentiality to ensure the trust and safety of the coaching relationship. Manager-coaches must set clear boundaries to protect the team member's well-being and maintain confidentiality. Confidential information shared by team members should not be disclosed beyond agreed upon conditions or misused. Manager-coaches should also be transparent with team members about the limits of their role and the purpose of any self-disclosure.

Manager-coaches must be vigilant to avoid imposing their values, beliefs, or agendas on team members (Knights & Poppleton, 2008). The use of self should enhance the team member's autonomy and self-determination rather than steer them toward the manager-coach's perspectives or preferences. Consultation with peers, leaders, human resource partners, and professional coaches provides a space to examine challenging cases, ethical dilemmas, and potential boundary violations. It allows manager-coaches to receive feedback and guidance on the appropriate use of self.

Strategies for Developing Effective Use of Self

The use of self in coaching is a multifaceted concept encompassing a manager-coach's ability to consciously employ their own experiences, emotions, and perspectives to benefit the coaching process. It involves a deliberate and strategic sharing of one's self without overshadowing or intruding upon the team member's journey. The use of self recognizes that the manager-coach's authentic presence and engagement can significantly impact the team member's self-awareness, learning, and growth. The use of self can include various aspects such as self-awareness, self-regulation, self-care, and building rapport.

Self-awareness is the first and most important aspect of using self in coaching. It refers to the manager-coach's ability to be aware of their thoughts, feelings, and behaviors and how they may impact the coaching relationship. Self-awareness is crucial because it allows manager-coaches to be more intentional in their communication and behavior and more responsive to the team member's needs. For example, a manager-coach aware of their biases and assumptions can avoid projecting them onto the team members and provide a more unbiased and objective coaching experience. Self-awareness can be developed through various means, such as self-reflection, mindfulness, and seeking feedback from others (Palmer & Whybrow, 2018). Self-reflection involves reflecting on one's thoughts, feelings, and behaviors and how they may impact the coaching relationship. Mindfulness, the practice of being present and aware in the moment, can help manager-coaches be more aware of their thoughts, feelings, and behaviors. Seeking feedback from others, such as colleagues or supervisors, can also help coaches develop self-awareness by providing them with a different perspective on their behavior.

Self-regulation is another essential aspect of the use of self. It refers to the manager-coach's ability to control and manage their thoughts, feelings, and behaviors. Self-regulation is critical because it allows coaches to remain calm and composed in challenging situations and to respond to the team members in a supportive and helpful way. For example, a manager-coach who can regulate their emotions can avoid becoming defensive or argumentative when the team member expresses frustration or disappointment. Self-regulation can be developed through various means, such as emotional intelligence, stress management techniques, and practical communication skills (Whybrow & Palmer, 2018). Emotional intelligence is the ability to understand, manage, and express one's emotions, and it can help manager-coaches better regulate their emotions. Stress management techniques such as exercise, meditation, and time management can help you manage your stress levels and better regulate your emotions. Practical communication skills such as active listening, empathy, and assertiveness can help coaches communicate more effectively with their team members and better control their emotions.

Self-care is another important aspect of the use of self. It refers to the coach's ability to care for their physical, emotional, and mental well-being. Self-care is vital because manager-coaches who are not taking care of themselves may be unable to provide the best possible service to the team members. For example, a manager-coach who feels stressed or overworked may be unable to give the team members the needed attention and support. Self-care can be developed through various means, such as regular exercise, healthy eating habits, and time management (Whybrow & Palmer, 2018). Regular exercise can help manager-coaches reduce stress, improve mental clarity, and boost energy levels. Eating healthy can help coaches maintain their physical and psychological well-being. Time management can help manager-coaches balance their workload and make time for self-care.

Building rapport and establishing a solid connection with team members fosters openness, transparency, vulnerability, and trust. Rapport refers to the harmonious and empathetic relationship established between individuals. It is characterized by mutual trust, respect, and understanding, which create an atmosphere of openness and cooperation. Building rapport is not a one-size-fits-all approach but a nuanced process that varies based on context, personality, and cultural factors. Rapport-building fosters trust, a cornerstone of effective use of self. When individuals perceive someone as genuine and reliable, they are more likely to share their thoughts and feelings openly. This trust enhances credibility, which is crucial in professions like counseling, where team members must have faith in the therapist's abilities. Building rapport involves active listening and empathetic communication. When individuals feel heard and understood, it paves the way for deeper connections. For instance, manager-coaches must understand their team members' emotions and experiences to offer effective support. In leadership and management roles, conflict is inevitable.

Building rapport equips leaders with the skills to navigate disputes constructively. Leaders can de-escalate situations and find common ground by demonstrating empathy and understanding. Building rapport is a skill that can be honed through practice and self-reflection. Here are some practical strategies:

1. **Active Listening.** Give attention to the speaker, show interest through verbal and nonverbal cues, and avoid interrupting or judging.
2. **Empathetic Communication.** Practice putting yourself in the other person's shoes and validating their feelings and perspectives.
3. **Cultural Competence.** Be mindful of cultural differences in communication styles, body language, and values to build rapport across diverse backgrounds.
4. **Authenticity.** Be genuine and transparent in your interactions, as authenticity fosters trust.

Some Ways to Continue Developing Use of Self in Coaching

Developing the use of self is a continuous journey. Feedback, experiences, reflection, and a mindset of openness and learning engage the manager-coach to evolve in their effective use of self. Here are four specific actions that can assist manager-coaches.

1. **Continuous Self-Reflection and Feedback.** Manager-coaches should constantly self-reflect to deepen their self-awareness and refine their use of self. Seeking feedback from team members, peers, or supervisors can provide valuable insights into the impact of using self on professional practice.
2. **Cultural Competency Training.** Professionals in culturally diverse contexts should prioritize cultural competency training. Training programs can enhance manager-coaches' ability to navigate cross-cultural interactions sensitively and effectively. Cultural competency training should be an ongoing commitment.
3. **Peer Supervision and Collaboration.** Regular peer supervision about your management and coaching offer manager-coaches opportunities to discuss challenging situations, ethical dilemmas, and the nuances of using self (Bernard & Goodyear, 2019). These interactions promote ethical practice, skill development, and self-awareness.
4. **Professional Coaching.** Ongoing work with a professional coach can provide opportunities and support for professional development, including using self, role modeling, and coaching about situations managers face as coaches for team members.

There are many ways to develop self. Regardless of the process, several elements are essential for effectively developing the use of self:

–   Increasing awareness
–   Building acceptance of self
–   Engaging with others for challenge, support, and feedback

- Adopting new behaviors and perspectives
- Integrating those behaviors and attitudes into a more conscious and unconscious competence
- Developing mastery, the state of competence at which behaviors are natural, reflection and ongoing learning occurs, innovation occurs, and learning agility is demonstrated. (Bennett & Bush, 2014)

Summary

The concept of use of self, deeply rooted in humanistic and psychodynamic theories, plays a pivotal role across various professional fields. Practitioners leverage their experiences, emotions, beliefs, and values to build authentic connections with team members, foster trust, and enhance team member outcomes. Self-awareness, ethical considerations, and continuous self-reflection are foundational to effective use of self.

Preparing to engage in coaching conversations is essential. Coaching conversations are not chitchat. They have purpose and focus. They require skills. And they need the manager-coach to show up as a guide. Coaching is a discovery process focused on the other person's development, performance, and transformation. Coaching conversations are action-oriented and outcome-focused.

Here are some tips to help manager-coaches be their best and provide the best support for their team members:

1. **Take care of your physical needs**—food, water, and restroom. If you are hungry, thirsty, or need to use the restroom, you will be distracted. Remove these potential negative impacts on your ability to focus on the person you will coach and your work with them.
2. **Remove distractions**—sights, sounds, and any competing priorities.
3. **Center yourself.** This involves letting go of distracting thoughts and emotions and focusing on how you will bring the best available version of yourself to the coaching conversation.
4. **Identify assumptions you may have about the person being coached.** Take a few minutes and think about (and write down or record) any assumptions you have about your team member and yourself as a manager-coach, as well as the likely topics of the coaching conversation (if you know them). By capturing your assumptions, you are more likely to be aware of them during the coaching conversation. You will recognize when you are operating based on assumptions versus evidence and facts.
5. **Gather materials** related to your team members and others you may need during the coaching session. This may be the overarching goals for the coaching engagement and any related materials (e.g., personality or emotional intelligence assessments), as well as your notepad and pen to use during the session.

6. **Review any notes from previous coaching conversations.** Reviewing your notes about the topics discussed in earlier coaching sessions will help you focus on your team member.
7. If you are new to coaching, **review the coaching conversation framework you will use**—e.g., the six-step process described in Chapter 3.
8. **Take a deep breath** (or two) and fully engage with your team members.

A Conversation with Cherie Swarthout
Director of Athletics
Queens University of Charlotte

This conversation was recorded and transcribed, then edited for clarity and conciseness.

John Bennett (JB): *In your role as athletic director, how do you use coaching?*

Cherie Swarthout (CS): I used to be a lot more directive, more telling than asking. I didn't listen as well. I was always trying to figure out what to say next to whatever the situation was. I have much more authentic conversations. In conversations, I use what the other person says so that they feel heard and noticed. I guess I use more of my senses—what they're saying and how they're coming across. And I'm also not afraid to be in those moments that are very awkward and difficult. Sometimes I shy away from difficult questions or conversations, or emotional pieces.

I work in a very emotional industry where a lot of passion flies around. Recently I had a [sports team] coach in here, and we were talking about the budget for the upcoming season. I could tell he was getting uncomfortable. Instead of just glossing over it or playing the top-down approach of telling him what to do, I just paused and said, "I can tell this is making you really uncomfortable. Can you share what you're feeling?" It took the conversation to another level. It peeled away more layers so that you could get to the root cause. He became highly emotional but it was not a combative conversation. It was a tough thing that he was experiencing, and we talked through that. And because we were able to uncover that, fast-forward eight weeks later, oh my goodness! He's hitting home runs on the thing holding him back that was creating so much stress and distress. We were able to work through it, get to a different level because he was vulnerable. I was vulnerable. I wasn't afraid to ask the question. He's like my superstar right now.

JB: *How did you make that transition, so that you could show up like that?*

CS: I mean, the classes I took [at Queens] were just unbelievable, just pivotal. And I think the coaching curriculum was key because it really boils down to self-awareness. To me, it's a skill set, certainly, but you can have a skill set and not be self-aware and not be able to effect change, and so to me, it has been a discovery process of creating more self-awareness for myself. But what are the things that you know cause me distress? How does that show up when that happens and when? What are my overt behaviors when I am under stress, you know? And I think it was just being open to better understand myself, which has helped me embrace the necessary skills. I'm not afraid of the conversation. I'm not afraid to go there. Very little shuts me down or gets to me, if that makes sense.

JB: *What I'm hearing is that idea of vulnerability but a self-awareness that allows you not to be triggered, or blind to, or overly excited about something that somebody's saying, or steer away from it because it's something that you're uncomfortable with. So that's great. How have you continued to develop that skill and mindset as you've been in this practitioner role of leader and manager?*

CS: I'm much more self-aware than I have probably been. I continue to evolve in that area. I'm much more comfortable with my strengths in the spaces I need to grow. There's always that gotcha moment, and as soon as I get outside of what I should be doing, I overreact. I talk before I listen. I don't get all the information. It always comes back and kicks me in the tail, and it might not be a hard kick, but it's an "uh-huh." And I am constantly replaying almost every conversation in my head. I asked, "What did I do? What didn't I do? What could I have done better?" But there's always that moment that I don't know. I'm in the people business, and I work with a lot of fascinating and unique personalities, and they all are very different. I'm constantly in training, learning how to maximize them because our athletic programs are only as good as our head coaches, so I've got to be in a place where I can continue to help them evolve and do what I can to become more self-aware.

JB: *You've described a lot of self-reflection as you do this work, and you're in a somewhat different scenario than many people in that you're in a world where the word "coach" is used as an athletic coach. It's a sports coach. And then we're talking about coaching as a manager and leader. How do you see the similarities and differences between those two?*

CS: Well, our best coaches are the ones that are most self-aware. . . . It's the coaches who don't listen to their athletes, who think they have all the answers that tend to burn out and burn down. The ones that listen to that are relatable. Those are the ones who are the most successful. So it's not standing on the sideline yelling. They've got to have a relationship with the student-athletes.

JB: *And you're modeling that in terms of your work as a leader; it sounds like as you think about the role in playing this kind of manager-coach, leader-coach role that you play. How is that received?*

CS: I'm always very calm, just, yeah, until I'm not. Unfortunately, I have to fight to be a very direct communicator; being 6 feet tall and having very high expectations sometimes create a barrier for me with others because it may make me less approachable. I'll ask staff and coaches if they think that's the desired outcome. "How do we get to the desired outcome?" I've always got my foot on the gas. So that forces me to take everything I do, probably down a bit.

Sometimes people would like me to be more directive. Well, if I have to tell them what to do, I don't need them.

I deal with everybody as an individual. I may deal with my golf coach very differently than I deal with my women's basketball coach. Sometimes there's an inequity there. I treat everybody very individually. I think they appreciate it rather than being directive, you know, being kind of the top-down person, but I also can be that person when I need to be.

JB: *It sounds like you're also using a coaching approach in your relationships with peers. Not that you're coaching them, but you're using some of those skills and are self-aware. Am I putting words in your mouth with that?*

CS: Absolutely, and it's listening. And it's asking powerful and clarifying questions. I think because we frequently just want to be heard, and I just take it the other way, I just want to hear that I'm going to ask clarifying questions, and I promise you I'm going to be heard, but not before I have broken down those barriers where you know you've been heard. Now I can, whatever you've just said, take that and ask a powerful question and then say, "Well, have we considered this?" or "What are your thoughts about this?" I ask a lot of questions. They're so tired of me asking questions. But it takes away the animosity that I could create when I ask a question versus a directive.

JB: *Is there another example that you think of where you've used a coaching approach, how did you go about that, and what was the outcome?*

CS: You know, it's every day. We had a difficult situation with one of our coaches this fall. I brought him in and asked him, "What's going on?" He said, "What do you mean?" I said, "I've got some of these things that have happened there. There are some red flags for me. Can you talk about those?" He agreed. And I told him, "They're inconsistent with who I know you to be when I line those up. So you know, what else is there? What's going on?" And they would talk a bit, and I told him I understood there were challenges. Through asking powerful questions and guided discovery, he got to the place where he said he thought he needed some time away from work. And that's precisely what happened. But it was through listening and reflecting him—mirroring back to him what he had said that he got to that place. Through the conversation and the trust-building, we already had trust and vulnerability, and he reached his conclusion.

JB: *What advice would you give a leader manager who's considering using a coaching approach?*

CS: I think it starts with you. I think you have to have great self-awareness. You have to demonstrate that. I believe you have to show vulnerability. I think you have to be curious and kind. And I believe that those relationships' strength allows you to have challenging conversations. But if you don't have that foundation, it's very hard to have a difficult conversation and effect change where people aren't trying to jump ship. I think it creates better buy-in. With your staff, they feel heard and valued, which I believe is a byproduct of the coaching style.

JB: *Is anything else you want to share? Anything you want to emphasize? Add to?*

CS: I think everybody should learn to apply a coaching mindset and skills. I think it helps with everything. It's not just about what you do professionally. It helps with your parenting. It helps with relationships. If you use that approach, it makes everything better. It creates sensitivity, it creates intuition and a better sense of the moment in time, and there's always a time that you can circle back and say, "Let's talk about this," or "What didn't go well?"—you know, debrief on some things.

Part II: **Coaching Skills**

Chapter 5
Coaching Skills: An Overview

When a paradigm no longer provides reliable guidance for how to live in the world, the most common response is to grasp hold of it more firmly. As it dawns on us that we don't know how things work— that it's not working—we become more insistent that it has to work just as we thought it did. . . . We use our big brains and our powers of cognition to resist change. Our skills at manipulating information lead us to become more fundamentalist, more certain.

—Margaret Wheatley, 2017, p. 196

In research conducted by Graham et al. (1994), effective managers who used a coaching approach scored-highest in developing warm relationships, observing the performance of team members, and providing relevant information. They scored lowest on giving feedback, establishing performance expectations, and providing guidance.

This chapter explains the essential communication, interpersonal, and cross-cultural tools and knowledge required for coaching leaders at all levels. These tools and knowledge include listening for understanding, asking powerful questions, providing feedback, offering insights, planning action, ensuring accountability, and building support for achievement. This chapter addresses the following questions:

– What are the competencies of effective coaches?
– What are the essential skills/practices of coaches?
– How are these skills/practices applied?

Coaching is the practice of science in the form of art. There is both an art and a science to coaching. Learning the skills of coaching and the theories that inform coaching is one step toward becoming a manager-coach and coaching in the most effective way possible. Coaching also requires integrating knowledge and practice comfortably and effectively. Once this integration is accomplished, the next step is developing mastery.

Mastery starts with the coach. While many people can learn to coach and use the knowledge and skills employed by coaches, specific characteristics of those who do it well can be observed. There are a variety of coach competency models available, including frameworks developed by the Center for Credentialing & Education (CCE), European Mentoring and Coaching Council (EMCC), Graduate School Alliance for Education in Coaching (GSAEC), and International Coach Federation (ICF).

Kombarakaran et al. (2008) and Stern (2008) found that successful coaches

– are educated in the art and science related to coaching.
– understand contemporary organizational issues but not necessarily the detailed nature of the business.
– understand human motivation.
– understand the impact of emotions and interpersonal style on leadership.
– understand leadership and management issues from a multi-systems viewpoint.
– understand the political and economic realities within the organization.

https://doi.org/10.1515/9783111002415-005

- understand the competitive environment.
- are self-aware—they know their needs and do not depend on the coaching relationship to get those needs met.
- can maintain appropriate confidentiality.
- can maintain appropriate roles and behaviors between coach, executive, and stakeholders.
- can provide insights and help team members learn new skills through modeling.
- have a passion for helping others grow and perform.
- are comfortable around top management.
- can notice and deal with paradoxes.
- can demonstrate interpersonal sensitivity.
- can detect hidden agendas.
- can flex and be creative.
- demonstrate approachability, compassion, and the ability to relate well with others.
- can actively listen and reflect accurately on what is said.
- demonstrate high levels of integrity and personal honesty.
- build trust.
- ask powerful questions.
- provide emotional and motivational support.
- follow through.
- establish coaching goals with the client.
- monitor coaching results.
- develop themselves as human beings and in their roles as coaches.

While successful coaches share a well-defined set of characteristics, potential clients may not be able to observe these characteristics until a coaching engagement is underway. However, clients look for certain things when selecting a coach, including

- industry experience
- education
- work experience
- work at the appropriate level in the organization (leader and coach)
- personal developmental level
- coaching skills
- chemistry/style
- personality
- demographics: gender, race, age, sexual orientation, etc.

Coaching works in different environments and with other desires, frameworks, and assumptions when

- desired outcomes are defined.
- the organization supports coaching.
- the organization embraces a culture of feedback, development, and support.

– the coaching is developmental and not corrective.
– the team member is ready for coaching—that is, they are open to feedback, has the desire to change/improve, and can devote the time and energy to self-discovery and behavior shifts.

Positive and productive coaching relationships do not often occur spontaneously. They require the right conditions, skills, and knowledge from the manager-coach. Here are some of the factors for manager-coaches that are conducive to creating positive and productive coaching relationships:

– **Helper Empathy.** When a manager-coach possesses helper empathy, you attempt to see the world the same way the team member perceives it by looking from their internal frame of reference. You do this preliminarily by thinking *with* rather than *for* or *about* the team member. Empathy has two stages. Brammer and MacDonald (2003) refer to these as "feeling into" experiences of the client and being in the client's place, that is, seeing the world as the client sees it. In the second stage, the manager-coach becomes an alternative self for the team member, an emotional mirror. You enter this internal frame of reference by listening attentively and asking themselves questions such as: What is the team member feeling right now? How do they view the situation they face? To consider the external frame of reference, you might ask questions such as: Why is the team member concerned? What is causing the situation? An effective manager-coach tries to think and feel like a team member.
– **Helper Warmth and Caring.** When a manager-coach is warm and caring, you convey a closeness beyond professional or clinical distance. Manager-coaches demonstrate this through friendliness and consideration by smiling, maintaining comfortable eye contact, and other nonverbal behaviors. In addition, you reveal warmth and caring by showing compassion and sincere concern for the client.
– **Helper Positive Regard and Respect.** When a manager-coach possesses positive care and respect, you have a deep concern for the team member's well-being and respect for the client's individuality and worth. Rogers (1989) referred to this as "unconditional positive regard."
– **Helper Openness.** When a manager-coach possesses vulnerability, you share personal experiences in service of the team member's agenda by disclosing thoughts and feelings. You demonstrate this by revealing thoughts, feelings and insights. This disclosure results in genuineness, authenticity, and congruence with the client.
– **Helper Concreteness and Specificity.** When the manager-coach possesses concreteness and specificity, you communicate accurately and concisely. You demonstrate this by using contextually appropriate language the team member understands. You pay attention to interpreting their messages and seek opportunities to clarify when a team member does not understand what was communicated.
– **Intentionality.** When the manager-coach possesses intentionality, you select responses to team members from various options. Manager-coaches demonstrate this

by selecting statements, questions, and nonverbal responses based on the team member's cultural background, goals, personality, and learning style (Brammer & MacDonald, 2003).

In addition to establishing a trusting relationship with the team member and other stakeholders (e.g., manager, human resources), the manager-coach must be self-aware and personally and professionally evolving.

A quality coaching interaction cannot be pulled off with any amount of method expertise or dazzling command of theory. It culminates from deep personal work that the coach has done and continues to do to prepare for this kind of engagement. Heightened alertness to one's natural biases, tendencies, and impact is necessary, along with a nimble ability to choose (Storjohann, 2006).

Coaching Competencies

Currently, there is no universally agreed upon competency model for coaching or for coaching within any specialty area, such as career, personal, or performance coaching. Instead, organizations such as CCE, EMCC, GSAEC and ICF have developed a variety of models. Considering that coaching is a helping relationship grounded in many professions and professional practices, it is essential to note that the competencies that demonstrate proficiency may take many forms.

Beyond coaching, the helping practices include consulting, facilitation, management, mediation, mentoring, pastoral care, teaching, therapy, and counseling. Competency is the ability to do something successfully and consistently get a desired beneficial outcome (Lawley & Linder-Pelz, 2016). To successfully coach, manager-coaches need to adapt their behavior skillfully and flexibly to the specific needs of the team members. This agility will engage the coach to apply various skills to the team members' varying needs.

Newsom and Dent (2011) reported one of the most comprehensive studies on contemporary coaching competencies. They identified several groups of activities:

–   **Professional coach activities,** which include assessing practice needs, promoting/marketing your coaching business, evaluating your coaching process, and engaging in self-development activities.
–   **Goal setting and attainment activities,** which include directives aimed at behavioral change, such as discussion of work-life balance issues, sharing an understanding of wellness, using knowledge of current business trends, and discussing obstacles to progress.
–   **Related activities,** such as clarifying an understanding of client concerns and challenges; establishing trust, honesty, and respect in the coaching relationship; assessing team members' strengths and development needs; and using knowledge of theories and techniques.

A review of these models resulted in the finding that 11 common elements across the models inform the practice of coaching. These 11 elements include:

1. **Ethics** (See Chapter 15)
   - Practice according to an established and recognized code of professional conduct.

2. **Self-awareness** (See Chapters 4 and 16)
   - Demonstrate awareness of own values, beliefs, behaviors, competence, and experiences.
   - Recognize how values, beliefs, behaviors, competence, and experiences impact the practice of coaching and client engagements.
   - Use self-awareness to manage meeting the client's objectives, and, where relevant, the stakeholders'.
   - Use self-awareness to inform self-development.

3. **Self-development** (See Chapters 4 and 16)
   - Build and maintain professional knowledge.
   - Understand and appropriately apply theory and knowledge.
   - Seek and use feedback to improve as a manager-coach.
   - Obtain and maintain professional credentials.
   - Engage in professional associations and networks.

4. **Contracting** (See Chapter 2)
   - Define key stakeholders.
   - Identify the coaching client.
   - Define the work to be accomplished.
   - Define the process that will be used.
   - Define the scope of the work.
   - Define boundaries.
   - Define measures of success and processes for monitoring.
   - Define terms of remuneration, if any.
   - Define roles and responsibilities.
   - Define the terms of informed consent and confidentiality.

5. **Relationship Building** (See Chapters 2, 4, and 5)
   - Establish effective working relationships with the client and key stakeholders.
   - Establish and maintain credibility and trust while building a professional reputation.

6. **Essential Coaching Skills** (See Chapters 5–12)
   - Communicate and listen for understanding.
   - Reflect.

- Ask powerful questions.
- Provide insight and feedback
- Use assessments.
- Explore possible actions.
- Action planning.
- Gain commitment.
- Explore and address obstacles to success.
- Ensure accountability.
- Develop networks of support.

7. **Coaching Process Skills** (See Chapters 2 and 12)
    - Plan and set goals.
    - Identify courses of action and analyze the consequences of each.

8. **Getting to Desired Results/Outcomes** (See Chapters 2, 5, and 12)
    - Manage progress and accountability.
    - Facilitate the team member's desired goals during the coaching process, including monitoring team member progress, decision-making, and use of resources.

9. **Using Models and Tools** (See Chapters 2, 3, 5–14)
    - Identify and consciously apply models and tools appropriately to serve clients.
    - Use assessments to support client goal achievement.

10. **Organizational Acumen** (See Chapters 2, 5–14)
    - Understand the organizational context and apply it to the coaching engagement.
    - Understand and apply key terms and concepts associated with the organizational setting.

11. **Evaluating** (See Chapter 16)
    - Assess personal performance as a coach.
    - Assess impact of the coaching.
    - Assess competence.

Jake Weiss (2020) defined nine managerial coaching behaviors in his research about employee coachability and managerial coaching. They are:
1. Personalize learning using examples, analogies, and scenarios.
2. Provide feedback based on observations, reflections, and third-party input.
3. Seek feedback from the team member being coached related to their progress toward goals.
4. Provide resources, information, and materials to the team member being coached to support learning and remove obstacles.

5. Frame questions to help the team members think through issues.
6. Prompt team members to think outside of the box by encouraging them to see other points of view and by providing different perspectives and experiences.
7. Establish goals and expectations with team members and communicate the importance of those goals.
8. Create an environment for learning by engaging in meetings, fostering mentoring relationships, and providing stretch assignments for growth.
9. Build and foster working relationships based on rapport, trust, respect, and mutual benefit.

Essential Coaching Skills

From the 11 common elements that inform the practice of coaching explored in the previous section, Bennett and Bush (2014) propose that there are six essential coaching skills. These essential coaching skills can be split between foundational and applied skills. Foundational skills involve listening for understanding, identifying and asking powerful questions, and helping the client reframe or broaden the possibilities for awareness and action. These serve as a basis for the applied skills and are used more frequently during coaching conversations. Applied skills involve providing feedback and insight, which help the client develop understanding and commit to action. Another applied coaching skill is building partnerships for support to continue to sustain and evolve behavioral change.

Essential coaching skills:
– Listening for understanding
– Asking powerful questions
– Reframing
– Providing feedback
– Offering insight
– Building support

The six chapters that follow will further define these essential coaching skills. To put these skills in perspective, the following table (Table 5.1) shows each of the six steps in the coaching conversation process defined in Chapter 2 and maps the six coaching skills to those steps. Listening for Understanding and Asking Powerful Questions are applied in each step. The use of the other four skills varies.

Schwarz's (2013a) mutual learning model was introduced in Chapter 3. That framework can be applied to the six steps in the coaching process described in Chapter 2 and the six coaching skills presented in this chapter. Table 5.2 illustrates when the mutual learning behaviors are most likely to be applied to the steps and skills.

Table 5.1: Coaching Skills Mapped to Change Coaching Steps.

	Current Situation and Context	Needs and Desired Goals	Gathering Information	Possible Actions	Action Planning	Summary and Agreement
Listening for Understanding	X	X	X	X	X	X
Asking Powerful Questions	X	X	X	X	X	X
Reframing			X	X		
Providing Feedback			X	X	X	
Offering Insight			X	X	X	
Building Support				X	X	

Axioms for Change Coaching

Coaches in roles ranging across the spectrum from professional executive coach to manager-coach have gained insights from hard-won experience. Their insights have given rise to these axioms, among others:

- Never work harder than your client.
- Follow the process, use it as a guide for the coaching conversation.
- Keep in mind what about you may be holding you back, as well as what might be propelling you forward.
- If you don't know what to ask next, it is probably because you have not been listening.
- The presenting issue or agenda for coaching is rarely the real issue.
- It is nearly impossible to coach without a shared understanding of the client's goal/agenda for the coaching session.
- Avoid colluding with your client.
- A crucial role of the coach is to help the client go where they would not go by themselves.
- If you ask a powerful question, it is worth waiting for the response. Allow at least seven seconds after asking a question.
- Keep your questions to 15 words or less.
- Behind every statement is a question, so do less telling and more asking.
- Coaxing is not coaching.
- The job of the coach is to put themselves out of a job by supporting independence and interdependence versus dependence on the coach.

Table 5.2: Linking Coaching Process and Skills to the Mutual Learning Model.

Mutual Learning Behaviors[*]

	State Views & Ask Genuine Questions	Share All Relevant Information	Use Specific Examples & Agree on What Important Words Mean	Explain Reasoning and Intent	Focus on Interests, Not Positions	Test Assumptions & Inferences	Jointly Design Next Steps	Discuss Undiscussable Issues
Coaching Skills[**]								
Listening for Understanding			X			X		
Asking Powerful Questions	X	X	X	X		X		X
Providing Feedback	X	X	X	X		X		
Reframing			X			X		X
Offering Insights			X	X	X	X	X	X
Building Support							X	
Coaching Process Steps[**]								
Situation & Context	X			X				X

(continued)

Table 5.2 (continued)

Mutual Learning Behaviors*

	State Views & Ask Genuine Questions	Share All Relevant Information	Use Specific Examples & Agree on What Important Words Mean	Explain Reasoning and Intent	Focus on Interests, Not Positions	Test Assumptions & Inferences	Jointly Design Next Steps	Discuss Undiscussable Issues
Agenda & Goals	X							
Gather Information	X	X	X	X	X	X	X	X
Possible Actions	X		X			X		
Action Planning	X		X			X		
Summary & Next Steps	X							

*Schwarz, R. (2013). *Smart leaders, smarter teams: How you and your team get unstuck to get results.* Jossey-Bass.

**Bennett, J. L., & Bush, M. W. (2014). *Coaching for change.* Routledge.

- Listen for what is said (words, actions, emotions, etc.) and what is not being said.
- You've got to do "your work" to help others do "their work."
- Ask yourself and the people you coach: How does who I am (as a person, leader, coach) support what I'm trying to accomplish? How does it hold me back?
- Focus on what the client is saying and doing (or not) and less on what you want them to say or do, or your assessment of it.
- Change usually involves resistance and often comes in increments.
- With so many "transformations," why is there so little change?

Summary

Six coaching skills can be applied to the six-step coaching process to support team members as they develop capabilities, improve performance, and experience transformation. These skills align with the standards set by various professional associations and credentialing organizations.

Chapter 6
Coaching Skill: Providing Feedback

Feedback is always about the person giving it. And, sometimes, it is about the person receiving it.
—Charlie Seashore, Ph.D.

Feedback is data given in the present about past behavior. Feedback is a gift. Like all gifts, the receiver assesses feedback regarding their needs and desires. Sometimes, gifts are accepted but not used. Other times, they are deflected or re-gifted and sometimes rejected.

All of these are among the reasons the manager-coach must give the proper feedback in the right manner and at the right time. Feedback is often the beginning of a managerial coaching conversation. Providing feedback is an essential aspect of coaching as it allows manager-coaches to help team members identify areas for improvement, understand how others perceive their behavior, and make progress toward their goals. Feedback is information provided to an individual about their performance, behavior, or results to help them improve. It can be provided in several formats, such as verbal, written, or observation.

This chapter defines feedback and its importance in the context of coaching. It discusses the impact of feedback-rich cultures and how to foster them. It also describes several approaches to providing feedback, explicitly focusing on the Context, Behavior, Impact, and Request (CBIR) framework. This chapter links personal interest in improving and receptivity to feedback. It offers examples and tools for preparing and delivering feedback, including some considerations for providing unpleasant feedback and how to address team member responses. Lastly, it offers some helpful reminders.

We often use the term "performance management" without realizing that the origin of the concept of "management" was to control. The manager's role—not the coach's—is to focus on managing performance. Manager-coaches need to reframe your attention to equip, empower, enable, and enhance performance. As a manager-coaches your intent is to support: "performance enhancement," "performance empowerment" or "performance enablement." Ongoing coaching from one's manager is critical for performance management because it facilitates providing feedback, setting goals, and monitoring progress toward those goals. As such, coaching is closely linked to the feedback process and specifically to feedback from one's manager (Steelman & Wolfeld, 2018).

Feedback may be provided at any of three points in the coaching process. First, feedback can and often is offered before engaging in the coaching process to increase awareness and help the team member identify a need or goal for coaching. This feedback may come from the manager-coach or other sources. Second, it may be provided during the coaching conversation, especially during Gathering Information (Step 3), Possible Actions (Step 4), and Action Planning (Step 5). Finally, feedback may be provided after the coaching conversation as the manager-coach observes the team mem-

https://doi.org/10.1515/9783111002415-006

ber's behaviors related to the goals of the coaching relationship. The team members may also receive feedback from other sources, such as the impacts of their efforts, customers, team members, and surveys.

In coaching and professional development, feedback can serve many purposes. It can increase awareness of strengths and areas for development and growth, facilitate development by reinforcing behaviors, guide continuous improvement by providing evidence of the impacts of behaviors, and achieve development goals, which can be used to refine goals and adjust behaviors. It can also help increase motivation and engagement and build trust and respect between the manager-coach and team members.

By creating a culture of continuous feedback, team members are more likely to respond to and become actively engaged in their work and the organization. Frequent, developmental, and reinforcing feedback allows team members struggling to meet expectations to understand their direction, receive input, and discover how to improve their performance. This enables higher-performing team members to become stronger and excel, benefiting the organization (Bender, 2022). Feedback can serve to validate or invalidate self-perceptions and support. In addition, feedback can support a culture in which feedback is sought, used, and appreciated, and the sending and receiving of feedback are honed.

Team members are more likely to be receptive to feedback from any source when they trust and respect the person giving it, find it helpful, seek it, or have time to process it. It also helps team members hear the message when they have been told that the feedback is being offered before it is delivered, have time to prepare to receive it, and when the message is not overly personal. Of course, most of us prefer to receive positive, supportive, and encouraging feedback. And while receiving redirective or developmental feedback can be helpful, team members may not accept it as intended if they have a natural resistance to or concern about showing weakness. It is essential that feedback is delivered as soon as practical after the event or behavior and that developmental feedback be given in a private versus public setting to avoid embarrassment or shaming.

These leading practices will help you have the impact you intend when you deliver feedback:

- Provide the recipient with advance notice that feedback is coming. This may be a simple statement like, "I would like to provide you with some feedback about XYZ" or "May I provide you with some feedback about XYZ?"
- Prepare before you start giving feedback. This includes selecting specific examples of the behaviors you wish to provide feedback about, selecting the most suitable time and place to share the feedback, crafting your message, and being prepared for a range of possible responses from the recipient.
- To be most effective, provide feedback as close as possible to the event or behavior in question (Kluger & DeNisi, 1996). This allows clients to understand the context of the feedback and take immediate action to make improvements.

As a manager who recognizes the value of feedback, you can encourage team members to seek and use feedback from various sources, including

- direct feedback based on the manager-coach's observation of words and behaviors that are or are not aligned with the team member's goals for change.
- multi-rater (360-degree) feedback reports.
- comments (written and verbal) received from peers, direct reports, managers, customers, and other key stakeholders.
- self-reflections, such as feelings, thoughts, experiences, ideas, etc.
- observations in completing an assignment or as an "after action" analysis of what worked well and what could be changed.

Feedback may be delivered verbally, via email, body language, surveys, and in formal performance reviews.

Manager-coaches may find it helpful to encourage team members to develop the skill of receiving feedback. Here are some points the recipient can practice:

- Remember that the messenger is probably doing their best, and delivering this message is not easy for them. Thank the person who offered the feedback. They took the time to provide feedback for your benefit.
- Acknowledge what you heard and seek to understand the message. Be curious.
- Seek clarification, as needed, about the feedback. Seek to understand what the person providing the feedback observed or experienced and the impacts on yourself, others, and the organization.
- Take time to process the message before reacting. It is easier to make a statement later than to deal with the regret and damage caused by an impulsive comment.
- Consider the implications of your behaviors on yourself (e.g., goal achievement, reputation, growth, advancement), on others (e.g., your relationship with them, their ability to do their job) and on the organization (e.g., business goal achievement, use of resources, impacts on customers).
- Identify your strengths and past experiences that you can draw on and apply in this situation. Remember to take an inventory of what you have at your disposal and to avoid focusing only on what may have been taken away.
- Consider your options. We usually have options and can make choices. In this case, the options may be limited, so identify as many as possible and carefully select the most impactful.
- Seek support from others. Use them to help vent your emotions (sadness, anger, fear, anxiety, etc.). Ask them for the help you need. Look for resources such as an Employee Assistance Program (EAP), your network of colleagues, your healthcare provider, a job assistance program, or unemployment benefits.
- Develop a plan to act on the feedback. To paraphrase Victor Frankl, you may not control the situation, but you have control over how you respond. Even if a fully developed plan is impossible (yet), what are the next two or three steps that will help you respond productively?

– Implement the action (e.g., more feedback, direct action, no action).
– Seek feedback to confirm what you learned from implementing the action plans you implemented as a result of the feedback.

Fostering a Feedback-Rich Culture

Creating a work environment where feedback is regular and not primarily negative can improve performance. It fosters learning and growth, enhances communication, encourages trust, and makes feedback easier to give and receive. Subordinates whose managers have a high feedback orientation perceive those managers as developing favorable coaching relationships and exhibiting effective coaching behaviors. These managers value feedback for themselves. They promote an effective feedback and coaching process and are viewed as better coaches. Managers with a strong feedback orientation should be more likely to provide sound guidance and clear feedback and develop a constructive coaching relationship with their subordinates. Managers who value feedback will probably establish a context that supports and promotes feedback and coaching. They use effective coaching behaviors, form high-quality relationships with subordinates, and promote a favorable environment.

Feedback-rich cultures in organizations support giving and receiving high-quality feedback and view feedback as nonthreatening and behaviorally focused. Coaching is used to help team members interpret and use feedback. There is a strong link between performance improvement and valued outcomes (London & Smither, 2002; Steelman & Wolfeld, 2018). Effectively coaching team members involves communicating performance expectations, providing coaching feedback (guidance), helping employees analyze situations and solve problems (facilitation), and challenging employees to realize their full potential (inspiration) (Steelman & Wolfeld, 2018).

An Approach to Delivering Feedback

Many of us have been taught to provide feedback using a "sandwich" approach. This involves telling the feedback recipient one or more things they have done well, then sharing the corrective or redirective feedback, followed by more praise. This approach may appear to provide a balanced message and help the person delivering the feedback feel good about the conversation, but it can confuse the recipient. The critical message may be lost and does not provide a clear direction for making changes.

CBIR

One approach to delivering feedback is known by its acronym CBIR, which stands for:
- Context: When was the behavior for which feedback is being offered observed or experienced?
- Behavior: What behavior(s) were observed or experienced?
- Impact: What was the effect of those behaviors?
- Request: What, if any, requests for action are you making? (Bennett and Bush, 2014)

Here are two examples of how CBIR can be used as a practical framework for delivering feedback in a coaching context:

Example 1:
"Yesterday, in the meeting about the new project (context), I noticed that you spoke up more than usual and offered several useful questions and suggestions for the team (behavior). This input helped us see the project differently and develop strategies that had not been considered (impact). Please continue to speak up and share your questions and ideas (request). Doing so will help all of us do a better job."

Example 2:
"I've noticed over the past three weeks (context) that you have been making more mistakes on the reports you have been analyzing for the team (behavior). Your sales reports have had both content and grammatical errors. In addition, the level of analysis has not been as thorough as you have performed in the past or that we expect (behavior). As a result, the reports have been returned to you for additional work. I have had to review them more often and thoroughly than expected, and we have been late distributing our weekly reports (impact). Please tell me how you can correct this going forward (request).

To help you prepare to deliver feedback, consider what you know and what you assume about the team member. Table 6.1 asks you to consider six factors as you prepare to construct and deliver your feedback message.

Table 6.1: Known and Assumed.

Known		Assumed
	What are the performance/behaviors/results?	
	What are the motivations and drivers of the behavior?	
	What are the growth goals?	

Table 6.1 (continued)

Known		Assumed
	How well does the recipient trust you?	
	Are you interested in receiving feedback from me regarding this topic?	
	What have been the responses to feedback in the past?	

Feedback may focus on reinforcing behaviors or developing existing or new behaviors. We intentionally do not use the phrase "constructive feedback." If we refer to positive or reinforcing feedback as "constructive," then feedback intended to stop, start, or change behaviors would need to be called "destructive." None of the feedback offered should be destructive. That is why positive feedback intended to encourage and support behaviors is called "reinforcing feedback," while feedback designed to shift, change, or stop behaviors is called "developmental feedback."

Figure 6.1 illustrates reinforcing and developmental feedback on the vertical axis and the feedback provider and recipient on the horizontal axis. Aspirations and wishes for others can be powerful. They can also be centered on the manager-coach's expectations for the team member and not considering their goals and aspirations. This can lead to resistance or a lack of commitment to change behaviors or improve performance. Manager-coaches should focus feedback in terms of the recipient's goals. On the right side, the focus is on what the feedback recipient wants to be or do. It is focused on what they perceive their ideal or desired self to be.

Building on self-regulation theory, this framework defines the likely responses to reinforcing and developmental feedback from the perspectives of both the "ought" self and the "ideal" self. (DeNisi & Kluger, 2000; Higgins, 1987; London, 2003) Looking at the left side of the graphic, the feedback recipient has little incentive to develop if the feedback is reinforcing and from the giver's agenda. In the lower left quadrant, the feedback recipient will likely avoid disappointing others (particularly the feedback giver) when the feedback is developmental. So, while the recipient might change their behavior, those changes are made to avoid disappointing others and are not as likely to be internally motivated or fulfilling. In the upper right quadrant, reinforcing feedback is based on the recipient's goals, priorities, and intentions. Recipients are more likely to implement that feedback to continue improving performance and growth. In the lower right quadrant, development feedback is based on the recipient's goals, priorities, and intentions, emphasizing what the recipient could learn, develop, shift, release, or stop doing.

This model requires the feedback giver and feedback recipient to understand motivations and drivers for feedback to be effective. For the feedback giver, this includes understanding the differences and similarities between their goals for the recipient and the recipient's pursuits. For the feedback recipient, clarity about what is essential

Reinforcing Feedback

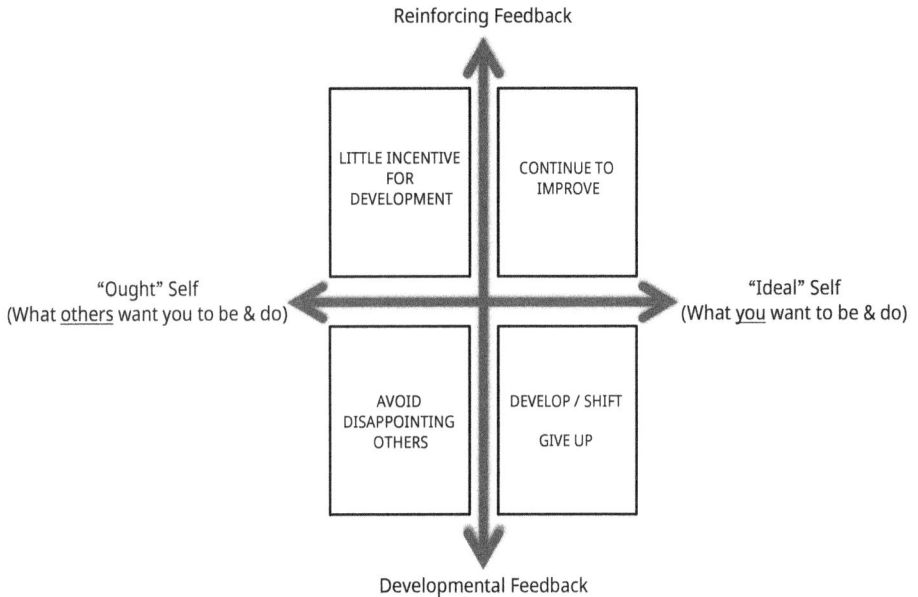

LITTLE INCENTIVE FOR DEVELOPMENT

CONTINUE TO IMPROVE

"Ought" Self
(What <u>others</u> want you to be & do)

"Ideal" Self
(What <u>you</u> want to be & do)

AVOID DISAPPOINTING OTHERS

DEVELOP / SHIFT

GIVE UP

Developmental Feedback

Figure 6.1: Self-Regulation Model of Feedback.

can help facilitate a rich understanding of, appreciation for, and ability to process feedback. For manager-coaches, this requires understanding, appreciating, and using what drives the team members so that feedback can be tailored to meet their goals in the business context. It means minimizing feedback focused on the manager-coach's goals. The manager-coach should take special care and devote time and attention to helping team members discern and articulate goals. Of course, this still requires leaders to define expectations and managers to support achieving stated priorities.

Nohria et al. (2008) noted that four drives are hardwired into our brains, and the degree to which they are satisfied directly affects our emotions and, by extension, behavior. They are the drives to

- acquire
- bond
- comprehend
- defend.

Each of the four drives is independent; they cannot be ordered hierarchically or substituted for another. Manager-coaches cannot just pay their team members a lot. They hope they will feel enthusiastic about their work in an organization where bonding is not fostered, work seems meaningless, or people feel defenseless. Nor is it enough to help team members bond as a tight-knit team when they are underpaid or toiling away at deathly dull jobs. Manager-coaches can get team members to work under such circumstances—they may need the money or have no other current prospects—but manager-coaches will not get the most out of team members, and they risk losing team members when a better opportunity comes. To fully motivate their team members, manager-coaches must address all four drives. This can be done, in part, by tailoring feedback to team members' values—their drivers.

Another way to tailor your feedback for desired results is to consider the developmental stage of the team member. Kegan (1982) and Berger (2012) developed a model of human development tied to the ego. This was presented in Chapter 4. Drago-Severson & Blum-DeStefano (2016) relate that framework to feedback. Table 6.2 illustrates how to tailor feedback using the CBIR model in the context of the recipient's form of mind. Because most adults exhibit the Socialized Mind and some exhibit the Self-authored Mind and Self-transforming Mind, these are illustrated here.

Table 6.2: Forms of Mind Applied to CBIR for Feedback.

Forms of Mind/ Steps for Feedback	Socialized Mind	Self-Authored Mind	Self-Transforming Mind
Context (Provide context for the feedback that will be offered: time, place, situation.)	– Begin with a sincere expression of your value of the person's leadership/technical practices. – Remind the recipient that you are offering feedback intended for their growth and that you are doing so because you care about them. – Remind the recipient of expectations that have been established.	– Remind the recipient that you are offering feedback to help them reach their goals and that you hope the feedback aligns with their growth plans.	– Remind the recipient that the feedback may be a valuable insight into them and their practices. – Discuss how the recipient might learn from the feedback and become better.
Behavior (Identify specific behaviors that illustrate the focus of the feedback.)	– Validate progress and personal qualities. – Show appreciation for the work and their contribution. – Provide validation.	– Acknowledge the recipient's competence and expertise. – Provide an opportunity to discuss ideas.	– Offer your observations as a source of learning and growth. – Focus feedback at the level of self vs. surface behaviors.

Table 6.2 (continued)

Forms of Mind/ Steps for Feedback	Socialized Mind	Self-Authored Mind	Self-Transforming Mind
Impact (Identify the implications and results of the behavior for which the feedback is provided.)	– Focus on the needs, interests, desires, and wishes of the recipient (authority, loved ones, etc.) or society's expectations, values, and opinions about the self and their work and thinking.	– Focus on interpersonal and mutuality, the personal desire to learn and grow, align with the recipient's values, and smooth running of their internal system.	– Invite to collaborate in reflection on behaviors & exploration paradoxes (internal and systematic).
Request (Request behaviors to continue, change, or stop.)	– Requests may be readily accepted from the authoritative position of the feedback provider.	– Provide opportunities to discuss the recipient's ideas, develop their goals, and critique and design changes. – Invite the recipient into a leadership role. – Encourage the recipient to explore new and different ideas, values, and approaches—professionally and personally. – Provide opportunities to collaborate in idea generation and action planning.	– Offer support as the person makes sense of external and systemic contradictions and inconsistencies. – Focus on authorship, choices, and self-government. – Help the recipient develop ways to gather information and feedback from others.

Table 6.2 (continued)

Forms of Mind/ Steps for Feedback	Socialized Mind	Self-Authored Mind	Self-Transforming Mind
Guiding Questions (asked by the recipient)	– Will you (valued other/authority) still like/love/value me? – Will you (valued other/authority) still approve of me? – Will you (valued other/authority) still think I am a good person?	– Am I maintaining and staying true to my integrity, standards, and internal values? – Am I achieving my goals and being guided by my ideals and values? – Am I competent? – Am I living, working, and loving to the best of my ability and potential?	– How can other people's thinking help me to enhance my thinking and behaviors? – How can other people's thinking help me to develop and grow? – How can I seek information and opinions from others to help me modify my understanding?

The following table (Table 6.3) is a worksheet intended to help you prepare to deliver feedback. The first three columns help the manager-coach clarify the messages, the reasons they are being shared, and how to construct messages to meet the recipient's needs. Only the CBIR portion of the worksheet (last four columns) would be used as notes while the feedback is shared.

Table 6.3: CBIR Worksheet.

What is the key message(s) of the feedback?	Why is it important to you (the feedback giver?	Why is it essential to the recipient?	What is the context?	What is the behavior?	What was/is the impact of the behavior?	What request(s) are you making related to the behavior?

Here are two completed examples (Tables 6.4 and 6.5) of the worksheet (Table 6.3).

Table 6.4: Preparing to Deliver Feedback Example A.

Person	Key Message	Why is it Important to YOU?	Why is it Important to THEM?	Context	Behavior	Impact	Request
Joan	– Teaching lessons aligned with curriculum standards is expected – Managing student behavior is essential for learning	– Student achievement – Teaching behaviors conducive to learning – Want her to succeed	– Desire to be successful as a teacher – Frustrated with student behavior – Wishes to see students learn at grade level	– Observed class 3 times in 2 weeks – Assistant principal observed once during the past 2 weeks	– Lessons do not support objectives – Voice raised; students not responding	– Students do not demonstrate a basic understanding – Students are not responding to your instructions	– Teach the material – Gain command of the classroom before being instruction – Work with an instructional support team

Table 6.5: Preparing to Deliver Feedback Example B.

Person	Key Message	Why is it Important to YOU?	Why is it Important to THEM?	Context	Behavior	Impact	Request
Tyrone	– Acknowledge and praise the work completed. – Reinforce the approach taken – Recognize the growth in his leadership	– See the work completed – Help him grow – Prepare him for the following assignments	– Desire to be successful – Desire to be recognized for accomplishments – Seeks more significant leadership responsibilities	– XYZ project final product deliverable	– Work completed on time – High-quality product—creative solutions, responsive to needs – Strategically aligned with our priorities – W and Z (team members) took on additional responsibilities and provided creative solutions	– Team members expressed appreciation for your leadership – The client was pleased – Others recognized the value and quality of the work	– Continue providing leadership to achieve significant results in a high-quality and timely manner – Continue developing the members of your team

Delivering Feedback

When providing feedback to others, offering an opening for the feedback can help break the ice and prepare the team members to receive what the manager-coach is about to tell them. Here are examples of effective openings for feedback:
- Would you like some feedback?
- In the past, you've asked me to provide you with feedback . . . .
- I'd like to give you input about . . .
- I've noticed . . .
- I have an observation about . . .
- I have an insight that I think you might be interested in.
- I'd like to suggest if you are interested . . .
- May I provide you with some feedback?

Once you have opened the conversation, drawing from the kind of feedback language that has proven particularly effective over time can be helpful. Here are examples of effective feedback language currently in use:
- When you . . . I sense that you are/not . . . .
- I felt . . .
- I observed . . .
- You responded . . .
- You acted . . .
- You did . . .

When preparing to give feedback, consider the following:
- What about me is showing up in the feedback I want to offer?
- Is the recipient open to receiving feedback at this time?
- Am I the best person to deliver the feedback?
- What is the best way to convey the message?
- What evidence do I have to support the feedback I want to offer?
- What are my expectations of the person I am offering the feedback to?
- How will I respond to the recipient's potential reactions?

Some feedback is better than others. Bens (2012) suggests the following principles of good feedback:
1. Be descriptive rather than evaluative.
2. Be specific instead of general with facts. Don't just give impressions.
3. Ask permission to provide feedback rather than imposing it. Provide feedback as soon as possible after a situation.
4. Focus the feedback on what can be changed—what the person can implement.

5. Check the feedback to be sure it is accurate and fair.
6. Demonstrate care by offering feedback with the positive intent of helping the other person.

Confrontation and Unpleasant Messages

One form of feedback is confrontation, and it is best employed whenever you observe discrepancies or inconsistencies with what a person
- is saying versus doing.
- says now versus what was said earlier.
- behaves now versus earlier.
- reports versus what has been reported by others.
- did versus committed to do.

Delivering (and receiving) unpleasant news can be difficult. Managers may need to set different expectations frequently during fast-changing business environments. During the turbulence of the last few years, many managers have become uncomfortably familiar with the need to deliver news about layoffs, furloughs, and pay cuts—unpleasant news that immediately affects the recipient and ripples through their personal lives. Examples include information about job loss, health conditions, layoffs, furloughs, elimination of bonuses and pay increases, possible pay cuts, and different expectations. These messages have an emotionally negative impact. They disrupt. They prompt adjustment or change. They require sacrifice.

So, what can you do to prepare and deliver such messages? And what can you do to help yourself receive and process these messages? It will probably not be easy. As tricky as having to give this message is to you, it is perhaps not as problematic as it will be for the recipient. Consider the impacts—e.g., emotional, physical, and financial. You may not do it perfectly, but you will do your best.

Here are some steps you might take:
- **Prepare:** What is the key message? Why is this message being delivered? (Adults especially like to know "why?") If it helps, write the message down and practice providing it. Writing a note as if the meeting has already occurred may be helpful. This aligns with the practice of "start with the end in mind." If this message has corporate or legal implications, clearly understand those guidelines.
- **Schedule** a date, time, and place that is mutually convenient and as soon as practical. That will make the connection more personal, and you can read body language in response to your message being delivered.
- Be **sincere** and demonstrate **empathy** as you take the following steps:
  - State the message. Provide the context for the news, deliver the critical message, explain the rationale, and pause. Let the recipient process the message.

- Ask the recipient to restate the message. This will help to ensure there is a shared understanding.
- Tell them what, if any, support is available to them. This might include an Employee Assistance Program (EAP), outplacement services, paid time off, etc.
- Tell the recipient that they may have questions and that you will do your best to answer them or get the answers. Then, ask them what, if any, questions they may have. Respond to those you can and commit to getting answers to the others.
- End the conversation. While it may be challenging to end the conversation with the person being upset, there is a point where you need to allow them to process the message without you.

Responding to Feedback

Feedback is offered to help the team member change. That change may range from continuing a behavior being developed, shifting to a new behavior, making sense of an event or feeling, or opening new possibilities for consideration. The responses may include denial or rejection, anger related to the facts and perceptions of the feedback, or bargaining about the data. Indeed, the intent of the manager-coach in offering the feedback is to help the team member gain new awareness that can be used to develop skills and shift the team member's mindset and behavior. You need to be prepared for a wide range of responses and the possibility that the initial response will not be the longer-term response.

Team members may take one of several approaches to dealing with the feedback being offered to them. Consider that feedback may be disconcerting, empowering, or affirming. Team members may have initial responses that change as they consider the feedback and develop ways to address it positively and constructively.

It is essential that manager-coaches deliver feedback and then pause. Allow the team member to receive the feedback and process it. Do not over-explain the feedback, and do not try to soften the message.

Feedback orientation is "an individual's overall receptivity to feedback. Feedback orientation influences how team members receive, process, and apply feedback. Elements that make up a feedback orientation include liking feedback, belief in the value of feedback, a tendency to seek feedback and process it thoughtfully, feeling accountable to act on feedback, and a sensitivity to others' views of oneself (London & Smither, 2002).

Someone with a strong feedback orientation is likely to value feedback, be more attuned to feedback in their environment, and be more apt to act on the feedback they receive. On the other hand, a team member with a weak feedback orientation will generally be more resistant to feedback, tend to ignore feedback in their environment, and be less likely to respond to received feedback (Linderbaum & Levy, 2010).

Upon hearing the manager's feedback, the team member faces several choices for how to react or respond. Managers with even the barest experience delivering feedback will have noticed that some recipients welcome feedback, others resist it, and many fall in the middle somewhere. Team members may or may not know how they attributed their choices. Edie Seashore, a pioneer in organization development and the use of self, developed a theory of choice awareness that offers a framework for processing feedback and making choices. She calls this the Choice Awareness Matrix (Patwell & Seashore, 2006). (See Figure 6.2)

	Choice Attributed to Self	Choice Attributed to Others
Aware	*Accountable*	*Blame & Praise*
Unaware	*Automatic*	*Socialization & Inheritance*

Figure 6.2: Choice Awareness Matrix.

Team members make choices about how they attribute decisions and actions. The attribution may be to themselves or others. These choices may be made consciously or unconsciously (aware or unaware). If the choice is attributed to others and is in the unaware category, it is called socialization, which may include following the norms of a group, organization, or social culture. Phrases that illustrate this approach include: "That's the way we do things around here" or "In America, we . . . ." Automatic attributions of choices are in the lower-left quadrant. In this case, the choice is attributed to one's self. However, the team member is unaware of the choice—it is not intentional. Automatic attributions may include doing something the same way it has been done for many years without consciously deciding to do it that way or considering other options. A person in this mode is unaware of his actions; reactions are automatic. Phrases that illustrate this approach include: "That's the way I do it" and "I've always done it that way."

In the upper-right quadrant is attribution to others and awareness of choice. This choice can be illustrated by phrases such as, "I would have done it, but . . .," "I've only been here a year," and "I'm new." This quadrant is referred to as the blame quadrant.

The fourth quadrant is where accountability for choices resides. The team member is responsible for the choices they make and the impact of those choices. Phrases that illustrate this mode include "I made that decision" and "It was my choice to feel/act that way." The manager-coach can use this framework to understand the team member's level of understanding and commitment to feedback and their choices. The manager-coach can then help team members take responsibility for their feelings and behavior, including being accountable for results.

An overarching goal of coaching should be to help team members use feedback from various sources to learn and develop continually. They are receiving and applying feedback results in increased self-awareness and the opportunity to develop. The critical point is that feedback allows one to consider a different perspective and determine what adjustments are needed or desired.

When a manager-coach avoids conflict or confrontations or is challenged to process feedback from others, they will probably have difficulty providing meaningful and timely feedback to team members. You must seek to understand your own responses to feedback as you develop the skill of giving feedback to team members in the context of coaching relationships.

In her research about mindsets, Carol Dweck (2000, 2007) identified two dominant perspectives that people have. One is a "fixed mindset" focused on performance, and the other is a "growth mindset" focused on learning and development. The fixed or performance goals-oriented team member tends to be most concerned with measuring ability. They emphasize demonstrating or validating superior competence by seeking favorable assessments of ability while avoiding unfavorable judgments. They are likely to ask, "Is my ability adequate or inadequate?" and consider outcomes to be a chief source of information relevant to this concern. Failure outcomes may readily elicit the helpless attribution that ability is inadequate. A team member with the growth or learning goals mindset tends to be most concerned with increasing their capacity and extending their mastery. They emphasize acquiring new skills, mastering new situations, and working hard. They will likely ask, "What is the best way to increase my ability or achieve mastery?" and consider outcomes that will provide information about whether one is pursuing an optimal course and, if not, what else might be necessary. Failure means that the current strategy may be insufficient for the task and require upgrading or revision. A person with a growth mindset is more likely to be receptive to feedback and see failures as opportunities for learning and growth. As a manager-coach, you may have opportunities to help team members see their operating mindset and embrace a learning and growth mindset. Those who receive feedback might follow these steps to process the gift of feedback:

1. Thank the person who offered it.
2. Seek clarification as needed.
3. Consider the implications.
4. Develop a plan of action.
5. Implement the action (e.g., more feedback, direct action, no action).
6. Seek feedback.

In their study of the effects of coachee characteristics (i.e., learning goal orientation and developmental self-efficacy) and coaching relationships (i.e., coach credibility and perceived similarity) on feedback receptivity, Bozer and Joo (2015), learning orientation and coach credibility were the strongest predictors for feedback receptivity. When leaders have a higher goal orientation and perceive their coach as credible, they are more receptive to feedback. So, manager-coaches should find common ground (e.g., goals, priorities, interests, leadership styles) with team members and help the team members develop and maintain a growth mindset. This will foster receptivity and growth.

Points to Remember

Here are some points to remember when providing feedback in the context of the role of manager-coach.
- Feedback is a gift, although it may not always be received as intended.
- Develop a keen awareness of one's responses to feedback (giving and receiving) to improve effectiveness and impact.
- Team members expect managers to provide feedback: Just do it.
- Once feedback is given, allow the recipient the opportunity and support to make meaning and act on the feedback.
- Own the feedback offered.
- Use facts to support claims about the team member's observed behavior observed. Do not judge the person.
- Be specific.
- Always be aware of the intent of offering the feedback. Make sure it is positive and constructive.
- Not all feedback is effective feedback. To be effective in providing feedback to coaching team members, consider applying the following principles:
- Be descriptive rather than judgmental or evaluative. Tell the team member being coached what behavior was noticed or what happened. Focus on behaviors and impacts.
- Be specific instead of general. Describe what was observed, heard, or experienced so that facts, not impressions, form the basis for the feedback.
- Time it. Feedback should be given as soon as practical after the situation described.
- Use hypotheses. Offer hypotheses to test one's impressions and conclusions.

- Focus on what can be changed. Make suggestions for change that clients can implement and are aligned with their goals.
- Check the feedback. Make sure one's understanding is accurate and fair. Check with the client to avoid misjudging the situation or behavior.
- Demonstrate care. Offer feedback with the positive intent of helping the other person.

Summary

Feedback is a gift. It may or may not be accepted. The feedback provider must be prepared for the feedback they offer to be rejected, as well for it to be used. The timing of feedback is essential. Provide it as soon as reasonable and when the circumstances are conducive to providing it and conducive for the recipient to receive it. Consider who is best suited to provide the feedback: usually, a person with firsthand knowledge of the behavior. However, sometimes that person may not be available, or the relational dynamics between the giver and receiver are not conducive to the feedback being received as intended. Consider the power dynamics between the giver and receiver. If you are the recipient's manager, you have great power by the nature of your position. Consider how that may impact how the feedback will be received. Carefully consider your intentions in giving feedback. Ask yourself: "What impact do I want to have due to the feedback?" Finally, the message itself is critical, so take the time to prepare to provide feedback. Use the CBIR model.

A Conversation with Kathy Elling
Chief School Performance Officer & Associate Superintendent (Retired)
Charlotte-Mecklenburg Schools

This conversation was recorded and transcribed, then edited for clarity and conciseness.

John Bennett (JB): *Please tell me about some of the ways you've used coaching.*

Kathy Elling (KE): I conceptualize it as just the way of work. For me, it is engaging in observation, reflection and practice with whoever I am working with. I try to model instead of rushing to a solution. When I see something happening, I can quickly think, "OK, here's the fix," so I must remember that's not my role. I feel like my orientation has always been as a developer of people. I think my skill set naturally lent itself to that.

JB: *How have you developed this mindset and skill set of coaching?*

KE: I came into the field initially with a school psychology background, and then I got a school counseling certification. I had some foundational skills. Going through the executive coaching certificate program [at Queens University of Charlotte] expanded my skill set, and it required practice to stay in that coaching mindset and framework. My personality and previous experience were heavily ingrained in "what's the diagnosis for what we're seeing?" And in my role, I thought I had to figure out how to fix things. And as a building principal, I was supervising teachers. I was expected to prescribe solutions.

Coaching, on the other hand, is about how to get people to a place where they can solve issues for themselves. The short answer is that I had to unlearn some practices and develop new ones. One of those was to be mindful of asking good questions and expecting a particular solution. I have learned to stay in the role of helping others problem-solve versus being the problem-solver.

JB: *I'm curious about how you see feedback fitting into this, both giving and receiving.*

KE: Very often, I'll give myself feedback before I get feedback from somebody else. I don't feel like I routinely do an excellent job of providing feedback. There's a way of giving feedback in a coaching model that draws upon what you're hearing and what the individual is saying, then paraphrasing it so that when you provide it back to them. They're going, "Ah. That's it. That's what I didn't get. That's what I missed." And there's more direct feedback, which says, "I hear that you've said X. I have the pleasure of seeing your work. I'm seeing you do this, this, and this. So, how does that land on you? How does that come together for you?"

I think of my work with individuals and in a coaching way as a mirror. We both have to be in the mirror. I have to see what you see, and you have to see what I see. And the folks that I have struggled most with are those people that can't get in the mirror. They can't see themselves in a uniquely distinct way and are locked into that perception, and they're not able to integrate how others see them. They are hard to work with because they just don't have an impetus to change how they see themselves.

I've not always worked in environments where feedback and growth were embraced. I do think it's a culture. You need to have a culture of developing people. If you're on my team, we are responsible for helping you grow and improve.

JB: *Let's go back to the feedback piece. I'm operating under a renewed commitment that a feedback-rich culture lends itself to a coaching culture. This requires both the manager and team members to accept and give feedback.*

KE: I agree. This reminds me of an experience that occurred early in my career. We had an art teacher who was an exceptional artist. She could not teach elementary art to save her life. My philosophy has always been that if I hire you and you are on our team, I will do everything possible to support you. We worked and worked and worked to help her. When it came time to talk with her about whether she should continue, I remember saying to her, "You know, you're an exceptional artist. There's being an artist, and there's being an art teacher. You are an artist. You're not an art teacher." You would have thought I'd given her a winning lottery ticket. She said, "You're correct. This is not for me. I need to resign." And she was grateful. I delivered the message in a way she understood. She left and became a successful artist.

JB: *What do you see as the value of using a coaching approach as a leader manager?*

KE: I think the value is in succession planning. If you invest in people and develop their leadership capacity, you're engaging in a way that enables the organization to sustain.

JB: *What advice would you offer a leader manager who's considering using a coaching approach?*

KE: Learn some foundational practices. And try them out; practice with someone open and willing. I would approach it like I'm trying on a new set of skills. I feel like this is the way we're going to be able to work together, and this is the way I want to work. Try the new practices and get feedback from that individual about what was helpful (and not) to them.

Chapter 7
Coaching Skill: Listening for Understanding

Consider how long you think you could bear to be quiet and let someone think out loud. With only the occasional benign murmuring and nod and smile of understanding from you and the occasional question requesting ever more thoughts, a person in your presence might just turn into a genius— at least, for that moment.

—Nancy Kline, 1999, p. 53

Listening is fundamental to communication and coaching. While hearing is passive, listening is active. Manager-coaches need to develop the skill of listening to themselves and their team members. Listening to yourself involves paying attention to what you are saying and not saying, along with your thoughts and feelings. It consists of listening to those you coach by paying attention to what they are saying and not saying, doing and not doing, their body language, feedback, and reactions from others, etc. Think of a specific time when you felt someone listened to you. What did they do? How did you feel? How did you respond? Now, think of a specific time when you did not feel like someone listened to you. What did they do? What did they not do? How did you feel? What were the impacts of their ineffective listening?

Effective listening in the context of coaching allows the manager-coach to understand team members, respond to their needs, help them gain insights, and be aware of their impacts. Listening requires curiosity. Most leaders have taken a course in public speaking, yet very few have taken a course on private listening. The best speakers listen to their audience and craft their message and delivery to meet the audience where they are.

In coaching, the skill of listening is critical. In this chapter, listening for understanding in the context of coaching is defined, the importance of effective listening for understanding as a manager-coach is explained, and effective listening practices in the context of coaching are shared. In addition, common barriers to effective listening and best practices are described along with listening levels.

When asked to reflect on personal experiences in which someone truly listened, managers shared that the listener
- gave their full attention.
- was fully present, not distracted.
- demonstrated interest in what was being said by being curious and empathetic.
- cared about them and what was important to them, and showed genuine interest.
- suspended judgment.
- connected their personal experiences with what the speaker was saying while keeping the focus on the speaker—not the listener.
- did not cut them off, interrupt, rush, try to "fix," or resolve a problem for them.

https://doi.org/10.1515/9783111002415-007

As a result, the managers shared that they felt appreciated, embraced, heard, helped, included, reflected, respected, supported, understood, valued, willing to share more, ready to collaborate, and validated. When someone listens, the listeners may experience feeling calm, curious, eager, empathetic, engaged, helpful, informed, present, and trusted.

Contrast those positive feelings with how you felt when you were thinking out loud about a problem, and the listener jumped in with a solution before you finished. We have probably all had that experience.

One of the best ways to demonstrate respect for others is to listen to them. In coaching, listening is more than simply making sense of what the team member says. Listening involves detecting and making sense of what is not spoken by connecting data observed and gathered from other sources. Effective listening is essential for manager-coaches, allowing them to thoroughly understand their team members' concerns and goals. By actively listening, managers can gain insight into the team member's perspectives, identify underlying issues, and help the team member develop a plan of action. "As Arlene Mendoza, senior innovation program manager at Alum, so astutely proclaimed, 'Listening to understand is a whole different dynamic because it's about extracting and understanding what the other person is trying to communicate to you' " (Younger, 2021, p. 91).

Manager-coaches are constantly engaged in sending and receiving messages in many different forms to and from their teammates, and this process of sending and receiving messages is at the heart of communication in any context. Effective listening by manager-coaches allows them to create a safe and supportive environment for their team members and helps them to identify their strengths and areas for improvement.

Communication is two-way; receiving the message is as important as sending it. The key to receiving messages is listening for understanding. One challenge associated with communication is understanding the message being sent. When a person being coached communicates during a coaching session, a message is sent. However, the team member may have difficulty articulating the message, and the manager-coach may not perceive or understand it in the same manner it was intended. When that happens, the usual result is miscommunication or misunderstanding. Therefore, the manager-coach's role is to help team members form that message, clarify it for themselves, and effectively send it to the manager. The coach facilitates this discovery process by asking powerful questions and providing feedback—two coaching skills that will be explored in detail in other chapters.

To help put communication in the context of coaching in perspective, Adam Kahane (2021) offers four modes of listening and talking:

- **Downloading:** People say what they always say; involves advocating ("The truth is . . ."; "I have my truth.") People typically do not listening—they are reloading.
- **Debating:** Talking is a clash of ideas; everyone says what they think ("In my opinion . . ."). Listening is from the outside, factually and objectively; all parties engage in advocating and inquiring.

- **Dialoguing:** Self-reflective talking ("In my experience . . ."; "I think . . ."; "I feel . . ."; "I want . . ."). Listening occurs as if from inside themselves—empathetically and subjectively ("I hear where you are coming from.").
- **Presencing:** Sensing what is manifesting and being fully present—attentive and undistracted. ("What am I noticing here and now?")

Awareness of the filters the team member uses to communicate and the filters the coach uses to interpret the message may help reduce miscommunication and misunderstanding. Filters are the values, beliefs, and assumptions that consciously or unconsciously influence the message sent and received.

The coach may use all five types of listening Kratz and Kratz (1995) describe in their book *Effective Listening Skills*:
- listening to bond
- listening to appreciate
- listening to learn
- listening to decide
- listening to enable

In the coaching conversation, the manager-coach typically spends 70%-80% of their time listening to understand. In the role of coach, strive to speak no more than 20% of the time during a coaching conversation, allowing the team member to speak at least 80% of the time. Following this guideline will make the coach's statements and questions more impactful. Effective listening requires listeners to be aware of their experiences, values, mental models, biases, and prejudgments about topics and people. Otherwise, the listener will not be open to what is shared or be curious to explore issues with the speaker. "It's so easy to look and see what we pass through in this world, but we don't. If you're like me, you see so little. You see what you expect to see rather than what's there" (Buechner, 2017, p. 25).

Building on the teachings of Wilfred Bion, the manager-coach can develop the skill of listening without memory or desire. When the manager-coach listens with memory, you trap the team member in an old personal agenda. When the manager-coach listens with fascination, you tie team members to a present or future personal agenda. Listening with an agenda disrupts and hinders (which we do every day) authentic conversation. To avoid listening with an agenda, the manager-coach must recognize disruptive behaviors: interjecting at the wrong times, showing visible undisguised prejudgment, and nodding mindlessly. Then, the manager-coach can actively self-correct: abandon agendas, find the storyteller, and tune out the inner critic (Aguayo, 2014).

Rebecca Ripley and Kittie Watson (2014) noted that each person has a preferred listening style or combination of four preferred types.
- **People-oriented listeners** identify the emotional states of others and tend to be attracted to personal interests and stories. They have a strong desire to build caring relationships. As a result, this listener may demonstrate care and concern for

others, provide clear feedback signals (verbal and nonverbal), and notice moods in others. On the other hand, they may become over-involved with the feelings of others, internalize or adopt the emotional state of others, and tune out when something is not attractive.

- **Action-oriented listeners** focus intensely on the task, have clear expectations, value-focused and structured presentations and conversations with a few key points. As a result, this listener may get to the core of a matter quickly, give clear feedback about expectations, help others focus on what is important, and identify inconsistencies in the messages of others. On the other hand, they may be impatient with rambling speakers, ask blunt questions, appear critical, and minimize relational issues and concerns.
- **Time-oriented listeners** are direct in how they value time and encourage others to do the same. As a result, they manage time effectively, let others know the time boundaries of conversations, discourage wordy speakers, and send cues to others when time is wasted. On the other hand, they tend to be impatient with time wasters, interrupt others, rush speakers, and limit creativity in others by imposing time pressure. Ripley and Watson note that only 7% of people identify with this preference.
- **Content-oriented listeners** carefully evaluate everything they hear and prefer to listen to experts and other highly credible sources. As a result, these listeners are likely to value technical information, test for clarity about what they hear, provide analysis, and look at various sides of an issue. On the other hand, they may be overly focused on details and minimize the value of nontechnical information.

Similarly, Minehart et al. (2022) identify four listening styles:
- **Analytical listeners** aim to analyze a problem from a neutral starting point.
- **Relational listeners** aim to build connections and understand the emotions underlying a message.
- **Critical listeners** seek to judge the conversation's content and the speaker's reliability.
- **Task-focused listeners** shape a conversation toward the efficient transfer of important information.

Regardless of which of these four-item types of listening is occurring, manager-coaches (and everyone else) can take steps to improve their ability to listen. To be a better listener:
- Recognize your preferred listening style and adapt or leverage it appropriately for the coaching conversation.
- Be fully present. Remove distractions (mobile phones, email alerts, visual distractions, possible interruptions).
- Approach the conversation with an open mind. Note your assumptions and use them as a source of inquiry.

- Be aware of how well you are listening and make adjustments.
- Be curious and avoid quick judgments and conclusions. Ask genuine questions that help you understand and advance the conversation for the other person.
- Be prepared for a wide range of thoughts and emotions.

Challenges to Listening

Most people spend more time listening than on any other communication activity, yet many never learn to listen well. One reason is that they develop poor listening habits that stick with them throughout life. These are some of the most common poor listening habits:

1. **Not Paying Attention.** Listeners may allow themselves to be distracted or to think of something else. Also, not wanting to listen often contributes to a lack of attention.
2. **"Pseudolistening."** People often think about something else and deliberately try to look like they are listening. Such pretense may leave the speaker with the impression that the listener has heard some vital information or instructions offered by the speaker.
3. **Listening But Not Hearing.** Sometimes, a person listens only to facts or details or how they are presented and misses the real meaning.
4. **Rehearsing.** Some people listen until they want to say something. Then they quit listening, start rehearsing what they will say, and wait for an opportunity to respond.
5. **Interrupting.** The listener does not wait until the complete meaning can be determined but interrupts so forcefully that the speaker stops mid-sentence.
6. **Hearing What Is Expected.** People frequently think they heard speakers say what they expected them to say. Alternatively, they refuse to listen to what they do not want to hear.
7. **Feeling Defensive.** The listeners assume they know the speaker's intention or why something was said or expect to be attacked for various other reasons.
8. **Ignoring the Answer.** This involves behaving like you asked a question to hear yourself talk instead of listening for the answer.
9. **Listening for a Point of Disagreement.** Some listeners seem to wait for the chance to attack someone. They listen intently for points on which they can disagree.
10. **Misinterpreting the Response.** The listener thinks the respondent agrees with what was said simply because they answered your question (Berger 2014, 2018; Fadem, 2009; Marcic et al., 2000; Murphy, 2019).

A manager-coach should consider whether they use some of these habits in specific situations or with particular people.

Effective listening involves giving the client your full attention and responding in a way that shows you understand what they are saying. It involves paying attention to the client's words, tone, and body language and asking clarifying questions to ensure understanding.

Managers can do a variety of things to become better listeners, including applying the following tips for better listening:

– Remove distractions that may negatively impact listening.
– Give the speaker your full attention.
– Listen for context.
– Suspend assumptions and judgment. Listen with an open mind.
– Remain curious/interested. Avoid becoming emotional or defensive.
– Observe body language.
– Ask for clarification.
– Listen to others in the same way that you would prefer to be listened to.
– Demonstrate respect by holding the confidence of the speaker when asked.

Techniques to Enhance Listening

Jack Zenger and Joseph Folkman (2016) challenge listeners to consider which of six listening levels they function at when listening. What could you do to advance the level at which you are listening for understanding?

Level 1: The manager-coach creates a safe environment to discuss difficult, complex, or emotional issues.

Level 2: The manager-coach clears away distractions like phones and laptops, focuses attention on the team members, and makes appropriate eye contact.

Level 3: The manager-coach seeks to understand the substance of what the team member is saying. They capture ideas, ask questions, and restate issues to confirm their understanding.

Level 4: The manager-coach observes nonverbal cues, such as facial expressions, perspiration, respiration rates, gestures, posture, and numerous other subtle body language signals. These cues represent approximately 80% of what we communicate.

Level 5: The manager-coach increasingly understands the team member's emotions and feelings about the discussed topic and identifies and acknowledges them. The manager-coach empathizes with and validates those feelings in a supportive, nonjudgmental way.

Level 6: The manager-coach asks questions that clarify assumptions the team member holds and helps the team member see the issue in a new light. For instance, the manager-coach might inject some thoughts and ideas about the topic that could be useful to the team members without hijacking the conversation so that they or their issues become the subject of the dialogue.

Renowned psychologist Carl Rogers (1980) referred to listening as an active process. He described himself by saying, "I hear the words, the thoughts, the feeling tones, the personal meaning, even the meaning below the conscious intent of the speaker" (p. 8).

A variety of techniques are available to help develop listeners. Here are some of the most effective:

– **Attending** involves establishing and maintaining culturally appropriate eye contact with the team members while maintaining a natural, relaxed physical posture that demonstrates interest. This technique is supported by using natural gestures that emphasize the manager-coach's intended message and by using verbal statements that relate to the person being coached statements without interruptions, questions, or new topics. It is essential to convey that the manager understands the team member's thoughts and feelings before responding.

– **Paraphrasing** is a way to demonstrate to the team members that their thoughts are heard and understood. Reflective listening involves paraphrasing what the team member has said to confirm understanding and build trust. By reflecting on the team member's words, the manager-coach can help the client clarify their thoughts and feelings and better understand their concerns. It is a nonjudgmental way of validating that the manager-coach believes the ideas of the person being coached are legitimate and respected. Paraphrasing allows the team member to hear how their ideas are being listened to. Paraphrasing clarifies what is heard and encourages the team members to think aloud. Paraphrase means to restate the essence of the person's content in the manager-coach's own words. Paraphrasing might use language like this: "It sounds like you are saying . . ." or "Let me test my understanding of what I heard you say . . .". Once you paraphrase the team member's thoughts, wait for the team member to respond. The team member's response may take one or more of the following forms: agree, seek to clarify, disagree, extend what has been paraphrased, or shift the focus of the conversation.

– **Drawing people out** is another skill to support team members in clarifying, developing, and refining their ideas. Drawing out demonstrates support and helps others further explore what matters to them. It is advantageous when people have difficulty clarifying ideas and do not realize they are being vague and confusing to the listener. Drawing people out may also be used in coaching when manager-coaches are unsure they understand what team members are trying to say. Phrases that might be used to draw people out include:
- "Please say more about that."
- "What do you mean by . . .?"
- "How is that working for you?"
- "What thoughts/feelings does that bring up for you?"
- "How does that appear?"

– **Mirroring** is a structured, more formal version of paraphrasing that demonstrates the manager-coach's neutrality and builds trust. This technique is instrumental in the early stages of a coaching relationship or during a particularly challenging conversation. Mirroring can speed up the flow of the coaching conversation and can be used to facilitate idea generation. To mirror, repeat verbatim the team member's words. Restate the feelings and content of the team member's communication while demonstrating understanding and acceptance. Mirror the client's words, pace, volume, tone, and gestures. For example, the team member says, "I feel confused about the direction the company is taking with the change reorganization of responsibilities." The manager-coach might say in a similar tone and pace, "I hear you saying, '*I am confused about my responsibilities.*'"

– **Tracking** involves keeping track of various thoughts and feelings expressed by the team member in a coaching session (or over a series of coaching conversations). The team member may express multiple ideas or pose several challenges quickly, confusing the manager-coach and themselves. Tracking makes the thoughts and feelings visible to the team members and asks them to focus. Your task is to listen to those thoughts and feelings and help the team members focus on the most important ones to be addressed or considered. Tracking comprises a four-step process:
1. The manager-coach indicates you are going to summarize the conversation.
2. The coach names the topics or concepts that have been introduced.
3. The team member checks with the client for accuracy.
4. The manager-coach invites the client to determine how they would like to proceed.

In the form of statements, the manager-coach might say: "At this time, at least four topics are in the conversation. I want to make sure I am tracking with you and them. The points are A, B, C, and D. Am I hearing you correctly? (Pause for confirmation and clarification; do not defend what you said.) Now, how would you like to proceed with our conversation?"

– **Acknowledging feelings** is another skill that can be applied to listening for understanding. In this case, the manager-coach identifies an emotion and then names it to help the team member recognize and accept the feeling. This technique involves a three-step process:
1. The manager-coach pays attention to the problematic elements of the coaching conversation and the experiences being shared (and not shared) by the team member, with the manager looking for cues that might indicate the presence of feelings.
2. The manager-coach asks a question that names the feelings you see. (Examples include: "It sounds like you might be feeling worried/frustrated/angry, etc.?" or "From the tone of your voice, I wonder if you are feeling . . .?" or "Is that what you are feeling . . .?")
3. The manager-coach uses facilitative listening to support the team member in responding to the feelings the manager named.

– **Validating** is a practice that legitimizes the client's opinion or feeling without assuming a position of agreement or disagreement. Validating helps the team members be open and say more. Remember, the manager-coach supports the team member in expressing the team member's truth. Validating involves a three-step process:
1. The coach paraphrases or draws out the team member's opinions or feelings.
2. The manager-coach considers whether the team member needs additional support.
3. The coach offers support by acknowledging the legitimacy of what the team member said. Examples of this acknowledgment include:
   - "I see what you are saying . . ."
   - "I accept that this is important to you."
   - "Now I see your point of view."

– **Empathizing** is the ability to understand and share the feelings of another. Empathetic listening is understanding and sharing the team member's feelings. This type of listening requires the manager-coach to put themselves in the team member's shoes and understand their perspective, even if they disagree. There are many ways to empathize, which is essentially attempting to view the world from the other person's point of view. The manager-coach imagines what the person might feel and why and then forms any insights into a statement of acknowledgment and support. With empathizing, the coach attempts to identify with and share the actual feelings of the team member being coached. The primary approach is to name what the manager-coach believes the team member is experiencing (e.g., anger, disappointment, rage, sadness, happiness). The manager-coach may name the factors that led to the team member's experience (e.g., "With all the work you put into the project, I imagine you were delighted with the outcome."). Another approach is to identify concerns about sharing feelings with others. The coach might say, "I imagine it might be difficult to discuss this topic with your colleague." With each of these approaches, the manager-coach should ask for confirmation by allowing the team member to confirm or refine a shared understanding, as it is possible to misinterpret or misrepresent the team member's experiences. Empathizing can also help the team member reframe the experience to make an action plan.

– **Intentional silence** involves remaining silent after a team member has spoken for an extended period. Staying silent allows the team members to formulate thoughts, process them, and develop a follow-up statement. Employing intentional silence also allows the coach to reflect on what is happening in the coaching conversation and formulate a question or comment. Such silences also can be used to slow the pace of the coaching conversation.

– **Listening with a point of view** involves listening to what a team member is saying or observing actions taken, then attempting to interpret them from the perspective of a specific person, group, or role such as manager, team member, regulator, customer, or another person. An example of this would be when the manager-coach allows their mental models, values, assumptions, and knowledge to blind them to other points of view and seek information that confirms their original point of view. It could also take the form of listening based on your role as the team member's manager. The manager-coach might notice behaviors aligned or misaligned with organizational or team priorities, the team member's professional goals, or expectations established between the manager and team member.

– **Summarizing** involves restating what the team member has said, conclusions that have been formed, options that have been developed, or actions that will be taken. Summarizing is used to focus the coaching conversation, help the person being coached form a new perspective, or commit to a view that has formed. The manager-coach must use this technique sparingly to avoid doing the team member's work or inserting the manager's point of view. Asking a person being coached to summarize a portion of a coaching session, possibilities being considered, insights gained, or commitments to action that were made can also be an effective way to use the technique (Kaner, 2007; Bolton, 1979; Brammer & MacDonald, 2003).

Coaches listen with their ears and eyes, as well as with the other senses. People's thoughts are not directly observable, but their words and actions reveal their thoughts. Their emotions are often concealed and less visible.

Manager-coaches can help team members by listening to the words, observing behaviors, exploring thoughts, and accessing feelings in a manner focused on self-discovery to serve the team member's goals for coaching. The manager-coach's behavior will evoke the team member's feelings, thoughts, and behaviors in response. Intent plus action yields impact; behavior plus feelings comprises effects. In other words, the intended result occurs when the manager's intent to serve the team member is combined with the manager's supportive behaviors.

In consulting, counseling, problem-solving, and coaching, we often say, "The presenting problem is rarely the real problem." When coaching with an emphasis on solutions and less focus on problem-solving, this axiom may best be restated as "the presenting issues are rarely the real opportunities." Helping team members understand and accept the deeper issues and a willingness to address them will result in a more significant and longer-lasting impact on coaching. This approach requires listening and exploring.

Effective Listening: Manager-Coach

This mnemonic, LISTEN, may help you remember a few critical points about developing and practicing the art and science of effective listening for understanding:

–   **L**ook at the person talking to connect with them, show interest, and seek to understand what they are saying.

- Inquire by being curious and asking genuine questions for a deeper understanding.
- Practice Silence to allow the other person time to talk, think, reflect, and prepare to speak.
- Talk only after the other person has finished speaking. Choose words to demonstrate care, support, empathy, understanding, connection, and encouragement.
- Enthusiasm: Display appropriate emotions related to what the other person is saying and doing—e.g., excitement, energy, sadness, concern, and joy.
- Neutral: Suspend judgment when listening; seek to understand what the other person is saying.

Summary

Listening is an active skill that is essential to coaching. Listening is one of the most important ways to demonstrate respect for the speaker, and listening to understand is one of the greatest gifts you can give your team members. Here are some tips:
- Be fully present and give your full attention to the speaker.
- Be aware of your assumptions and mental models.
- Demonstrate care and empathy.
- Seek to understand what is expressed with words, body language, and emotions through the perspective of the person you are coaching.
- Ask questions for clarification.
- Make statements to support clarity.
- Be patient. The person you are coaching may have difficulty expressing themselves.
- Foster sense- or meaning-making on the part of the person you are coaching.

Chapter 8
Coaching Skill: Asking Powerful Questions

We fear the unknown because it is full of questions. Questions are dangerous, risky. They prevent us from settling in and feeling comfortable.
                                                —Aaron Mahnke, 2017, Episode 59: A Deep Fear

Many of us have taken courses and completed workshops on public speaking, yet very few of us have learned the importance of asking powerful questions. Asking questions demonstrates curiosity, shows interest, solicits answers, engages others, prompts shifts in thoughts and actions, fosters reflection, helps to reframe a situation, helps generate ideas and solutions, and builds rapport. In other words, questions perform many functions in developing ourselves and our relationships.

One of my favorite quotations is from the winner of the 1988 Nobel Prize in Literature, Naguib Mahfouz (n.d.), who said, "You can tell a man is clever by his answers. You can tell whether a man is wise by his questions." Be wise! And, as Bertrand Russell said, "In all affairs, it's a healthy thing now and then to hang a question mark on the things you have long taken for granted." Asking questions requires trust and vulnerability.

Too often, leaders are expected (by themselves or others) to have answers. Saying "I don't know" or "I don't understand" may be perceived as a sign of weakness. Yet, being trusted and willing to be vulnerable opens the possibilities for curiosity, exploration, relatedness, and creativity. The six-step coaching process described in Chapter 2 relies on questions.

This chapter explains the importance of effectively asking questions as a manager-coach and describes the types of questions used in coaching. And it concludes with tips that serve as reminders for manager-coaches.

The Power of Asking Questions

In every aspect of our lives, questions are powerful. Whether asked as a parent, friend, colleague, manager, leader, or professional coach, questions serve many purposes, including
1. opening up thinking.
2. directing and focusing thinking.
3. prompting understanding.
4. clarifying _____.
5. encouraging creative thinking.
6. demonstrating interest and curiosity.
7. fostering divergent and convergent thoughts.
8. calling to action.

https://doi.org/10.1515/9783111002415-008

9. helping us understand and empathize with others.
10. discerning choices and making decisions.

Manager-coaches must also demonstrate wisdom by asking powerful questions to help team members discover what is essential, gain self-awareness, develop solutions, take action, and reflect on and learn from experiences. Asking powerful questions is one of two coaching skills used in each coaching step for a change process.

As humans we tend to delete most of what we see, categorize the rest, and then file it away in long-term memory using categories. When provided with new or different data, we quickly make judgments, develop assumptions, and dismiss what does not fit with what we already know, believe, or assume. This is the opposite of having a "beginner's mind." Assumptions and biases may be embedded in the questions we ask. Our mental models help us to both process data and dismiss data. Remaining curious is critical to understanding, developing possibilities, making evidence-based decisions, and acting.

A good manager-coach does not tell you what to do. Instead, they facilitate a discovery process to help you figure it out for yourself. The manager-coach helps others get from where they are to where they want to go. This means the focus is on the team member's priorities, not the manager-coach's.

Asking powerful questions is arguably one of a coach's most frequently used skills, second to listening. Kilburg (2000) promoted the idea of "requesting permission to ask questions, explore issues, challenge or push the client" (p. 116). Manager-coach es ask questions for many reasons, including exploring, understanding, focusing on the team member being coached, helping them verbalize what they are experiencing, and self-generating.

Using questions to *explore* is designed to help team members examine their thoughts, feelings, skills, interests, goals, and perceptions. Questions help the manager-coach and team member *understand* what the team member is saying and help the team member make sense of experiences. Manager-coaches use questions to *put the focus back on the team member being coached* to support the independence and interdependence of the team member and to avoid dependence on the coach for answers or solutions. Questions may also *help the client verbalize* thoughts, feelings, concerns, or understanding. In this way, the team member is kinetically engaged in the process. Finally, manager-coaches use questions to help team members *self-generate* questions, allowing team members to process information and experiences.

Questions allow manager-coaches to gain deeper understanding and clarity, test gaps and perceptions, and engage the team members—to draw them out. We need to formulate questions that invite honesty, dignity, and revelation. There are many forms and purposes of questions. Below are some of the forms and types of questions, along with a brief definition and example.

- **Application.** A question that focuses on how an idea, skill, opinion, etc., can be used to achieve the desired outcome. Example: "How will you use this?"

- **Closed-ended.** A question with a specific answer is often one of several options. Example: "Which of those three topics would you like to focus on first?" These questions are instrumental in gaining commitment, clarifying points, and ending a step in the coaching process before moving to the next step.
- **Commitment.** A question that seeks commitment for a decision or course of action. Example: "What will you do by Tuesday?"
- **Contextual.** A question to understand what is happening or what is being discussed. Example: "What was happening when you made that decision?"
- **Convergent.** A question that focuses on reducing the focus of the conversation. Example: "Which of those options would you like to pursue?"
- **Divergent.** A question intended to shift away from a particular line of thought or feeling to consider another perspective. It recombines existing elements or ideas to create something new and original. Example: "What is possible if you look at X and Y, then combine them into something different?"
- **Expansion.** A question to expand thinking and consideration. Example: "What other possible actions can you identify?"
- **Open-ended.** A question that does not propose a specific answer. Example: "What are some options you might consider?" Highly effective leaders and coaches use many of these questions.
- **Reflective.** A question that focuses on what is happening, what has happened or will happen, aimed at making sense of it. Example: "What does this mean for you?"
- **Reframing.** A question to prompt a shift of perspectives. Example: "What would you do if resources were unlimited?"
- **Why.** A question to understand meaning, purpose, or value. Be careful with "Why" questions. They can prompt defensiveness or philosophical answers. Minimize your use of "why" questions in coaching. Example: "Why did you take that particular approach?"
- **Leading.** Seeking information and indirectly shaping the answer. This type of question does not align with coaching. It is too directive and does not empower the team members to make choices. Example: "Of those options, this one is best— right?"

Before you make a statement, consider what questions you could ask. Asking a question instead prompts the person to whom the question is directed to assess the situation and formulate a response. This builds independence and interdependence. In other words, we can practice being a fountain of questions versus a fountain of answers.

When asking powerful questions, you must allow sufficient time for the answers. This may require seconds, minutes, days, weeks, or even longer. If your question is worth asking, it is worth waiting for an answer. "By 'living with' a question, thinking about it and then stepping away from it, allowing it to marinate, you give your [or the other person's] brain a chance to come up with the kinds of fresh insights and 'What If' possibilities that can lead to breakthroughs" (Berger, 2014, p. 109).

Managers are encouraged to use open-ended questions because they tend to engage and draw out the team members. When coaching (as a manager or professional), here are a few things to keep in mind:

- Take time to develop your question after the other person stops speaking.
- Base questions on what the other person said and what you observed.
- Use questions to facilitate the conversation through the steps in the change coaching model.
- Be aware of your assumptions, values, mental models, and their impacts on your curiosity.
- Avoid contextualizing your questions. If you are in sync with the person you are asking, just ask the question.
- Keep your questions as brief as possible. Fifteen words or less is a guide.
- Wait for an answer. Seven seconds may seem like a long time to wait, but a thought-provoking question requires processing time.
- Experiment with questions. You don't have to hit a home run whenever you ask a question. Remember that some questions may not be as powerful as you wish.
- Be prepared for the answer to your question to take a different direction. If that happens, your question had an impact, just not what you imagined.

Linking Questions and the Change Coaching Process

The six-step coaching for change conversation model described in chapter two can be used in formal and informal coaching conversations. All coaching is about change, and manager-coaches can apply this dynamic framework. The steps flow in a sequence, but it may be necessary to move backward to move forward because coaching requires discovery. For example, as the team member identifies and explores possible action in a coaching conversation, additional information may be needed, taking the conversation back to the Information Gathering step. Or, while in the Action Planning step, it may be necessary to return to the Possible Actions step to identify additional possible actions before narrowing down the action plans that will support the client's agenda or goals for the session.

The following examples of questions correspond with each of the six steps in the coaching framework presented in chapter two. They are not intended to be prescriptive, a menu to follow, or an exhaustive list of possibilities. They should be used to help you develop your questions. It is important to note that agility is essential. While the manager-coach is facilitating a conversation using the steps, it is critically important that you move through the coaching process and adjust to the flow of the conversation. Appendix C contains additional sample questions organized around the coaching skills described in Chapters 6–7 and 9–11.

Step 1: **Current Situation and Context.** The focus of this step is to establish or reestablish the coach-client relationship, obtain an update from the team member about recent events in the context of the coaching goals, assess progress on previous commitments for action, and acknowledge successes and breakthroughs that may have occurred.
- What has happened since our last coaching session?
- What is going on in your world today?
- What are you concerned about?
- What is going on right now?

Step 2: **Needs and Desired Goals.** The focus of this step is for the manager-coach to gain an understanding of the team member's current reality, understand and agree on the goals for the coaching session, align those goals with the overall goals of the coaching engagement, and, if necessary, adjust the goals of the engagement.
- What would you like to focus our coaching conversation on today?
- In five years, what would you like to be doing?
- Which of the three things you've mentioned would you like to focus on first?
- What would you like to accomplish?
- How do you need to behave today to get better results in the future?

Step 3: **Information Gathering.** "The focus of this step is gathering information that serves the client's agenda, gaining a mutual understanding of that information, and identifying needs for additional data—which may become an action item for later consideration" (Bennett and Bush, 2014, p. 69).
- What do you know that will help you address that goal?
- What is keeping you from achieving your goal?
- What is going on right now?
- What have you tried before?
- What resources do you have at your disposal regarding time, people, skills, etc.?
- What is working?
- How does that make you feel?
- How are you different today because of the experience?

Step 4: **Possible Actions.** The focus of this step is to explore possibilities for action that will serve the team member's needs and desired goals for the coaching session. In this step, team members generate ideas for possible action, establish criteria to evaluate those options, consider barriers to implementing them, and establish priorities for action.
- What are some possible actions you can take?
- Who could you consult?

- How could you modify your actions/thoughts to reach a different conclusion?
- What is possible?
- What do you want to do next?
- What is needed here?
- What other options can we think of?
- What would happen if you do that?
- What is stopping you?
- I invite you to (consider, try) . . . .

Step 5: **Action Planning.** The focus of this step is to develop action steps ensure accountability and commitment for implementation, and determine resource and support needs as well as how those resources will be acquired. In short, the team member decides what they will do, by when, with what outcome, and with what support.
- What action will you take? By when?
- What is next?
- What is the most important next step?
- What would be an excellent way to accomplish your immediate goal?

Step 6: **Summary and Agreement.** The focus of this step is to review insights and commitments gained from this coaching session, identify possible agenda items for future coaching sessions, and reinforce that team members own the coaching agenda and actions.
- What have you gained from our coaching conversation today?
- What are you taking away from our conversation?
- Once again, what commitments for action are you making today?
- What are you committed to do? (Bennett & Bush, 2014)

Some questions may be well-suited for multiple steps in the six-step coaching for change process. These include:
- What else?
- What are you thinking?
- How do you feel?
- What is an example?
- Tell me more.

Challenges to Asking Questions

Of course, there are plenty of challenges to asking questions. Here are some of the most common:
- time pressures
- bias for action
- having an answer
- being an expert
- wanting to help
- seeking a specific answer
- wanting to "save" the client
- lack of interest in what the client is saying
- unclear purpose/desired outcome
- have not listened to the client

Some questions have a higher impact than others. High-impact questions are related to the team member's current situation, are focused on the client's agenda, are asked one at a time (i.e., not "stacked"), brief (15 words or less is a good rule of thumb), focused on the topic, asked in language the client understands, and are facilitative (do not prompt defense). Leeds (1987) suggests avoiding questions that begin with "why" to minimize defensive responses. In addition, asking "why" questions may lead to more abstract, philosophical responses from clients than asking "what" questions, which prompt clients to generate concrete options.

Yet sometimes, manager-coaches just do not know what to say or ask. That's often because they have not listened effectively. To help you get out of this bind, you may use this "Magic Question." This question can help the manager-coach regain focus, encourage team members to think about their situation from a different perspective and support team members in developing the skill of assisting themselves versus growing dependent on their manager-coach for all inquiries and insights. The magic question is: "What should I ask you next?"

Here are three questions to ask yourself to help you further develop and refine the practice of asking powerful questions (Bennett & Bush, 2014).

1. **What are some common challenges to asking questions?**
- Having a disjointed conversation because you have not been listening to and building on what they said.
- Demonstrating a lack of curiosity about what the team member is saying.
- Using questions to coerce or manipulate a conversation toward your agenda versus their goals.
- Hiding the reasoning and intent of the questions obscures the purpose.

2. **What makes a question powerful?**
- Building on a previous statement or topic.
- Providing or asking for clarity.
- Being brief (no more than 15 words).
- Being singularly focused, not staked with multiple topics.
- Engaging those who are asking the question.
- Minimizing defensiveness
- Prompting thoughts, feelings, or actions.

3. **What is required to ask powerful questions?**
- Listening with genuine interest to the other person.
- Considering the potential impact of the question as it's constructed.
- Being clear about your motivation in asking each question.
- Stating your question clearly.
- Waiting for a response before asking another question.
- Clarifying the question.

Summary

After listening, asking powerful questions is a manager-coach's most frequently used skill. Here are a few more suggestions for ways to ask more high-impact questions:
- Listen to what others say and develop your questions based on that. Pause to process what you heard.
- Tune in to your reactions (physical and emotional).
- Craft a question with a clear intention:
    - Inquire.
    - Encourage dialogue.
    - Draw out additional information.
    - Provide direction, not the answers.
- Ask simple, brief, focused questions—15 words or less.
- Avoid questions that require a lot of setup or context.
- Use "why" questions sparingly.
- Avoid leading questions.
- Use more open-ended than closed-ended questions.
- Embrace silence. Wait for the answers to your questions before you respond. Wait at least 7 seconds before you follow up.
- Remain curious.

Chapter 9
Coaching Skill: Reframing

as soon as you put a frame around anything, you set it off, you make it visible, you make it real.
—Frederick Buechner, 2017, p. 21

It is easy to get so focused that you do not see other perspectives. It is easy to get so committed to a response that you fail to see other possible solutions. Coaching helps team members recognize the limitations of their thinking and perspectives while assisting them to consider other options and possibilities creatively. This reframing can serve an immediate need and help develop skills for future use.

This chapter includes a definition of reframing in the context of coaching for change and reasons it is a crucial coaching skill. This chapter also offers reframing strategies, examples of reframing in coaching conversations, and remedies to common barriers to reframing.

A great deal of emphasis in coaching skills development is placed on asking powerful questions of the team member being coached. A helpful coaching tool is making statements to team members that enable them to see issues and solutions more clearly so they can take appropriate action. People seek coaching for many reasons, including knowledge, experience, insights, and perspective. The team member may not receive the help they seek if these are not provided.

Reframing is another essential coaching skill. It involves encouraging, guiding, and supporting the team members to discover different or multiple perspectives. It is beneficial when a team member tries to make sense of a circumstance or develop strategies for action. Reframing may be used at any point in the coaching process, but it will most likely be used during the Information Gathering (Step 3) and Action Planning (Step 5) phases of the Coaching for Change model. Reframing fosters creativity, innovation, self-reliance, and solution-finding.

Reframing is a powerful way to help team members identify new opportunities. Re-interpreting a situation or problem allows team members to see things from new angles and find solutions that they had not seen before. According to cognitive behavioral theorists, reframing can help team members change how they think about a problem, which can change how they feel and behave (Ellis, 1962). By reframing a problem, manager-coaches can help team members shift their focus from the negative aspects of a situation to the positive. That leads to more effective problem-solving and decision-making.

One of the most common ways to reframe is through positive language. Imagine how differently the team member might respond when the manager-coach asks, "What can be improved?" instead of asking, "What's wrong?" This small change in wording shifts the focus to opportunities for growth and development and away from problems.

https://doi.org/10.1515/9783111002415-009

Another technique is to reframe a problem as a challenge. A team member may see a difficult task as an obstacle. By reframing it as a challenge, they can focus on the skills and abilities they need to develop to meet the task. Or reframing the obstacle as a puzzle might tantalize a team member who loves to solve puzzles. Just watch their eyes light up. This can help team members see a problem as an opportunity for personal growth and development rather than a source of stress and frustration.

As a manager-coach, you can also reframe a problem by helping the team members see the bigger picture. For example, a team member may focus on a specific problem at work. By reframing it in the context of the organization's overall goals and objectives, the team member can see how their situation relates to the organization's success. This can help team members see how their actions can positively impact the organization, which can motivate them to act.

Reframing can also help team members see how their actions are related to their values and beliefs. For example, a team member may be struggling with a difficult decision. By reframing it in terms of the team member's values and beliefs, the manager-coach can help the team member see how (and whether) their actions align with their values. This can help team members make decisions consistent with their values and beliefs, which leads to greater satisfaction and fulfillment.

Another reframing technique is the "Third Alternative" (Fisher et al., 1991). This approach helps team members see that there are often more options available than the two that are immediately obvious. By exploring the "Third Alternative," team members can find new solutions they may not have considered before. That leads to more effective problem-solving and decision-making.

Framing is naming an issue, challenge, situation, conflict, dilemma, etc. Naming it focuses the team member on how to address it. *Reframing* involves questioning the existing frame or perspective. When reframing, the manager-coach helps the team member develop and understand multiple perspectives, learn new perspectives, create new insights, get "unstuck," challenge assumptions/beliefs, overcome fear, create a new vision of the future, and shift from tactical to strategic thinking.

The manager-coach can help the team member reframe perspectives, assumptions, beliefs, data, timeframes, outcomes, and resources. To do this, the manager-coach uses tools that include metaphors, analogies, role plays, envisioning the future, multiple perspectives, reflection, and time stretching (See Table 9.1).

You can reframe with a statement, question, or pause. Reframing works well when the coach can relate to the culture, experiences, and knowledge of the person being coached and perhaps even share them in common, such as

- professional experiences
- books read or movies seen
- job changes
- family experiences
- hobbies or interests such as cooking, gardening, golf, travel

Table 9.1: Reframing Strategies.

Reframing Strategy	Statements/Questions by the Manger-Coach
Metaphors	– What image comes to mind when you think about your experience? – If you considered a color or animal that might represent your feelings, what is it? – If you were to make a map of your journey, what would be your next stop along the way?
Analogies	– That sounds like . . . – I experienced a situation that may relate. May I share it? . . . In what, if any, ways does that relate to what you are experiencing?
Role Plays	– I will be the employee whose performance you are concerned about. You play yourself. Let's have the conversation you need to have with the employee. – If __ were sitting in front of you right now, what would you like to say to him/her?
Envisioning the Future	– What would you like to be doing in five years? – How would you imagine feeling if you could achieve this goal for yourself?
Multiple Perspectives	– Who has gone before you and done well with this challenge? How did they approach it? – What is another way you could look at the issue? – Put yourself in the other person's position on this issue. What do you see? – How would you feel if you heard someone tell you what you want to say to this person?
Reflection	– Think of a time when you used that skill and it worked well.
Time Stretching	– What would it look like five years ago if you were accomplishing your dream? – How will you have changed if you fast-forward to six months from now? – Imagine it is five hours (or days, weeks, months, years) from now. What will have happened?

Managers using a coaching approach may find this skill challenging for several reasons. You may not know enough about the team member to easily relate nonwork experiences and interests to the coaching focus. You can overcome this by inviting team members to share personal and professional goals and interests.

Team members may not naturally reframe for themselves, making reframing a different way of thinking about issues. To overcome this, help team members recognize their interpretation of events, point of view, or mental model. Then, you can help the team member look at issues from the perspective of others or gain awareness of the possibilities of other points of view.

Manager-coaches may not be skilled in identifying opportunities for reframing. This can be overcome by noticing your frames of reference, perspectives, values, and ways of approaching work. This awareness may help the manager-coach recognize the closely held frames of reference of team members, which can be used to help the team members reframe for themselves.

Here are four examples of reframing (see Table 9.2) to illustrate how the strategy might be applied. Each coaching situation is described along with a reframing approach and an example of how the reframing might be used.

Table 9.2: Examples of Reframing.

Situation	Reframing Strategy	Example of Application
Jeff is preparing for a conversation with a colleague with whom the relationship is new, and the request he will be making is significant. He is concerned about his approach and asked his manager to provide him with some coaching. The manager-coach and Jeff agree that a coaching versus a directive approach would be best as it will allow Jeff to identify several options and develop his solutions.	**Role Play**	As the manager-coach, you help Jeff identify several possible approaches to the conversation. Then, Jeff selects a process that he thinks will be most effective, plays to his strength, and is likely to help build the working relationship while getting a favorable response to the request. The manager-coach suggests that she and Jeff role-play the conversation to help him prepare for the conversation with the colleague. At the end of the role-play, the manager-coach asks Jeff how he thought it went, what he might retain and do during the conversation, and what he might change. Jeff better understands how his colleague might respond to his approach. Jeff identifies that he has a good strategy, but that he might be better positioned to have the conversation with a few changes.
Asbury meets with their manager-coach to discuss a work-related problem that has absorbed time and resources.	**Envisioning the Future**	The manager-coach asks Asbury to talk about the desired outcomes for the problem. As Asbury speaks, the manager-coach realizes that Asbury is focused on the immediate issues and solutions with short-term impacts. So, the manager-coach asks Asbury to think beyond the current issues and to consider what they would like the answer to be one year from now, and to consider those possibilities without any constraints on time or resources. Asbury's energy and enthusiasm shift, and new ideas begin to flow.

Table 9.2 (continued)

Situation	Reframing Strategy	Example of Application
		Asbury describes a future state. Then, the manager-coach asks Asbury to consider how to work through the current issue with this longer-term, desired state in mind. This results in Ashbury having a new perspective on the issues and potential next steps. In addition, Ashbury realizes the value of thinking longer-term—more strategically—when solving issues.
Jane leads a team of 150 people and has six people reporting directly to her. The team members are diverse and represent several distinct functional areas and skill sets. In the past, Jane has used a one-size-fits-all approach, which has resulted in resistance to change. She comes to her manager to discuss a proposed change.	**Multiple Perspectives**	Jane's manager-coach asks her to identify the stakeholders involved and impacted by the proposed change. Then, the manager-coach asks Jane to determine what may interest or concern each stakeholder group. As this conversation unfolds, Jane realizes the need to tailor her messages and approaches to meet the needs and interests of the stakeholders. She also recognizes the value of looking at the change through multiple lenses. As a result, she adjusts her messages and reconsiders some elements of the proposed change.

Summary

The manager-coach's role is to help the team members see situations differently, gain new awareness and then process that new meaning in order to learn something, gain new insights, or generate new possibilities. The manager-coach helps the team member develop action steps.

Reframing is a powerful skill used in coaching to help team members shift their perspectives and identify new opportunities. It can help team members change how they think about a problem, which can change how they feel and behave. Manager-coaches can use reframing techniques to help team members see problems as opportunities for growth and development, see the bigger picture, and align their actions with their values and beliefs. This can lead to more effective problem-solving and decision-making, which can help leaders at all levels achieve their goals and be successful in their roles.

Chapter 10
Coaching Skill: Providing Insights

Quit the foreplay; just say it.

—Charlie Seashore, Ph.D.

Team members *hold the answers,* and the coach *helps uncover* or discover these answers by asking questions. This approach is purely a nondirective one. The powerful questions a manager-coach asks can guide the team member to seek answers by looking inside, gathering data, and making meaning of what they find. In addition to helping uncover the team members' responses, the manager-coach is often called upon to provide insights that the client might not be able to access by questioning alone. Providing insights is a skill that is essential for effective executive coaching. It involves helping clients gain a deeper understanding of themselves and their behavior to identify areas for improvement and progress toward their goals. Insights can be provided through various methods, such as observation, reflection, and feedback.

This chapter defines the coaching skill of providing insights, differentiates between feedback and insights, describes common barriers to delivering insights, offers potential solutions, and gives examples of providing insights in coaching conversations.

Providing Insights: Defined

Effective coaching involves "challenging" the team member to reflect more deeply, and to examine their values, beliefs, assumptions, perspectives, and actions. Challenging may involve seeking clarity, discovering blind spots, understanding meaning, or testing assumptions. Where a challenge is concerned, the approach aims to use intrinsic motivation (DiClemente & Prochaska, 1998; Miller & Rollnick, 2012). A model of "supportive challenge" is used in the therapy literature.

In general, the manager-coach needs to be friendly without being a friend, balance high support with a high level of challenge—holding the team member accountable—and encourage deeper reflection and stimulate a change in circumstances that will enhance the drive to act. Although this level of challenge may be appropriate for individuals with high levels of resilience and who are highly functional, providing such a level of challenge to vulnerable or dysfunctional individuals would be unethical (Passmore, 2009).

Providing insight may involve drawing on a manager's knowledge and experience base. In the context of coaching, this approach may help identify areas for exploration. Providing insight may also lead to ways of helping team members discover solutions, insights, and resources for themselves. A word of caution: This skill should be used sparingly. Remember, the primary focus of coaching is to help clients discover for themselves the agenda, solutions, actions, and resources required to achieve their

https://doi.org/10.1515/9783111002415-010

goals. Offering too many insights or offering them too frequently can lead to the client depending on the coach to "do the work." Manager-coaches should help team members develop independence from the manager and interdependence with the team member's support network (Bennett & Bush, 2014).

Preparing to Provide Insights

Insight should be offered as a nonjudgmental description of behavior in clear and concise words and be grounded in observations of that behavior. The insight should be focused on the real issues versus some obscure or self-serving agenda. Stay focused on the client, not others involved in the client's situations or issues. Your voice can and should be heard in the coaching conversation. While using silence, asking powerful questions, and supporting the team member as they discover and act are essential for effective coaching, offering the wisdom and insights of the coach is also valuable.

One of the critical ways that manager-coaches can provide insights is through observation. By observing a team member's behavior, manager-coaches can gain a deeper understanding of the team member's strengths and weaknesses and identify patterns of behavior that may be impacting their effectiveness as a leader. For example, you might observe a team member during a meeting and note that they tend to interrupt others or dominate the conversation. This insight can help team members develop strategies to improve their communication skills.

Another way that you can provide insights is through reflection. Reflection is thinking deeply about an experience or behavior to understand its meaning. For example, a manager-coach might ask a client to reflect on a difficult decision and consider the factors that influenced their decision. This can help the team member better understand their decision-making process and identify areas for improvement.

Feedback is also an essential tool for providing insights. As mentioned earlier, feedback is information provided to an individual about their performance, behavior, or results to help them improve. Feedback can be provided in several formats, such as verbal, written, or observation (Kluger & DeNisi, 1996). For example, you might provide feedback to a client on their presentation skills, pointing out specific areas to improve. This can help the team member better understand their strengths and weaknesses and progress toward their goals.

A critical aspect of providing insights is to focus on the team member's strengths and potential. That way, manager-coaches can help them to build confidence and motivation. For example, you might show team members that they can inspire and motivate others and help them develop strategies to leverage this strength in their leadership role.

Another critical aspect of providing insights is to be nonjudgmental. Manager-coaches must avoid judging a team member's behavior or performance and instead focus on providing constructive and objective feedback. This can help create a safe and supportive coaching environment where team members feel comfortable discussing their weaknesses and taking steps to improve. It is also essential for manager-coaches to consider the cultural background of the team member when providing insights. Cultures may have different norms and expectations regarding feedback, and coaches should be aware of these differences to provide sensitive and appropriate feedback.

Providing insights is a skill that is essential for effective executive coaching. It involves helping team members better understand themselves and their behavior to identify areas for improvement and progress toward their goals. Manager-coaches can provide insights through observation, reflection, and feedback. It is essential to focus on the team member's strengths and potential, be nonjudgmental, and consider their cultural background when providing insights. Insights can help team members build confidence, motivation, and effectiveness as leaders.

Providing insights to a team member is not a skill used in every coaching conversation. When it is used, here are steps to take:

1. Prepare.
2. Send an insightful message.
3. Wait in silence for a response.
4. Listen for the response: accepting or defensive.
5. Recycle the process, beginning with Step 2.
6. Focus the client on meaning-making, possible actions, and action planning.

Here are some essential things to consider when providing insight:

– Listen for understanding.
– Consider whether and how what a coach observes and offers as insight to the client reflects who the coach is.
– State the insight in as few words as possible (target: 10–15 words or less).
– Be respectful and objective.
– Once the insight has been offered, stop talking. Wait for a response.

Example of Providing Insight

Consider this example of how a coach can help a client develop insights. Jerome is a middle manager with an employee (Jane) new to a role that requires building and maintaining effective relationships with peers across the organization. Jerome described his situation with Jane to his manager (Susan). Knowing that Jerome recently attended a leadership workshop in which the Situational Leadership Model was taught, Susan was able to help Jerome identify how he perceived Jane in terms of the kind of support she might offer Jane. As Susan listened to Jerome consider his options for action in helping Jane develop relationships, Susan observed that Jerome could be treating Jane in a manner that was not in alignment with Jane's placement in the Situational Leadership model. After several attempts to get Jerome to identify alternative approaches to working with Jane, Susan asked Jerome if she could offer an observation. After Jerome agreed, Susan said, "Jerome, based on your assessment of Jane, she is in a place where supporting her discovery of possible ways to develop these important relationships is possible. And I noticed that the solutions you identify are more directive in nature. Would you agree?" Jerome said, "Yes. Perhaps Jane needs me to be more of a manager-coach than a supervisor. If I shift my behavior in the following ways . . . maybe it will allow me to improve the impact of my interaction with Jane."

Summary

Offering insights can be a useful coaching skill that helps team members see challenges, opportunities, and behaviors in different ways. Ask if you can offer an insight: Make an offer rather than a declaration. Ground insights with data whenever possible, and base your observations on low-inference data. After you suggest insights or offer a hypothesis, ask the team member to respond based on their observations and insights about themselves. Be willing to be wrong or to have an insight that the team member is unprepared to hear or act on. Take ownership and responsibility for the insights you offer.

Here are some tips to remind you of key points from this chapter:
- Provide insights rarely.
- Use your insights to advance the agenda of the team members.
- Avoid insights that are judgmental.
- Share insights in a way that will be understood and accepted.

Chapter 11
Coaching Skill: Developing Support

I think of my work with individuals and in a coaching way as a mirror. We both have to be in the mirror. I have to see what you see, and you have to see what I see. And the folks that I have struggled most with are those people that can't get in the mirror.

—Kathy Elling

Effective leadership goes beyond giving orders or overseeing tasks in today's rapidly evolving business landscape. It involves nurturing talent, fostering growth, and maximizing individual and team potential. Managerial coaching has emerged as a critical approach for leaders to achieve these objectives. At the heart of successful coaching is the skill of developing support, which creates an environment where employees feel valued, motivated, and empowered to excel. Managerial coaching is a critical competency that enables leaders to empower their teams, foster growth, and enhance organizational performance. Among the multifaceted skills required for effective coaching, developing support stands out as a pivotal element. This skill involves creating a supportive environment where individuals feel encouraged, valued, and motivated to achieve their professional and personal goals.

This chapter delves into developing support as a managerial coaching skill by highlighting its significance, core principles, practical strategies, potential challenges, and real-world applications. This chapter will define what it means to provide support in the context of the manager-coach relationship. It will describe common barriers to developing solutions and will provide remedies. It will also provide examples of developing support in coaching conversations for manager-coaches, and show ways to build and encourage self-reflection.

Significance of Developing Support in Managerial Coaching

The skill of developing support is integral to managerial coaching. First and foremost, it strengthens the leader-follower relationship, which is pivotal in today's collaborative work environments. Supportive managers are more likely to earn the trust and respect of their team members, which, in turn, can lead to increased employee engagement and commitment (Eisenbeiss et al., 2008). Furthermore, developing support is tied to creating a positive work culture, which directly impacts organizational performance.

A supportive work environment can boost employee morale, motivation, and job satisfaction. In contrast, lacking support can lead to disengagement, increased turnover rates, and decreased productivity (Eisenbeiss et al., 2008; Lambert et al., 2012). Thus, developing support is a soft skill and a strategic imperative that can significantly affect an organization's bottom line.

https://doi.org/10.1515/9783111002415-011

Key Components of Building Support

Two aspects of building support are essential in the context of coaching. First is the supportive relationship between the manager-coach and the team member. Chapter 2 discussed building trust and rapport between the manager-coach and the team member. This chapter adds insights and suggestions. The second context for building support is the work the team member should do to support their work outside of the relationship with the manager-coach. Support can be defined as the provision of encouragement, assistance, or resources to help an individual achieve a desired outcome. This coaching skill is often used in Action Planning, Step 5 in the change process. It may also be applied in Step 4, Possible Actions, as the needs for support may be identified. The coach-manager should also be tuned to support systems that are mentioned (or not) during Step 3, Information Gathering. This information may be helpful later in the coaching conversation as manager-coaches help the team member identify existing supports and gaps where supports may be beneficial.

A support system is a resource pool drawn selectively to support the team member in moving in the direction of choice, which leaves the person being coached stronger. Building and using support is a critical skill in the context of coaching. It helps the manager create a positive and supportive coaching environment that enables team members to achieve their goals. Building support involves creating a relationship of trust and understanding between you and the team member and providing the team member with the resources and tools they need to succeed.

A critical aspect of building support is to create a positive and encouraging coaching environment. This can be achieved by giving the team members regular positive feedback and encouragement. For example, a you might point out to a team member when they have made progress or achieved a goal and provide specific feedback on what they did well. This can help build the team member's self-confidence and motivation.

Another aspect of building support is giving the team members the tools and resources to achieve their goals. This can include providing the team members with specific strategies or techniques for achieving their goals and access to relevant information, research, or experts in the field. For example, you might give team members information on a new leadership development program or introduce them to a mentor who can provide guidance and support. Building support also involves creating a relationship of trust and understanding between the manager-coach and the team member. This can be achieved by being open, honest, and nonjudgmental when communicating with the team members.

It is crucial for the team member to develop, access, and use a support system, so that they can reduce their dependence on the manager and can function effectively when the manager is not present. As the team member explores possibilities, develops action plans, provides feedback, or establishes partners for accountability, they may also identify individuals or groups with whom they can access information, role models, resources, and feedback. Many sources can provide support, including peers,

mentors, spouses/partners, other family members, friends, and professional association colleagues.

Establishing, maintaining, and effectively using a support system is a skill. Support systems can be challenging to set up, counterproductive, disappointing, and un-
predictable. They require energy and effort to maintain. And they require courage to
access and use.

Dependence, independence, counter-dependence, and interdependence are critical concepts in coaching and social interaction. These terms refer to different ways
individuals relate to others, and it is essential to understand them to develop healthy
relationships and avoid problematic behavior patterns.

Dependence refers to a state in which an individual relies on others for emotional and practical support. Dependent people may be unable to meet their needs
and look to others for validation, comfort, and assistance. This can manifest in several
ways, including seeking constant attention and approval, being overly clingy in relationships, and having difficulty making decisions independently. Dependence can be
problematic when it becomes excessive and interferes with a person's ability to function independently.

On the other hand, **independence** refers to the ability to be self-sufficient and
care for oneself without relying on others. Independent people can meet their own
needs, make decisions, and navigate life's challenges. Independence is generally seen
as a positive trait but can also be problematic when taken to extremes. Overly independent people may have difficulty forming close relationships and may push others
away, leading to feelings of loneliness and isolation.

Counter-dependence refers to a pattern of behavior in which individuals react
against dependence and strive for independence. Counter-dependent people may
avoid close relationships and reject relying on others, even when doing so would be
helpful. They may also resist feedback and criticism, seeing it as an attack on their
independence. This can lead to difficulties in personal and professional relationships,
as others may feel rejected or unvalued.

Interdependence is a state where individuals are connected and interrelated but
maintain a sense of self and individuality. Individuals can foster supportive and fulfilling relationships by developing a healthy sense of interdependence. In interdependent relationships, people can support each other while retaining autonomy. This
allows for a healthy balance of support and independence, leading to more robust
and satisfying relationships.

Challenges in Developing Support

While developing support in managerial coaching is essential, it has challenges. Manager-coaches may encounter obstacles such as:

- **Time Constraints.** Managers often juggle multiple responsibilities, leaving limited time for coaching and support. Finding a balance between coaching and other duties can be challenging (Clutterbuck & Megginson, 2005). However, prioritizing coaching as a leadership activity is crucial for long-term team development and success.
- **Resistance to Feedback.** Some employees may resist feedback, especially when it involves constructive criticism. Managers must address this resistance by fostering a culture of continuous improvement and learning (Whitmore, 2009). Building trust can also mitigate resistance to feedback. See Chapter 6 for additional information and guidance related to giving feedback.
- **Cultural and Organizational Barriers.** Organizational culture and norms can impact the effectiveness of developing support. In some cultures or organizations, there may be a reluctance to give and receive feedback openly (Whitmore, 2009). Managers must navigate these cultural and organizational barriers while promoting a supportive coaching environment.
- **Skill Gap.** Not all managers possess the necessary coaching skills, including developing support. Addressing this skill gap requires training and development programs that equip leaders with the knowledge and tools to be effective coaches (Clutterbuck & Megginson, 2005).

Core Principles of Developing Support

To effectively develop support within a managerial coaching context, leaders should adhere to several core principles:
- **Empathy: Understanding Employee Needs.** Empathy is a cornerstone of developing support. Managers must strive to understand their team members' unique needs, aspirations, and challenges. This requires active listening, open communication, and a genuine interest in their employees' well-being (Cherniss, 2010). Leaders can tailor their coaching approach to provide the necessary support by recognizing and acknowledging individual concerns and aspirations.
- **Trust-Building: Establishing Credibility.** Trust is fundamental in any coaching relationship. Managers must demonstrate trustworthiness by following through on commitments, maintaining confidentiality, and consistently displaying ethical behavior (Cherniss, 2010). When employees trust their leaders, they are more likely to be receptive to coaching and guidance, fostering an environment of support.
- **Feedback and Recognition: Reinforcing Positive Behavior.** Regular feedback and recognition are essential components of developing support. Employees need to know how they are performing and where they can improve. Constructive feedback should be balanced with acknowledgment and praise for accomplishments (Gentry et al., 2012). Recognizing and celebrating achievements not only boosts morale but also reinforces positive behavior and performance.

- **Tailored Support: Individualized Coaching.** Practical support is not one-size-fits-all. Managers should tailor their coaching to each team member's unique needs and aspirations. This requires a deep understanding of individual strengths, weaknesses, and goals (Eisenbeiss et al., 2008). By providing personalized coaching, managers can help employees reach their full potential.

Helping Team Members Seek Support

Team members may need assistance from the manager-coach to know what support is required and how to ask for it. Remember that there are power dynamics at play in this relationship. The manager-coach is in a more powerful position, and the team member is in a potentially vulnerable place to ask for help (Schein, 2009).

Here are four types of support team members might seek, and some guidance for team members as they develop the ability and willingness to seek support.

1. **Learning/Development Support**
   - What it is: Teaching, reflecting on experiences, role-modeling, attending training.
   - When it is most helpful: There is a knowledge or skill gap.
2. **Informational Support**
   - What it is: Facts, guidance, or advice that help team members make decisions and act.
   - When it is most helpful: If team members are unsure what to do next or know what they want to do but are unsure how to do it.
3. **Practical Support**
   - What it is: Hands-on help, such as making a decision or an introduction to a colleague.
   - When it is most helpful: When team members know what they want to do but could use a hand in following through.
4. **Emotional Support**
   - What it is: An opportunity for team members to voice their thinking and/or feelings and get understanding and encouragement in response.
   - When it is most helpful: If team members are stressed, worried, lonely, or struggling after a setback.

Here are some guidelines for team members as they build the capacity to ask for support:
- **Acknowledge care and effort.** Everyone likes to feel appreciated. Before making a request, thank the support giver for caring and all they do to help. When a team member asks someone to do something new or different, they may feel that their current behavior is being criticized, which can trigger defensiveness. To avoid that, the team members should focus on what they need and how it would help.

Start your request with "I." For example, "I'm trying to do X. I would appreciate it if you could tell me or provide me with Y."

- **Be specific in terms of time.** The team member should clarify whether the request is for today, this week, or sometime in the next three months. Otherwise, they may become frustrated that the other person is not following through within the necessary time frame.
- **Offer to do something in return.** Relationships are two-way streets. When asking colleagues or managers to change for them, the team member might suggest something they could do for in return. For example, you might tell your partner, "I'd appreciate it if you'd X in the morning. In return, I'll do the Y for you."
- **Say "thank you," even if they don't say yes.** No matter how the potential support provider responds, thank them for listening and considering the request. The team members should tell them they do not expect them to say yes to every request, but they appreciate knowing it is okay to ask.

Strategies for Implementing and Developing Support

Implementing the skill of developing support in managerial coaching requires a thoughtful approach. You can use the following questions to foster partnership and build support, independence, and interdependence:

- What, if any, support could help you implement your action plan?
- What is important to you in an accountability partner?
- From whom could you seek that information?
- Who in your network may have had a similar challenge and would be willing to provide you with information about their experiences?
- How might you ask someone to work with you?
- What are you doing right now that might be improved upon by developing a new partnership?

Here are some tips to keep in mind and to practice as a manager-coach to help team members develop and use their support systems:

- Help team members identify opportunities to develop partnerships for support and accountability.
- Help team members identify needs for role modeling and ways to gain from the experiences of others.
- Remember that coaching aims to help team members develop independence from the manager-coach and interdependence with others.

Practical strategies that manager-coaches can employ include:

- **Active Listening.** Effective support begins with active listening. Managers should actively engage in conversations with their team members, asking open-ended

begin?stop

questions and demonstrating genuine interest in their concerns (Whitmore, 2009). Active listening helps managers understand employee needs and makes employees feel valued and heard.

- **Regular Check-Ins.** Frequent check-ins are essential for maintaining a supportive coaching relationship. Managers should schedule regular one-on-one meetings with their team members to discuss progress, challenges, and goals (Gentry et al., 2012). These check-ins allow managers to provide guidance, offer feedback, and promptly address issues.
- **Goal Setting.** Setting clear and achievable goals is a crucial aspect of developing support. Managers should work with their employees to establish SMART (Specific, Measurable, Achievable, Relevant, Time-bound) goals (Locke & Latham, 1990). This process ensures that employees have a clear sense of direction and purpose, which can enhance motivation and commitment.
- **Feedback Framework.** Managers should establish a structured feedback framework with positive reinforcement and constructive criticism. Feedback should be specific, timely, and focused on behavior rather than personality (Whitmore, 2009). Creating a feedback-rich culture encourages continuous learning and improvement.
- **Recognition and Rewards.** Recognition and rewards play a vital role in developing support. Managers should regularly acknowledge and celebrate the achievements and contributions of their team members (Gentry et al., 2012). This can be verbal praise, awards, or other forms of recognition that align with the organization's culture.

Summary

The managerial coaching skill of developing support is a powerful tool that manager-coaches can use to empower their teams, foster growth, and enhance organizational performance. By adhering to core principles such as empathy, trust-building, feedback, and tailored support, managers can create a supportive work environment that boosts morale, motivation, and job satisfaction. Time constraints, resistance to feedback, and cultural barriers present challenges to developing support. Leaders can overcome obstacles with the right strategies and a commitment to prioritizing coaching. In today's dynamic and competitive business world, organizations that invest in developing support as a managerial coaching skill are more likely to attract and retain top talent, drive innovation, and achieve sustainable success.

Questions to ask as you help the team member identify, secure, and use the support they need to implement their action plans:
- What is it you need to support? (e.g., starting, stopping, changing, or continuing something)
- What kind of support do you need? (e.g., expertise, funding, expertise, accountability)

- When do you need the support? (e.g., when you need it to start, how long do you anticipate needing it, on one or more specific occasions)
- How do you want to receive the support? (e.g., in person, email, budget resources)
- How will you ask for the support? (e.g., directly to the potential resource provider, or to someone who can help you secure the support)
- Who can provide the support? (e.g., manager, peer/colleague, direct report, consultant, coach, family member, or friend)
- What will you do to secure the support you need? (e.g., ask for it, write a proposal, purchase it)

Chapter 12
Integrating Coaching Skills into the Process

My focus, for example, is not just on the individual agenda. I'm always working in the context of the organization, what results the organization needs.

—Michele Langford

Numerous professional practices support sustainable behavioral change. At its core, all coaching is about change—for performance, development, or transformation at the individual, group, or organization levels. Skilled manager-coaches are familiar with the coaching process described in Chapter 2 and the coaching skills related to it in Chapters 5–11. With a foundational understanding of coaching, the role of the manager as coach, and the skills involved in coaching for change, it is time to integrate those components into leadership and management practices.

This chapter begins with some common challenges faced by managers who want to help team members excel. Next are some principles to guide manager-coaches followed by some challenges manager-coaches face and possible solutions. The chapter concludes with two case examples to illustrate the application of the six-step coaching process and various coaching skills.

Challenges of Helping

As human beings, we often strive to be helpful. We may do this in one or more of our roles as a friend, colleague, manager, peer, coach, consultant, parent, sibling, etc. In his book *Helping*, Schein (2009) wrote about the imbalance that occurs when a helping relationship emerges. This imbalance involves the person being helped as a "down" or "subordinated" position. (Note: This is not "subordinate.") Most of us want to be helpful, to be valued, and to provide to others. However, our desire to help may not match the needs or desires of those we seek to help. Here are some reasons our help does not always work:

- **Rejection of help.** The person we are trying to help may not want help, want the assistance we are offering, or want help from us. Make sure the person you want to help wants help from you and in the way you want to offer it.
- **Misunderstanding the need for help.** We may not understand the needs of the person we are trying to help. Clarify the actual needs and desires of the potential recipient of your help by inquiring.
- **Projecting our needs.** We may project our impressions, assumptions, conclusions, and needs on the person we are trying to help by trying to help them based on a misunderstanding of their needs. Be mindful of what you want for the other person compared to what they want for themselves or are ready to accept from you.

https://doi.org/10.1515/9783111002415-012

– **Projecting our solutions.** The person we are trying to help may want our help but not the specific version of the help we are offering. Gain agreement about the assistance you are offering. Be sure you are providing the aid they are willing to accept, in the form(s) they are eager to take, at the time and place they are ready to receive it from you. Avoid giving them what we want or think they need. Don't impose your solution.

– **Creating dependence.** We may provide help in a way that makes the recipient dependent on us, the helper. However, doing so does not help the person develop independence. Avoid becoming a crutch, so that you "put yourself out of a job" as the helper. Support the person you are helping to be more independent, and less dependent on you or others for help. This allows them to be more interdependent —making choices about the assistance they need from various sources and asking for what they need, how they need it, and when they need it.

– **Doing to others.** This can be a tough one. In our efforts to help, we may be doing something *to* the person we are trying to help versus doing it *with* them. You may have noticed yourself taking a task away from someone because you think you can do it better or faster than the person you are trying to help. You may have done something for another person in the spirit of assisting without their permission assuming they wanted it done. A simple question like, "May I help?" or "Would you like my assistance as you do ___?" could make the difference between doing something *to them* versus *with them.*

In conclusion, do help. But check your motives and the desire of those you want to help. Seek ways to help the person you are helping build their capacity for independence and interdependence. Everyone needs help, and most of us do want to be helpful. Here are a few questions to help you consider your role as a helper:

– Do I understand the needs of the person I want to help?
– Am I the best person to provide this help?
– What's the best way to assist?
– What is driving me to help this person at this time?

Powerful Lessons and Impactful Shifts

Experience and observation tell us some potential lessons that can shift mindsets and behaviors to improve the manager-coach's work with team members. Whether you are an experienced professional coach or a manager-coach, paying attention to your thoughts and reactions has the potential to provide new insights and further development. (See Appendix B for a questionnaire on self-awareness.) The Change Mastery Model (See Chapter 3) can be applied to the novice or expert manager-coach.

Table 12.1 describes actions to address common challenges manager-coaches face.

Table 12.1: Common Challenges Manager-Coaches Face.

As a Manager-Coach, If I Think . . .	The Possible Basis for the Thought May Be . . .	What I Could Consider Then . . .
I think the team member needs my help, so I naturally (or automatically) operate as a mentor.	– Desire to help – Seeing the team member as a junior – Wanting to provide answers – Rushing to solutions	– Reframe what it means to be a helper – Apply coaching skills – Stay focused on developing independence and interdependence vs. dependence
I don't know what to say or ask.	– Desire to help – Listening – Desire to add value – Inadequacy	– What did the team member just say or do? – What can the team member do to refocus or reframe their thoughts now?
But if they would only . . .	– Desire to provide answers/ solutions – Having an insight or perspective team members have not recognized for themselves	– What makes my solution best for the team member? – How can I help the team members identify options for themselves?
I must respond quickly to the team member, so I process and respond rapidly.	– Not comfortable with silence – Concerned about keeping the conversation moving quickly – Naturally process information faster than the team member	– Embrace silence – Allow yourself time to consider what was said by the team member as you prepare your following statement or question – Do not focus on your performance: Take risks
Why can't they see what is going on?	– No paying attention – Ineffective listening – Lack of awareness of what is happening – Paying too much attention to details and not seeing a more comprehensive perspective	– What can I do to help the team member gain a new perspective? – Is this the best time to share my feedback or insight?

Table 12.1 (continued)

As a Manager-Coach, If I Think . . .	The Possible Basis for the Thought May Be . . .	What I Could Consider Then . . .
I have a solution for them.	– Desire to "fix" – Desire to help – Desire to avoid discomfort	– Why do I think my answer is better than what the team member could develop with my help? – Why am I trying to do team member's work for them? – How will giving them my solution help the team members grow and develop? – What makes me uncomfortable?
I'm not doing an excellent job.	– Self-doubt – Desire to help – Noticing an area for development	– What prompts me to doubt my skills? – Am I doing my best? – What could I have done differently (stopped, started, continued)?
I don't like this team member.	– Personal values and beliefs – Desire to have a personal relationship/friendship with team members – Desire to be liked	– Do I need to enjoy the team members? – What about me is showing up in the team members? – How is this impacting my ability to work with this team member? – Am I the best coach for this team member? – Would someone else be a better coach for this team member?
Can they make the behavioral changes they need to make?	– Manager-coach's priorities vs. the team member's priorities – Questioning team members' motivation – Asking the team member's capacity for change	– Am I doing the best I can? – Is the team member doing their best? – What could I help the team member become aware of that might positively impact them? – What progress is the team member making?

Table 12.1 (continued)

As a Manager-Coach, If I Think . . .	The Possible Basis for the Thought May Be . . .	What I Could Consider Then . . .
They are so resistant!	– Desire for change – Ability to convince or persuade – Impatience	– What is holding the team member back? – What does the team member need to understand? – What is comfortable about the current state? – How much is the team member willing to change?
I'm not an effective coach.	– Self-doubt – Lack of confidence – A recognized skill gap	– What would the best version of my coaching skills look like in this situation? – What risk could I take that might make a positive difference? – What are my skill gaps that need to be developed?
Why did I just say that?	– Making statements when a question would be more effective – Making assumptions – Inserting a judgment	– What question could I ask that would help the team members discover the answer for themselves? – How are my values, beliefs, and experiences influencing the statements I make and questions I ask? – How can I help the team members explore the topic for themselves?
Not sure how to reflect after the coaching conversation to support your development as a manager-coach	– Viewing learning to apply a coaching approach as different from learning other skills – I am not sure how to reflect – Thinking that reflection is a waste of time	– Schedule time after coaching sessions to review what transpired and reflect on your work with the team member – Ask yourself: So? So what? What's next?

Principles of Manager-Coaches

Managers and leaders at all levels are critical allies on their team members' personal and professional development frontlines. They play a crucial role in individual and team development toward mastery by providing feedback and coaching. Manager-coaches are people to whom others report and who use coaching skills with those who report to them.

Definitions of manager-coach coalesce around the thought that the role of a manager-coach is to empower employees, help improve individual and team performance, develop employees to increase their ability to achieve career goals, enhance the quality of work, and retain top performers within organizations (Joo et al., 2012).

Traditionally, managers have been defined as telling, judging, controlling, and directing, and coaches as empowering, helping, developing, supporting, and removing obstacles. Coaching as a management function involves a nondirective, humanistic, motivating, and empowering approach to fostering the achievement of personal and professional development in alignment with organizational priorities. Coaching involves helping the person being coached identify their goals, discover possible actions, create a plan, and be accountable for the results. It involves increased self-awareness and learning to evolve as an individual, team member, and contributor to the success of others and the organization. To achieve mastery, the manager-coach can effectively and efficiently apply the mindset and skills of coaching with consistently high proficiency, improvise when necessary, reflect on their performance to continuously improve, and support others in developing the mindset and skills.

Here are seven principles to guide manager-coaches to effectively support others in their growth, development, and performance through the application of a coaching mindset and skills:

1. **Create a Safe and Brave Space.** Manager-coaches are responsible for creating a safe environment where the team being coached can share, take risks, experiment, and learn. To accomplish this, the coach-manager needs to be trusted. The manager must accept what is shared without prejudgment and bias while encouraging the team members to be vulnerable.
2. **Focus on the Team Member's Agenda.** Manager-coaches may be tempted to impose an agenda on the team member being coached. However, a key tenet of coaching is that the team member sets the focus of the work—not the manager-coach. This makes the coaching self-directed and coach-guided. As the manager of the team member being coached, you may have suggestions or preferences that can be shared to inform the selection of the most important and impactful goals for coaching. Help the team member select and articulate the desired outcomes for coaching in general and for each coaching conversation.
3. **Facilitate and Collaborate.** As an experienced professional, you may have profound and rich expertise in the work of the team members. This wisdom should serve to inform the manager-coach but should not be used to impose their views

on team members. Managers who coach develop the skills to partner with team members to guide them through discovery, experimentation, learning, and performance. As Alison King wrote (1993), the teacher (in this case, the coach) should be a guide on the side, not a sage on the stage. This means the manager-coach should be selective about being directive and use a more facilitative approach.

4. **Promote Mastery Through Self-awareness.** The goal of any manager should be to foster the development of others toward mastery. Mastery includes the ability to skillfully execute, reflect, and learn from experiences, improvise as needed, demonstrate agility, function interdependently, and support the development of others. This requires both reflection and feedback. You have a front-row seat to observe and offer feedback, which should support an existing goal for the team member or provide new awareness of opportunities for coaching, development, and application.

5. **Balance Personal Development and Organizational Priorities.** Manager-coaches may work with team members whose personal priorities do not align with the organization's goals. This places you in a potentially awkward position of trying to support competing priorities. The manager-coach's objective is to support the organization's needs while helping team members align to those priorities and develop as an asset to the organization. This may require the manager-coach to clarify their responsibilities as a manager before using their coaching skills to help the team member discover alignment or misalignment and a path forward.

6. **Promote Learning and Growth from Experiences.** Past experiences can provide worthwhile learning opportunities. Manager-coaches are encouraged to help team members think about experiences from the perspectives of what worked well, what could have been changed to improve the situation, what role they could have played to foster a better outcome, etc. This process of reflecting can help team members develop awareness, as well as the ability to reflect as events occur so they can adjust and gain additional insights for future applications. This reflective process helps sustain learning and creates a feedback loop for continued developmental learning.

7. **Model What You Coach.** Manager-coaches are responsible for demonstrating the leadership and job skills that the team member is trying to develop. This role modeling—including vulnerability, experimentation, learning, and even working with a coach—builds trust and confidence and teaches others by example. With feedback as a critical component of the effective team-member/manager-coach relationship, the manager should regularly seek feedback and use it to improve their performance and periodically provide feedback to others.

Developing and applying coaching skills requires learning, practice, feedback, and reflection. These seven principles provide a foundation for managers to use coaching to
help team members improve performance, develop capabilities, and transition in their
roles, careers, and lives. The self-awareness questionnaire in Appendix B can help.

Case Examples

Below are two coaching conversations between a manager-coach and a team member.
They are fictionalized and designed to illustrate the six-step coaching process and
some coaching skills. Additional examples are provided in Appendices D and E.

Example 1

This coaching dialogue between a manager and a team member who supervises a
team illustrates the six-step coaching process and the coaching skills of listening for
understanding, asking powerful questions, providing insight, and developing support.
See Table 12.2.

Table 12.2: Coaching Case Example 1.

Dialogue	Coaching Process Step	Coaching Skill(s) Applied
Team Member: Good morning. I hope you had a good weekend. I've got something I want to talk with you about today. I hope you can help me. **Manager-Coach:** *Good morning. Yes, it was a good weekend. The weather was great. I got to play a round of golf. I hope you had a good weekend as well.* **Team Member:** It was lovely. I spent time at the park with my family on Saturday. We hadn't done that in a long time.	Step 1: Current Situation and Context	Listening for Understanding Asking Powerful Questions
Manager-Coach: *You mentioned that you had something you wanted to talk with me about. What is it?* **Team Member:** I'd like to focus on building a high-performing team despite the challenges posed by varying performance levels.	Step 2: Goal/Desired Outcome	Listening for Understanding Asking Powerful Questions

Table 12.2 (continued)

Dialogue	Coaching Process Step	Coaching Skill(s) Applied
Manager-Coach: *Let's delve deeper into that. Can you elaborate on the difficulties you face?* **Team Member:** I find maintaining a high-performing team challenging when some members don't meet expectations. It's particularly tough with the mediocre performers. **Manager-Coach:** *How do you perceive your leadership style affecting the team, especially when dealing with varying performance levels?* **Team Member:** I believe my empowering style works well with good performers, but I tend to take over tasks when dealing with mediocre performers. **Manager-Coach:** *How does that impact their growth and the team's overall performance?* **Team Member:** I might inadvertently hinder their growth by not letting them handle their responsibilities independently. **Manager-Coach:** *I've noticed that sometimes you seem to get directly involved in the work of some team members. I wonder what's going on in those situations.* **Team Member:** Yes, I do. Sometimes, it is because I'm very interested in their actions. In other cases, it is because I don't have confidence in their ability to develop a good outcome. Thank you for raising that. I have not always been aware of when I'm getting overly involved and why. I need to work on that.	Step 3: Information Gathering	Listening for Understanding Asking Powerful Questions Providing Insight
Manager-Coach: *That might be another topic for us to focus on. What do you think?* **Team Member:** It is. Let's continue with the team members' performance. I'll make a note to return to my tendency to get overly involved. **Manager-Coach:** *OK. If we don't have time to discuss that today, we can pick that up during our next meeting.*	Step 2: Goals & Desired Outcomes	Listening for Understanding Asking Powerful Questions

Table 12.2 (continued)

Dialogue	Coaching Process Step	Coaching Skill(s) Applied
Manager-Coach: *To support the development of all team members, how can you adjust your approach to empower both high and mediocre performers?* **Team Member:** I could start by setting more explicit expectations and providing additional support and guidance to the underperformers without taking over their tasks entirely. **Manager-Coach:** *That's a positive step.* **Team Member:** I could create a development plan tailored to each team member's needs. I can identify specific areas for improvement and work with them individually on action plans. **Manager-Coach:** *I wonder if there is a way to get your team members involved in developing these plans.* **Team Member:** Wow. I realized I would do all the work, and they might not buy into the plans. I need to involve them in creating individual plans. **Manager-Coach:** *How could you do that?* **Team Member:** I could share my observations with them, then ask them to identify one or two things they could do to improve or enhance their work on the team. Then, they could draft an action plan to review with me.	Step 4: Possible Actions	Listening for Understanding Asking Powerful Questions
Manager-Coach: *You have identified several possible actions. What are you willing to commit to doing?* **Team Member:** I think I will start with three team members by meeting with them this week. I will share it with them. I'll ask them to identify actions they will take to address the feedback. Then, I'll ask them to create a development plan by the end of next week. **Manager-Coach:** *How will you address this with the other team members?*	Step 5: Action Planning	Listening for Understanding Asking Powerful Questions

Table 12.2 (continued)

Dialogue	Coaching Process Step	Coaching Skill(s) Applied
Team Member: I'll use the first three team members as a pilot. I think I'll start with the people most likely to resist the feedback and action planning. Then, I can adjust my approach, if necessary, before meeting with the other four members of my team. How does that sound?		
Manager-Coach: *It sounds like you have a clear plan in mind and plan to learn and adjust along the way. Is there anything you need to prepare for these meetings?*		
Team Member: Yes. I need to block time on my calendar to identify the specific feedback I want to provide each person. I'll use the CBIR model to frame it as I prepare for the one-on-one meetings. You know, I will use these action plans as a topic of discussion during my ongoing one-on-one sessions with each team member. This will help foster accountability.		
Manager-Coach: *We have a few minutes remaining. I'd like to hear what you've gotten from this conversation and what you plan to do.*	Step 6: Summary and Agreement	Listening for Understanding Asking Powerful Questions Developing Support
Team Member: I realized I would do all the work and not encourage my team members to create action plans. I have a clear plan to pilot my approach by meeting with three members of my team this week. I will apply the CBIR feedback model to guide my conversations.		
Manager-Coach: *Anything else?*		
Team Member: This has been very useful. I was feeling overwhelmed. You've helped me find a way forward and boosted my confidence. Oh, and let's return to my tendency to get overly involved during our next meeting.		
Manager-Coach: *Well, you did the work. I'm glad this was helpful. Let's schedule a follow-up meeting in two weeks to discuss the development plan's progress and any adjustments needed.*		
Team Member: That sounds good. I'll track the progress and make necessary adaptations.		

Example 2

This illustrates the six-step coaching process for a coaching conversation between a manager and a team member. The steps in the coaching process and the coaching skills of listening for understanding, asking powerful questions, and reframing. The team member approaches their manager for help with a person the team member supervises. See Table 12.3.

Table 12.3: Coaching Case Example 2.

Dialogue	Coaching Process Step	Coaching Skill(s) Applied
Manager-Coach: *Good afternoon. How are you today?* **Team Member:** I'm great. I do have something I'd like to discuss with you. It relates to how I can better supervise a member of my team, Sarah.	Step 1: Current Situation and Context	Listening for Understanding Asking Powerful Questions
Manager-Coach: *I'm glad we're having this coaching session today. What's the specific goal or area you'd like to focus on improving?* **Team Member:** I want to enhance my ability to motivate one of my team members—Sarah. Sometimes it feels like I'm not connecting with what drives them, affecting their performance. **Manager-Coach:** *Great, understanding their motivation is crucial. Let's dive deeper into this.*	Step 2: Needs and Desired Goals	Listening for Understanding Asking Powerful Questions
Manager-Coach: *What strategies have you already implemented to motivate them?* **Team Member:** I've set clear goals, offered rewards, and provided positive feedback regularly. But there's a disconnect. Sarah doesn't respond as positively as I'd hoped. **Manager-Coach:** *It's good to know what you've tried. How well do you understand Sarah's personal motivations and goals?* **Team Member:** I have a general idea, but I think I need to delve deeper into understanding what truly drives them. **Manager-Coach:** *Have you had a similar experience with an employee? If so, what have you done in those situations?* **Team Member:** No. I've never faced this before.	Step 3: Information Gathering	Listening for Understanding Asking Powerful Questions Reframing

Table 12.3 (continued)

Dialogue	Coaching Process Step	Coaching Skill(s) Applied
Manager-Coach: *Have you observed another leader deal with a similar situation?*		
Team Member: No. I've never faced this before.		
Manager-Coach: *Have you observed another leader deal with a similar situation?*		
Team Member: Now that you mention it, I recall my former manager faced a similar situation with a member of their team. They met with the team members and shared their observations, then asked the team members what would be needed to get them engaged.		
Manager-Coach: *What does that experience tell you that might help you here?*		
Team Member: It tells me that this situation is not unique. I have more confidence based on what I observed my former manager do.		
Manager-Coach: *How do you think you could gain a better understanding of their motivations?*	Step 4: Possible Actions	Listening for Understanding Asking Powerful Questions
Team Member: I'm considering scheduling a one-on-one meeting to discuss Sarah's long-term career aspirations and how their current role aligns with those goals.		
Manager-Coach: *That sounds like it could be a good thing to do. Is there anything else you can think of that you might be willing to do?*		
Team Member: I could observe Sarah to see what appears to excite her when she shows curiosity and when she is less energized. This might be helpful as I get to know her better, and it might give me some data that I can share with her.		
Manager-Coach: *That sounds like several possible action steps. What specific actions do you plan to take based on this insight?*	Step 5: Action Planning	Listening for Understanding Asking Powerful Questions
Team Member: I'll schedule a meeting with Sarah within the next week and actively listen to understand their aspirations better. Then, I'll adapt my motivational strategies based on what I learn.		
Manager-Coach: *How do you plan to sustain these changes in your approach to keep Sarah motivated?*		

Table 12.3 (continued)

Dialogue	Coaching Process Step	Coaching Skill(s) Applied
Team Member: I'll ensure ongoing communication and revisit these discussions regularly to align Sarah's motivations with our team's objectives.		
Manager-Coach: *How will you evaluate the effectiveness of these new strategies?*		
Team Member: I'll track Sarah's engagement, productivity, and overall attitude to see if there's a positive shift after implementing these changes.		
Manager-Coach: *That's a comprehensive plan. I'm confident these structured steps will guide you toward a more practical approach to motivating Sarah.*		
Manager-Coach: *Does this conversation meet your needs to develop a plan to help motivate Sarah?* **Team Member:** Yes. It was exactly what I needed. **Manager-Coach:** *Great! So, as we wrap up, please summarize your insights from this conversation and your action plans.* **Team Member:** I've gained some confidence in my approach. I plan to observe Sarah more carefully, meet with her to share my feedback and work with her to create a plan of action. I will also ask her what, if any, support I can give her.	Step 6: Summary and Agreement	Listening for Understanding Asking Powerful Questions

Summary

Change coaching is a helping relationship focused on helping individuals and teams develop capabilities, apply those capabilities to improve performance, and transform individually and collectively. The six-step coaching process and six coaching skills can be used to effect sustainable behavioral and organizational change. Manager-coaches encounter numerous challenges that can be overcome by shifting mindsets, applying a coaching process and skills, and continuously developing.

Manager-coaches who adhere to these seven principles of coaching mindsets can effectively support their team members' growth and development:

1. Create a safe and brave space.
2. Focus on the team member's agenda.
3. Facilitate and collaborate.

4. Promote mastery through self-awareness.
5. Balance personal development and organizational priorities.
6. Promote learning and growth from experiences.
7. Model what you coach.

A Conversation with Michele Langford
Healthcare Executive with an Integrated Healthcare System

This conversation was recorded and transcribed, then edited for clarity and conciseness.

John Bennett (JB): *In addition to leading a team of about 40 people, a large part of your job is to work with executives across the healthcare system. Both probably involve a lot of coaching in both formal and informal ways. Is that correct?*

Michele Langford (ML): It is just part of what I do every day. . . . It's informal, yet it has been very intentional as part of my leadership approach.

JB: *How are you approached, and how do you approach others?*

ML: I will approach others, and then others approach me. Many times I will have somebody reach out and ask if I have a few minutes to talk. It could be something as small as something that just happened in a meeting, and they want to debrief their experience and talk about what happened and how that may look different. . . . There are team members across the organization that will reach out and say, "I just need somebody to talk to as a mentor or for advice." My natural approach to these conversations is to use a coaching mindset, skills, and process. It just comes naturally in interactions throughout every day.

JB: *How do you show up so that people would even want to reach out to you, particularly those not in your direct line of responsibility and accountability?*

ML: I've been with the organization for an extended period, and people know me and know that about me. . . . One way I show up is I am very open. I am not judgmental. People know that they can talk to me about anything. I'm also trustworthy in that I don't share that information outside. And I think I'm known for being able to navigate organizational complexity. I believe that my leadership brand is what draws those conversations to me.

JB: *And when you're having that kind of conversation, how would you assess if you've been effective?*

ML: I am a big believer in feedback, so I often will ask for feedback. But instead of just saying, "Give me some feedback about what I just said to you," I have adopted the question, "What do you take away from this conversation?" And I have an opportunity to observe behaviors. Because I know what they're working on, I can watch for that and gather additional data throughout the organization. I also notice if I get a second call from the person. Do they call and say, "I want to tell you I'm excited about what just happened," or "I tried that first option we discussed, which didn't work so well. Can you help me think through option B?"

JB: *How did you develop your skills in coaching?*

ML: First and foremost, I have been coached. That's a great way to learn the value of such skills. I have completed graduate courses related to coaching and completed a certificate in coaching at Queens University of Charlotte. That program gave me a framework and theories to consider coaching as a discipline. So that helped develop those skills and mindsets. I have observed and learned from other coaching-oriented leaders. I've learned from what works; sometimes, I've been not so good, and those have been very powerful. I was learning to refine those skills and do something better the next time. I have pursued training where there are other coaches, such as Enneagram training. I have put myself in communities of other coaches. This is a great way to continue learning and have individual conversations with them. And then the other two things: feedback and reflection. I've mentioned the power of feedback. And I have developed coaching skills based on feedback that I have been provided. And one of the most powerful things I've done is to stay in a state of reflection and continue learning about coaching, mindset, skills, and ways of being.

JB: *You've talked about having a coaching mindset. What does that mean?*

ML: A coaching mindset is about approaching a situation with the mindset of asking more questions than telling, so it's a mindset of curiosity. . . . It's a mindset of meeting the individual or the team where they are and not directing them to an answer that I have already come up with. I think it's a mindset of openness and just showing up and being present.

JB: *Thank you! In a busy organization with so much activity and pressure for continuous improvement and growth, I'm curious how coaching as a manager shows up. How is the role of the manager-coach embraced?*

ML: In the past five years, the organization has developed a coaching for leaders program and curriculum. We are trying to show what it means to be a coach as a leader of people. So there has been some use of the word and some content created. It's not used daily, but the organization embraces coaching. Even though it's not formal, we're adopting a coaching mindset. Leaders who use this mindset are consistently identified as strong leaders and leaders with significant leadership competency. It is about coaching for results, which is a tricky balance. My focus, for example, is not just on the individual agenda. I'm always working in the context of the organization, what results the organization needs.

JB: *It sounds like you and other leaders are expected to keep the business's outcomes and performance in mind and develop the capabilities of the people doing the work.*

ML: That is correct. And I see every task as an opportunity for that.

JB: *What challenges have you observed or experienced using this approach as a manager/leader?*

ML: There are a few. One is a challenge of expectations. When team members reach out and say they want to have this conversation, often they do not understand how the coaching conversation will be handled or what to expect. So, I'll talk with them about what the conversation really is going to be and what they can expect. Often, team members will say they are coming to me because they want to tell me the answer to a question and what to do. I think that's a challenge, and the conversation has to be navigated appropriately to say, "Here's the purpose of this conversation" or "I've heard what you're asking. This is how I am planning to approach this [which does not include providing you with an answer] . . . . Is that OK?" That can challenge the person coming to me for help because they were expecting an answer, and I plan to help them discover a solution for themselves.

Another is the challenge of time. As we've already acknowledged, there is a balance of developing people, asking questions and getting a job done, delivering results, and producing outcomes in a particular period. Time pressures often challenge the coaching approach. Given the compressed timeline, a more direct leadership approach or style is often necessary. I think the other challenge is when performance issues are well beyond the need for coaching. So when it is time for disciplinary action, there's always the challenge of having to flex styles to say this is needed. . . . This leadership approach needs to be more directive and less coachlike.

JB: *You are describing the movement between coaching and managing. It seems like a continuum.*

ML: That's right. There are times when I need to expect an immediate shift in behavior or a situation where I need to direct action as a leader. As a strong leader, you work that full continuum. You . . . have to understand what the situation requires of you, and you know it comes back to your best use of self.

JB: *I'm guessing that continuum you describe would have coaching on one end and directing on the other end, there are probably some things like teaching, supporting, and nurturing that go in between.*

ML: I think that's right. I think advising fits in there. I believe . . . even the word consulting could be in there.

JB: *You've discussed how people come to you for coaching and how the organization values a coaching approach. How have others responded to your use of coaching in your manager role?*

ML: So first, I would say appreciative of the time, the openness, and holding of space for a conversation. I think people are empowered, feel energized, and feel ready to act. They feel unstuck, prepared to move forward, and respond with greater confidence in what they're preparing to do. And one of the most incredible responses that I have experienced is seeing others start to adopt that coaching approach when leading others.

JB: *Can you think of a time when you used coaching as a manager and give me an understanding of that experience?*

ML: I have examples of team members seeking to develop, enhance their performance, and transform.
    For a focus on development, I had a new team member, a new college graduate, and he was incredibly curious about what work life and the work world were all about. He was still in this discovery mode of who he was and what he wanted to do. So I used lots of conversations to help him identify what he was interested in and what he would like to do, and he developed the plan for exploration, making sure that he didn't pigeonhole and think that he had the answers at such an early stage of his career. The plan included getting to know other leaders, learning from their experiences, exploring other jobs, and having different positions within the organization. That led him to go back to school and be around other folks. He changed jobs, and he has carried that framework with him. I have watched him accept several positions and try different hats, and he continues to come back to me to want to check in, tell me what he's done, and learn from all of those experiences.
    I have a direct report who has been given feedback about finding his voice. He got feedback about how skilled he is. He's an expert. However, I don't hear his voice in meetings, and I used a coaching approach to share that feedback and then explore ways that feel natural to him to use his voice in meetings. The outcome is that people are wowed by what he says in meetings. I observe people listen to what he says he has seen as their thought partner on many issues, and that stems from the change he made in finding his voice to being more comfortable, particularly in a room with executives.
    In terms of transforming, I think about a leader I have worked with who was promoted to a much more significant role. And through a coaching process and conversation helped her identify a framework for what it means to move from a manager of a facility to a manager of the markets. We worked

to determine what skills would be required. The leader created a way to get feedback from her direct reports and others, then stayed focused on those necessary skills. This provided a foundation for her development to operate successfully at a higher level.

JB: *What is the value of coaching in your leadership and management role?*

ML: Number 1, I believe it's a way to value others. It feels like an investment in a team member or the team. That's one of the most significant values, but others include instilling confidence, creating trust, helping others grow, and developing other leaders for the organization. I take great pride in growing leaders for the organization. And I think using this approach is a valuable way to get there. It gives me more and broader insights. Being open to a conversation and hearing what others are experiencing gives me insights that I can be an even stronger leader and learn and grow from those experiences. I think the value is in authentic connections and engagement. Overall the value, for me personally, is being a better leader of people.

JB: *What advice would you offer someone who's a leader manager who's considering using a coaching approach?*

ML: Dive deeply into understanding a coaching approach and how it differs from others. Another suggestion is to realize that as leaders, we've got to use a variety of approaches. . . . Understand it can't be all coaching.

Part III: **Special Considerations**

Chapter 13
Coaching Across Differences

Men often hurt each other because they fear each other, they fear each other because they do not know each other; they don't know each other because they can't communicate; they can't communicate because they are separated.

—Rev. Dr. Martin Luther King, Jr.

We live and work in a global society. Organizations and the communities in which they are based are more diverse than ever. Manager-coaches work with leaders from various cultural backgrounds and all experience levels. It is, therefore, increasingly important that manager-coaches understand differences and how they influence the mindsets and behaviors of the manager, team members, and organizations.

Coaching is a powerful tool used to help individuals reach their full potential. Coaching across differences is the practice of coaching individuals who come from different backgrounds, experiences, cultures, and identities. Coaching across differences can be challenging due to the differences in communication styles, values, and expectations of the coach and the team members. However, coaching across differences can also be rewarding as it helps the manager-coach and the team members develop a deeper understanding of each other's perspectives and values.

As human beings, we have many identities. Individual identities are how we see ourselves—e.g., accountant, lawyer, teacher, professional, caring, kind, and thoughtful. Cultural identities include our communication style, conflict style, preference for individualism or collectivism, task and relationship orientation, and leadership style. A third set of identities is social. This is how others see us and ascribe meaning to those identities in the context of society. The value of one identity group over another is defined socially, meaning it varies by culture—e.g., the United States, Western Europe, and Asia. The social identities differentiated in the U.S. include race, gender, sexual orientation, class, religion, nationality, age, and ability. Preference may be afforded to one dimension of one of these identities over another—e.g., U.S. citizen over immigrant; white over black, people of color and indigenous people; male over female. These socially constructed differences lead to privilege or power for the dominant social identities compared to the subordinated social identities.

Inequity, exclusion, covering, and a sense of not belonging are rampant in organizations of all sizes. As Radd et al. (2021) note, ". . . the problem lies in the system and the inequalities are symptoms and results. In other words, although Inequality breeds inequity, it is not the cause but the result of a system set up to produce inequities" (p. 9). Inequality is a systemic issue that permeates relationships at various levels of organizations, including the individual and interpersonal, institutional, structural, and historical.

At the individual and interpersonal levels, racism and other forms of discrimination involve overt, intentional acts of personal meanness, exclusion, and unfair treat-

https://doi.org/10.1515/9783111002415-013

ment. Everyone carries unconscious biases, which contribute to negative judgment, exclusion, and discrimination. Equality means everyone receives the same treatment and access. Equity means people get the treatment they need and access tailored to meet them where they are. At the organizational level, the laws, rules, processes, and organizations we use to engage in schooling and other aspects of our lives all work to continue historical and current patterns of inequity. At the structural level, how our system of education, and our entire society for that matter, are built and organized predictably leads to the types of disparate outcomes that exist today. And at the historical level, the problems we face today have their roots in centuries of human experience. Histories inform what you think, how you feel, and how you react. Leaders at all levels are responsible for actively fostering cultures of equality, inclusion, and belonging.

This chapter explores the challenges and opportunities of coaching across differences. It discusses the importance of cultural competence and empathy in coaching across differences and defines and describes various terms and concepts related to diversity, equity, inclusion, and belonging. It identifies and describes nine common social identities and explains why and how differences matter. It explores these concepts and identities in the context of coaching by managers. In also discusses the dynamics of differences between manager-coaches and team members, as well as challenges and strategies for coaching across differences.

Opportunities for Coaching Across Differences

To be valid, a perspective on culture needs to be of practical value in helping individuals 1) navigate a broad spectrum of differences, 2) understand the fundamentals of various cultures and cultural interactions, and 3) translate this understanding into personal behaviors and organizational expectations. Awareness of culture at the individual, group, and organization levels can help a manager-coach observe and work with team members on specific behaviors or attitudes that affect their success, both positively and negatively.

Coaching across differences also presents many opportunities for the coach and the client. Some of the possibilities include:

- **Learning:** Coaching across differences allows the coach and the team members to learn from each other. The coach can learn about the team member's culture, experiences, and values. The team member can also learn about the manager-coach's culture, experiences, and values.
- **Empathy:** Coaching across differences requires empathy from the coach and the team member. Empathy is the ability to understand and share the feelings of another. When the manager-coach and the team members demonstrate empathy toward each other, it can strengthen the coaching relationship and lead to tremendous success.
- **Diversity and Inclusion:** Coaching across differences can promote organizational diversity and inclusion. When managers coach individuals from different

backgrounds and cultures, it helps create a more inclusive and welcoming environment for everyone.

- **Improved Communication:** Coaching across differences can help improve communication skills for both the coach and the team members. By working with individuals from different cultures and backgrounds, manager-coaches can better understand how to effectively communicate with people with varying communication styles.

- **Personal Growth:** Coaching across differences can also promote personal growth for the manager-coach and the team members. By working with individuals with different perspectives and experiences, manager-coaches can challenge their assumptions and beliefs and develop a greater sense of empathy and understanding.

- **Increased Creativity:** Coaching across differences can also improve creativity and innovation. When individuals with different backgrounds and experiences work together, they are more likely to generate new ideas and solutions.

- **Cultural Competence:** Coaching across differences requires cultural competence from the manager-coach. Cultural competence is understanding, appreciating, and effectively working with individuals from diverse cultures. When the manager-coach demonstrates cultural competence, it can lead to a deeper understanding of the team member's experiences and needs. Cultural competence involves developing an awareness of one's own cultural biases and assumptions, as well as learning about and respecting the cultures of others. This skill is becoming increasingly important in today's globalized world.

According to Sue et al. (2022), cultural competence involves five essential elements:

1. **Self-Awareness:** Manager-coaches must first develop an awareness of their cultural biases, assumptions, and values
2. **Knowledge of Difference Cultures:** Manager-coaches must learn about the cultures of their team members and develop an understanding of their experiences, beliefs, and values.
3. **Understanding of the Dynamics of Power and Privilege:** Manager-coaches must understand how power and privilege can impact the coaching relationship and the experiences of their team members.
4. **Cross-Cultural Skills:** Manager-coaches must develop skills to effectively communicate and work with individuals from diverse cultures.
5. **Commitment to Social Justice:** Manager-coaches must be committed to promoting social justice.
6. **Improved Organizational Performance:** Coaching across differences can also improve organizational performance. When manager-coach can effectively coach individuals from different backgrounds and cultures, it can help improve teamwork, collaboration, and productivity within organizations.

Coaching across differences presents many opportunities for the coach and the client to learn, grow, and improve. By embracing diversity and working with individuals from different backgrounds and cultures, coaches can develop a greater sense of empathy and understanding, which can help create more inclusive and effective organizations.

Challenges of Coaching Across Differences

Coaching across differences can present many challenges for the manager-coach and the client. Some of the challenges include:

- **Communication Styles:** Communication styles can differ across cultures. For example, some cultures prefer indirect communication, while others prefer direct communication. This can create misunderstandings and misinterpretations.
- **Values:** Values can also differ across cultures. For example, some cultures may value individualism more, while others may value collectivism. This can affect the goals and expectations of the coaching relationship.
- **Expectations:** Expectations of the coaching relationship can also differ across cultures. For example, some cultures may expect the coach to be more authoritative, while others may desire the manager-coach to be more collaborative. This can affect the coaching style and approach.
- **Identity:** Identity can also affect the coaching relationship. For example, individuals who identify as LGBTQ+ may have different experiences and challenges than individuals who identify as heterosexual. This can affect the goals and approach of the coaching relationship.
- **Power Dynamics:** Power dynamics can also affect the coaching relationship. The employer-employee power dynamics are present in any managerial coaching relationship. Manager-coaches from a dominant culture may have more power in the relationship than clients from a marginalized culture. This can magnify any trust and rapport issues.
- **Unconscious Bias:** Manager-coaches may have unconscious biases that affect their ability to effectively coach team members from different backgrounds and cultures. These biases can lead to assumptions and stereotypes about the team member's experiences and perspectives, which can affect the quality of the coaching relationship.
- **Lack of Cultural Competence:** Manager-coaches may lack the necessary cultural competence to effectively coach team members from different backgrounds and cultures. This can lead to misunderstandings, misinterpretations, and a lack of empathy and understanding between the manager-coach and the team member.

Coaching across differences can be challenging due to the differences in communication styles, values, expectations, identity, power dynamics, unconscious bias, and cultural competence. However, by acknowledging these challenges and developing strategies to address them, coaches can effectively coach clients from different backgrounds and cultures and help them achieve their goals.

Key Terms and Concepts

Terms and concepts related to diversity, equity, inclusion, and belonging continue to evolve and may not have a universal understanding. Here are some key terms and concepts with definitions that you should be familiar with as you work with team members.

Ally: Someone who advocates and supports a community other than their own. Allies are not part of the communities they help. A person should not self-identify as an ally but instead show that they are one through action.

Belonging: ". . . your sense that you are part of something greater than yourself that you value and need and that values and needs you back. In other words, belonging creates a strong sense of connection, reciprocity, and shared value. . . . A culture of belonging is built on access, reciprocity, and sharing of power and opportunity. It is not a culture that excludes anyone based on social identity, though it might set clear parameters around employee orientations, motivations, and aspirations" (Miranda-Wolff, 2022, p. 8).

Bias: A preconceived or irrational tendency, trend, inclination, feeling, or opinion. Prejudice is taught by the socialization practices one is exposed to.

BIPOC: Black, Indigenous, and People of Color.

Class: A social stratum sharing essential economic, political, or cultural characteristics and having the same social position.

Covering: This is downplaying your differences relative to mainstream perceptions in ways that are costly to your productivity and sense of self in the workplace.

Cultural dominance or dominant social identity: Supremacy on a given dimension of diversity. The condition of being culturally dominant. Cultural dominance equals rule, control, power, and authority.

Culturally subordinated or subordinated social identity: A status imposed by a culturally dominant social identity group onto another group it deems inferior to itself. Subordination is done to a group. No group voluntarily subordinates itself.

Critical Race Theory (CRT): What began as a legal theory in the 1970s is now a collection of activities and scholars who study transformational relationships among race, racism, and power. This approach has spread to other disciplines, such as political science, ethnic studies, sociology, theology, and healthcare (Delgado & Stefancic, 2017). Today, CRT is a cross-disciplinary examination of how laws, social and political movements, and media shape, and are shaped by, social conceptions of ethnicity and race. The word *critical* in the name is an academic reference to critical thinking and critical theory rather than criticizing or blaming people.

Diversity: The de-facto state of differences among human beings in social space. The practice or quality of including or involving people from various social and ethnic backgrounds and different races, genders, sexual orientations, etc.

Dominant: Supremacy on a given dimension of diversity, such as culture or social identity. Cultural dominance equals rule, control, power, and authority.

Equity: Everyone gets what they need; fairness, impartiality, absence of favoritism.

Ethnicity: An ethnic-social group with a distinctive culture, values, religion, language, etc.

Exclusion: The opposite of inclusion. It involves conscious and unconscious acts that place some individuals or groups of individuals outside the sphere of power, knowledge, opportunity, collaboration, partnership, decision-making, and career advancement.

Gender: A socially constructed system of classification that ascribes feminine or masculine characteristics to people.

Gender identity: A person's internal sense of themselves as a specific gender—girl/ woman, boy/man, etc.—irrespective of their biological sex.

Implicit bias: Having prejudice and stereotypes without intending to do so and acting based on the bias.

Inclusion: Allows individuals with different identities, skill sets, beliefs, and experiences to feel they belong within the group because they are valued, relied upon, welcomed, and empowered. Inclusion is also the ability to interact with people in a way that makes them feel they belong, are valued, and are welcome to be themselves.

Intersectionality: A term coined by law professor Kimberlé Crenshaw (1989) to describe how multiple systems of oppression interact in the lives of those with multiple marginalized identities. The notion is that no one can be identified by only one dimension of diversity and social group identity. Instead, each of us has multiple social group identities and lives from a nexus where all our identities intersect. Intersectionality examines the relationships between various marginalized identities and allows us to analyze social problems more thoroughly, shape effective interventions, and promote inclusive advocacy among communities.

JEDI: An abbreviation that represents Justice, Equity, Diversity and Inclusion.

Marginalize: To push someone out to the margins of social space or activity because of stereotypical assumptions about that person's intelligence, competence, capability, or overall desirability.

Microaggressions: Subtle but offensive comments or actions directed at a culturally subordinated group. Often unintentional or unconscious, they insult, invalidate, or exclude marginalized groups and reinforce stereotypes.

Prejudice: A preconceived unfavorable opinion or feeling about someone formed without knowledge, thought, or reason. It is a "prejudgment about another person based on the social groups to which that person belongs. Prejudice consists of thoughts and feelings, including stereotypes, attitudes, and generalizations that are based on little or no experience and then are projected onto everyone from that group. Our prejudices tend to be shared because we swim in the same cultural water and absorb the same messages" (Diangelo, 2018, p. 19).

Privilege: Is ". . . unearned benefits given to individuals with particular socio-cultural identities—white privilege, male privilege, heterosexual privilege . . ." (Radd, et al., 2021, p. 51). It is the other side of oppression. Privilege and oppression affect each other, but they do not negate each other. Privilege describes what everyone should experience and is understood in the context of power systems. A person with privilege may have worked hard to earn their privilege.

Race: The Swedish botanist Carolus Linnaeus created a taxonomy of differentiated races within humanity in the mid-1700s. A German anthropologist, Johann Blumenbach, turned Linnaeus's taxonomy into a hierarchy, putting "Caucasian" at the top and "Negroid" at the bottom. Scientifically speaking, there is only one race: the human race. "Race," as currently understood, is a social construction.

Racism: ". . . a marriage of racist policies and racist ideas that produce and normalize racial inequities" (Kendi, 2019, p. 18). It is institutional, structural, and systemic.

Sexual orientation: A person's physical, romantic, emotional, aesthetic, and other form of attraction to others. Trans people can be straight, bisexual, lesbian, gay, asexual, pansexual, queer, etc., just like anyone else. For example, a trans woman who is exclusively attracted to other women would often identify as lesbian. In Western cultures, gender identity and sexual orientation are not the same.

Social identity: The portion of an individual's self-concept derived from membership in a social group.

Socialization: The process of learning how to behave in a way that is acceptable to society. It mostly happens in the context of family and home of origin.

Stereotype: A widely held but fixed, oversimplified, and to some extent erroneous image or ideas of a person or group. Stereotypes are based on very little data and are related to assumptions and implicit bias.

Structural inequality: The combination of privilege, exclusion, power, and oppression in all levels, facets, and functions of cultures, societies, systems, and organizations. When exercised, these factors confer favor, privilege, or benefit for one group (dominant) over other groups. Structural inequality is supported through visible and hidden policies, programs, rules, norms, assumptions, and attitudes. The behavior creates, sustains, and contributes to the existence and continuation of bias, discrimination, and dominance in all areas of society, culture, or system (Royal, 2010).

Dominant and Subordinated Identities

Human beings are comprised of many intersecting identities. For example, a person may be black, female, heterosexual, upper class, and Christian. Another person may be Hispanic, male, gay, and Buddhist. The combination of social identities intersects to form how people view themselves and are viewed by others.

Dominant identities—those with power and privilege—and subordinated identities—those with less power or privilege— are culturally defined. The dominant identity groups tend to seek to maintain the status quo. Their privilege and entitlement are invisible. They may not see other peoples' differences and different experiences, and they may believe everyone can achieve (meritocracy). "The concept of privilege violates everything we've been told about fairness and everything we've been told about the American Dream of hard work paying off and good things happening to good people" (Oluo, 2019, p. 63). Those with subordinated (not subordinate) identities use energy to manage themselves with the privileged group. They may work to conform to dominant group practices, internalize stereotypes and assimilation as a survival strategy, tend to seek support groups, and withhold feelings and thoughts to minimize risks. They may also collude with the dominant group.

Ijeoma Oluo (2019) notes the following examples of how those in subordinated identity groups are disadvantaged in the United States.

- "Black sounding name": 4 times less likely to be called for a job interview.
- White women make 83 cents for every white man's dollar.
- Hispanic women earn 58 cents for every white man's dollar.
- Black men earn 73 cents for every white man's dollar.
- Hispanic men earn 69 cents for every white man's dollar.
- An average of 16% of black and 7% of Hispanic students are suspended each year, compared to 5% of white students.

The following Table 13.1 lists nine social identities, dominant or privileged groups, and the subordinated groups.

Table 13.1: Big 9 Social Identities.

Dominant/Privileged	Social Identities	Subordinated
White	**Race**	People of Color
Angelo	**Ethnicity**	Indigenous
Cisgender male	**Gender Expression**	Cisgender female, nonbinary, transgender
Middle aged	**Age**	Young and ld
Heterosexual	**Sexual Orientation**	Lesbian, gay, bisexual
United States	**Nationality/National Origin**	Europe, Australasia, Middle East, Africa
Christian	**Religion**	Muslin, Hindu, Jewish
Able-bodied	**Ability**	Disabled
Executive, top 5% of wage earners, "white collar"	**Economic Status**	Hourly, "blue collar"

Practical Strategies for Coaching Across Differences

Everyone has preferences, makes assumptions, has mental models, and is biased. A simple example is how you like your food prepared. Some people like a steak cooked rare, while others like it prepared medium-well or well done. When our preferences are unmet, we may conclude the restaurant is not competent, so we stop going there or recommending it to others. At a personal level, our past experiences, values, and beliefs help shape our preferences. Some of these preferences may result from a conscious choice, while others are unconscious. These preferences lead to biases for or against something or someone.

These biases may draw us toward or away from options. Examples of affinity bias include decisions about who a leader decides to interview for an open position, who is promoted, and who gets special project assignments that will help advance their career. Less obvious affinity biases include who you invite to lunch or coffee, share information with, invite to social events, or offer to mentor. Subtle affinity biases include with whom you make eye contact during a meeting and the people you shake hands with, recognize as credible sources of information, or go to for advice. Manager-coaches should continuously seek to identify and address their biases while helping team members do the same.

As noted in chapter one, the goals or agenda for coaching can be organized into one or more of three categories: performance, development, and transformation. Table 13.2 shows examples of specific areas of focus related to coaching across differences.

Table 13.2: Examples of Focus for Cross-Cultural Coaching.

Focus of Coaching	Individual	Group or Team
Performing	– Developing the ability to lead or succeed in a diverse, multicultural environment (skills such as interviewing, managing performance, handling conflict, delegating, etc.). – Improving awareness or behavior in interpersonal communications and inclusion. – Performing effectively in a diverse, multicultural team. – Improving critical business skills in a diverse, global context (such as negotiation and selling skills, building and sustaining client relationships, etc.).	– Improving team performance in diverse, multicultural, or global settings. – Leveraging the effectiveness and business relevance of employee networks or resource groups. – Enhancing performance and innovation through expanded team membership (or alliances). – Increasing awareness of team members' differences, capabilities, and contributions, leading to improved effectiveness or productivity.
Developing	– Developing global leadership capabilities and building global mindsets. – Increasing strategic and global thinking. – Building effective networks and strategic relationships. – Examining "self as an instrument of change." – Identifying "stretch" opportunities. – Enhancing individual fit and performance in cultural transitions.	– Leading global teams. – Developing and sustaining practical team norms. – Developing or leveraging more-effective stakeholder relations/alliances with other teams or groups. – Enabling virtual cross-functional collaboration and teamwork. – Exploring team "self-management" (i.e., leaderless teaming).
Transforming	– Developing the ability to notice and adapt to various cultures and environments, to fit in easily and quickly, and to contribute at all levels of an organization. – Building capacity and bandwidth to function successfully with higher levels of responsibility and power. – Demonstrating successful contribution or leadership in a new or different arena (level, region, customer, product type, etc.).	– Building an effective global strategy. – Establishing effective alliances, collaboration, and teamwork at the trans-organization, multi-country, or cross-industry levels.

(Bennett and Bush, 2014, adapted from the TMC/Berlitz paper, "The Concept of Culture," 2009)

Manager-coaches can use several practical strategies when coaching across differences to ensure an effective coaching relationship. Some of these strategies include:

- **Develop Cultural Competence:** Manager-coaches should develop cultural competence, including understanding their own cultural biases and assumptions and being open to learning about other cultures. They can do this by attending training sessions, reading books, and engaging with individuals from diverse backgrounds.
- **Build and Maintain Rapport and Trust:** Manager-coaches should establish trust by building rapport and demonstrating empathy. You can do this by actively listening, asking open-ended questions, and respecting team members' experiences and needs.
- **Understand the Client's Context:** Manager-coaches should take the time to understand the team member's context, including their cultural background, values, and experiences. This includes awareness of any unique challenges or barriers the team member may face due to their identity or background.
- **Be Flexible:** Manager-coaches should be willing to adapt to the team member's communication styles, values, and expectations. This includes being open to adjusting your coaching style and techniques to better suit the team member's needs and preferences.
- **Use Inclusive Language:** Manager-coaches should use inclusive language, including avoiding assumptions about the team member's identity, using gender-neutral language, and avoiding language that may be offensive or insensitive.
- **Seek Feedback:** Manager-coaches should seek feedback from their team members about the coaching relationship and process to identify any areas for improvement and ensure the coaching relationship is effective and beneficial for team members.
- **Use Open-Ended Questions:** Manager-coaches should ask questions that encourage team members to share their experiences, perspectives, and goals. This can help build a deeper understanding of team members' context and create a more effective coaching relationship.
- **Avoid Stereotypes and Assumptions:** Manager-coaches should be open to learning about team member's unique experiences and perspectives.
- **Acknowledge and Address Power Dynamics:** Manager-coaches should actively work to create a more equitable coaching relationship.
- **Co-creating a Brave Space:** Adapting this approach from education, manager-coaches should invite and embrace controversy related to diversity, equity, inclusion, and belonging, and critically interrogate reasons people want to opt out of uncomfortable conversations. You should acknowledge when a perceived attack is, in fact, just a challenge, own your intentions and impacts on others, and "unpack the common wisdom of respect to investigate whether our concrete expectations of respect perpetuate social hierarchies . . ." (Pawlowski, 2019, p. 66).

Summary

Overall, coaching across differences requires coaches to be culturally competent, flexible, and adaptable in their coaching approach. Here's how to build those skills:
- Acknowledge your preferences, biases, prejudices, and privileges, and work to address them.
- Seek to understand the unique experiences of others.
- Foster trust and bravery for team members to bring their whole selves to work.
- Value differences.
- Adjust your approaches to meet the needs of subordinated identities.
- When in doubt about how to interact with another person, ask them from of a place of curiosity.

Practical strategies that manager-coaches can use to coach team members from different backgrounds include:
- Building rapport and trust
- Understanding the team member's context
- Using open-ended questions
- Avoiding stereotypes and assumptions
- Acknowledging and addressing power dynamics
- Seeking feedback

Chapter 14
Specialty Coaching

Empowering involves setting clear expectations, inviting risk-taking, and being a resource.
—Heather Younger, 2021

Leaders and team members have abundant opportunities to apply coaching principles and skills in their interactions with individuals and teams. In addition, managers and human resource professionals have opportunities to initiate coaching services using an internal or external professional coach for themselves or others. This chapter focuses on special coaching circumstances from the manager's perspective. These circumstances include peer coaching, team coaching, and supporting a coaching engagement conducted by an external executive coach. This chapter defines these situations and offers guidance for managers.

Coaching Peers

Peer coaching has emerged as a powerful tool in the realm of managerial leadership, blending the benefits of coaching with a collaborative and reciprocal approach. It examines the origin and principles of peer coaching, as well as its effect on professional growth and team success. This is a comprehensive understanding of the dynamics, challenges, and advantages associated with peer coaching for managers by exploring relevant literature, case studies, and empirical research.

The traditional hierarchical model of managerial leadership has given way to more collaborative and inclusive approaches. In this context, peer coaching has gained prominence as a valuable strategy for professional development. Peer coaching involves reciprocal relationships in which managers, serving as both coaches and coachees, engage in reflective conversations, share experiences, and collaboratively work toward individual and collective goals. Peer coaches encourage more experiential learning while mentors are expected to have a higher level of knowledge that they can pass on to the protégé. Parker et al. (2018) define peer coaching as "a focused relationship between individuals of equal status who support each other's personal and professional development goals" (p. 4).

Peer coaching draws inspiration from various coaching models and adult learning theories. Its roots can be traced to the principles of adult learning, where self-directedness, experience, and problem-solving take center stage (Knowles, 1980). Additionally, peer coaching incorporates elements of the change coaching model described earlier in this book, focusing on setting goals, exploring reality, generating options, and identifying ways forward. The essential principles of peer coaching encompass trust, reciprocity, confidentiality, and a shared commitment to continuous improvement.

https://doi.org/10.1515/9783111002415-014

The foundation of peer coaching lies in establishing trust between participants. Trust allows for open and honest communication and creates a safe space for managers to share their challenges, successes, and aspirations. Reciprocity is equally vital, as each participant takes on the dual role of coach and coachee. This reciprocal relationship fosters a sense of equality and shared responsibility for each other's professional growth. Peer coaching relies on the principle of confidentiality to ensure that discussions between managers remain private and secure. This creates an environment where individuals feel comfortable being vulnerable, seeking feedback, and exploring solutions without fear of judgment. The nonjudgmental nature of peer coaching enhances the quality of reflective conversations and contributes to a culture of openness and mutual support (Showers & Joyce, 1996).

At the heart of peer coaching is a shared commitment to continuous improvement. This emphasis aligns with the principles of lifelong learning and professional development (Hawkins & Shohet, 2012). Peer coaching provides a structured framework for managers to actively pursue their professional goals and refine their leadership practices.

Peer coaching provides a supportive framework for reflective conversations with peers that help managers gain a deeper understanding of their strengths, weaknesses, and leadership style. This self-reflection helps managers recognize the values, beliefs, and biases that may affect their decision-making and interactions with team members (Boud et al., 1985). The heightened self-awareness cultivated through peer coaching lays the groundwork for targeted professional development.

Peer coaching enables team members to identify specific skills and competencies that are crucial for their roles. Through collaborative goal-setting and feedback, team members can tailor their professional development plans to address specific areas for improvement. This targeted approach enhances the efficiency of skill development initiatives, leading to tangible improvements in leadership capabilities. Engaging in peer coaching builds confidence by providing team members with a supportive network for discussing challenges and testing potential solutions. As team members receive positive reinforcement and constructive feedback from their peers, their self-efficacy and belief in their ability to lead effectively are strengthened (Bandura, 1997). This increased confidence positively influences their leadership presence and decision-making. Peer coaching allows team members to leverage the experiences and insights of their peers. Learning from the successes and challenges of others accelerates the learning curve, enabling team members to navigate complex situations more effectively (Yorks & Kasl, 2002). The exchange of experiences fosters a culture of continuous learning and knowledge sharing.

A framework or structure for peer coaching can help guide the partnership between peers. Parker et al. (2018) apply a three-step model to peer coaching.

Step 1: Build the relationship by creating a positive holding environment through mutual and compatible selection, check-in, working agreements, and by being a critical friend.

Step 2: Create success by building self-awareness, developing relational skills, reflecting on process, and social skills.

Step 3: Make peer coaching a habit through transference to other contexts, deepening connections, mutual learning, and relational mindset.

Knowledge, Skills, and Abilities

Peer coaching requires the same knowledge and skills as other forms of coaching. As with all types of effective coaching relationships, the peer-coach should use effective listening skills, ask exploratory questions, build trust, and maintain tact, confidentiality, and diplomacy. Establishing a safe, nonjudgmental, and encouraging environment enables the client to explore all areas of development without fear of evaluation.

As the relationship deepens, the pair must preserve equality by providing developmental feedback to each other. Developmental feedback is focused on the team member's goals, builds on strengths (skills and competencies), and prevents bad habits from forming. Peer-coaching participants must actively work on the act of non-evaluation to achieve and sustain that environment of equality throughout the engagement. The ability to practice new learned behaviors is also critical to peer coaching's success. The opportunity to practice and reinforce new skills leads team members toward mastery.

Challenges and Solutions

While peer coaching offers many advantages, this type of coaching also presents some challenges. Table 14.1 presents some of the challenges that you may encounter when peer coaching, as well as potential solutions.

Table 14.1: Peer Coaching Challenges and Possible Solutions.

Challenges	Possible Solutions
Trust: Lack of trust between the peers.	– Develop a mutually supportive relationship. – Foster a culture of openness and trust by using trust-building behaviors (e.g., integrity, benevolence, and competence).
Knowledge, skills, and abilities: Lack of coaching competence; poor self-awareness or interpersonal skills leading to dominance or manipulation of the partnership; not understanding how to set and measure goals.	– Train team members how to coach, listen effectively and provide constructive, non-evaluative feedback. – Establish and measure progress toward goals. – Maintain equality in the coaching partnership. – Model coaching skills.

Table 14.1 (continued)

Challenges	Possible Solutions
Multiple roles: Dual roles of peer-peer and peer-coach can be confusing and can heighten power differences between teammates.	– Clarify the work that will be a part of the peer-coaching relationship. – Establish boundaries for the coaching; keep the coaching work in the setting of established coaching sessions. – Ensure regular check-ins to assess the peer-coaching process and adjust as needed.
Power inequality: The peer-peer relationship involves a nearly equal distribution of power, and they are no longer equals once one of them seeks help from the other.	– Ensure both participants are equal in role, tenure, and/or experience. – Allow participants to select a peer with perceived equivalence. – Ensure that sessions are divided equally in terms of time and attention to each partner's issues, and that coaching goals are similar in scope and duration. – Offer observation or supervision by a trained coach if the partners are concerned about equality issues. – Organizations must create structures that mitigate power differentials and ensure that peer coaching is truly a reciprocal and collaborative process.
Coaching process: Ensure that both partners are knowledgeable about coaching and committed to forming a strong, trust-filled peer-coaching relationship.	– Provide foundational coaching skills training and skill development. – Allow peer coaching participants to select their own coaching partners. – Ensure that regular "process checks" are built into the coaching process, and opportunities for both partners to discuss what is going well and what needs to be improved about the interaction.

(Bennett & Bush, 2014)

The impact of peer coaching extends beyond individual managers. It influences team dynamics, communication, and innovation. As organizations navigate the complexities of the modern business landscape, embracing peer coaching as a fundamental component of leadership development can position them for success. By addressing challenges, investing in coaching skills, and fostering a culture of trust and collaboration, organizations can leverage the power of peer coaching to cultivate a new generation of agile and effective managerial leaders. The case studies presented illustrate that peer coaching is not merely a theoretical concept but a practical and impactful strategy that can drive positive organizational change. Looking ahead, the continued exploration of peer coaching's potential and its integration into evolving leadership practices will contribute to the ongoing transformation of managerial leadership in the 21st century.

Coaching Teams

The role of managers has evolved beyond traditional hierarchical structures. Historically, the role of a manager was often perceived as a directive figure, issuing orders, and overseeing tasks. However, leadership has evolved as organizations have shifted toward flatter structures and more collaborative work environments. The traditional authoritative model is making way for a more participative and supportive approach, with an emphasis on coaching. The concept of a manager as a coach involves a shift from a command-and-control model to one centered on empowerment, guidance, and skill development.

A coach-style manager focuses on building strong relationships with team members, fostering their professional growth, and creating an environment that encourages continuous learning. This approach aligns with the principles of transformational leadership, which emphasizes inspiration, motivation, and individualized consideration (Bass & Riggio, 2006).

Successful organizations recognize the importance of fostering collaboration, communication, and a positive team culture. Adopting a coaching mindset is one effective way to do that. Consider that teams are more than a collection of individuals operating independently. Teams are people working interdependently toward a shared purpose using agreed-upon processes. This requires, for example, trust, leadership, communication, collaboration, commitment, and cooperation. Healthy teams can work through differences and address conflicts in the work, processes, and interpersonal relations. Teams do not just happen because members are assembled and given a task. They need to be formed, developed, and supported. Optimally performing teams take time to reflect and learn from their experiences to continuously improve individual and team performance.

Leaders should recognize that just as behavior occurs at the individual level, it also occurs at the team level. Leaders need to know when and how to intervene to support teams in accomplishing their tasks while applying effective team and interpersonal skills and processes. With much of the work in organizations done in teams, it is important to help teams perform at their best.

The terms "team coaching" or "group coaching" may be used interchangeably. A group often refers to a small assembly of people gathered for holistic goals or tasks. A team is more likely to refer to a group of people gathered for a specific coordinated purpose, which is usually task oriented. It focuses on using collective talents and resources to accomplish the team's work (Hackman & Wageman, 2005).

Team coaching focuses on helping individuals effectively work together toward a shared purpose while also focusing on the effectiveness of the team. This may involve clarifying focus or purpose, defining roles and responsibilities, applying agreed-upon working agreements or norms, addressing conflict, making decisions, focusing on assignments and tasks, presenting outcomes of the group's effort, learning through the experiences of working together, and decoupling or adjourning the team. David Clutterbuck et al. (2022) offer this definition, "Team coaching helps a team become more aware of the systems that affect its function, relationships, and/or performance. These systems may be internal, external, and/or boundary-crossing; and are consistently evolving. With understanding comes the ability to make better decisions that sustain the team and make it future-fit" (p. xvi).

Knowledge, Skills, and Abilities

Team coaching requires competence in coaching, facilitation, and interpersonal and group dynamics. A manager-coach needs to have knowledge of the client's agenda, be able to identify behaviors, and discern if there is a desire to change those behaviors. Many of the skills needed for individual coaching are the same.

A key difference is the capacity to be able to notice enough of what is happening in the team without deluging the team with so much that the team is rendered ineffective by information overload. The role of manager-coaches coaching teams is to protect the boundaries of the team, observe the team's interactions, represent authority or experience in the team, limit destructive behavior, and attend to the team's system administration, such as preparing the setting (Bennett & Bush, 2014)

Knowledge of team dynamics, combined with practical experience, is important. While coaching skills are essential, a coach's ability to be self-aware and introspective is crucial. Possibly the most challenging skill of a team coach is the coach's ability to transition the team to coach itself. Clutterbuck (2020) and Zeus and Skiffington (2001) suggest that the manager-coach monitors the team in designing goals and addressing both wins and obstacles. In addition, the coach coordinates the team by designing team activities and teaching.

Another important skill is that of noticing group behaviors that enhance and impede teamwork. By feeding this information back to the team, the manager-coach can prompt the team to reflect and attempt to interpret and make meaning of its behaviors. The manager-coach follows up by helping team members decide whether and how they wish to change behaviors.

Challenges and Solutions

While team coaching offers many advantages, manager-coaches who coach teams face many challenges. Table 14.2 summarizes some of the challenges as well as possible solutions.

The concept of managers as team coaches represents a paradigm shift in leadership styles by emphasizing collaboration, empowerment, and continuous learning. The benefits, such as increased employee engagement and performance, make the transition worthwhile despite its challenges. Key strategies for successfully implementing team coaching include building trust, listening actively, setting goals, providing constructive

Table 14.2: Team Coaching Challenges and Possible Solutions.

Challenges	Possible Solutions
Focusing the agenda: With multiple participants in the team, it may be difficult to establish agreement about the coaching agenda.	– Use consensus-building tools to develop a shared focus for the team and for coaching.
Building trust, credibility, and respectful interaction: The manager-coach must maintain boundaries so that team members who share something with them can trust them to maintain confidentiality.	– Identify ground rules for team sessions as soon as possible and address any behavioral deviations that arise. – Ensure that agendas and any pre-reading is sent out before meetings. – Start each meeting with a check-in to give each team member an opportunity to share an individual perspective and express themselves in the team.
Dual roles: Managers who coach teams they lead face the challenge of juggling their roles as manager, participant, and coach. This may involve determining which role to play at any given moment.	– Be clear with the team that you have multiple roles and how you may exercise them in the work of the team. – Seek input from the team about the implications of holding multiple roles and about potential solutions that will enable them to work with the manager-coach in their roles.
Maintaining a coaching approach: The manager-coach does not need to be an expert in all areas, nor should participants expect this. The manager-coach is there to help the team discover and live into the team's capacity.	– Call on experiences and knowledge from all team members. – Lay out the space in a way that fosters equity, inclusion, and belonging. – Implement checkpoints during work sessions to help the manager-coach stay on target. – Use evaluation forms for team feedback to help the manager-coach develop skills. This will model a culture of feedback and learning.
Working at multiple levels: Working with a group of individuals as well as the dynamics of the group. Personal, interpersonal, team, and organizational issues are always occurring within the ecosystem of a team.	– Employ collaborative and collective goal-setting methods and assess increasing the team's capacity for successfully completing tasks and solving problems. – Periodically evaluate the impact of coaching on the team. – Seek and address feedback about how the manager-coach is interacting with the team. – Be aware of multiple levels of circumstance that are impacting the team, and help the team be aware of and address them.

(Bennett & Bush, 2014)

feedback, and empowering through autonomy. By adopting a coaching mindset, managers can create a positive work environment that nurtures talent, fosters innovation, and contributes to the overall success of the organization.

As the business landscape continues to evolve, the role of managers as team coaches will probably become even more critical in building resilient and high-performing teams. Organizations that invest in developing coaching capabilities at all levels will be better positioned to navigate the challenges of the future and thrive in an ever-changing environment.

External Coaching

Organizations are increasingly recognizing the value of external executive coaching as a strategic investment in leadership development. While executive coaching primarily focuses on individual growth and skill enhancement, the role of managers is pivotal in ensuring that coaching outcomes are integrated into the broader organizational context.

The landscape of professional development has evolved, and organizations are increasingly turning to external executive coaching to nurture leadership talent. When a professional coach is engaged from outside the organization, managers play a critical role in ensuring that individual coaching goals align with broader organizational objectives.

Leaders who manage team members may have the opportunity to suggest, recommend, approve, or coordinate hiring an executive coach to work with a team member. Often this is done through a human resources professional and may involve independent executive coaches or coaches who are available through a coaching services provider with whom the company has negotiated an agreement.

Managers may recommend that a team member work with a professional external coach for various reasons, including the team member needs an objective person to support them, the manager lacks the time to provide in-depth coaching, or the manager lacks the specialized skills to coach the team member. Coaching works best when the team member is aware of their gaps and opportunities for growth.

Generally, external coaches should be engaged after the manager has provided feedback and there is a desire to invest in the team members to enhance performance, develop capabilities, or support a professional transition or transformation. Managers play an important role in providing feedback and helping the team member focus their goals for an effective engagement with the external coach.

While managers play a critical role in facilitating coaching outcomes, it is essential to address ethical considerations associated with their involvement. Managers must uphold confidentiality, avoid favoritism, and ensure equitable access to coaching opportunities. A commitment to fairness, transparency, and integrity is paramount in maintaining the trust and credibility of the coaching process. Managers of team members who receive external coaching should not expect the coach to tell them what the team member discusses with them. This level of confidentiality provides a safe environment for the team member to openly share with the coach. The team member may or may not want to share all their goals for coaching.

Supporting Matching Between Team Member and External Coach

In most circumstances, team members should interview two or three coaches before selecting one. Some organizations have a cadre of professional coaches that are familiar with the organization and regularly work with team members. In this case, one or more coaches may be recommended to the team member. Factors such as gender, race, sexual organization, language, experience coaching at the team member's level, specialization in the top priorities for coaching (e.g., interpersonal relationships, strategic thinking, transitioning into a role or the organization, preparation for career advancement, addressing external relationship, and executive presence), and knowledge of the industry may be factors to consider.

Keep in mind that that just as the team member needs to be comfortable the coach, the coach is also assessing the team member's fit as a potential client. Managers can help team members select and match with a coach by encouraging the team member to consider these questions before meeting with the prospective external coach(es):

1. What are your goals for coaching? Identify two to three goals on which you would like to focus the coaching work. In other words, what do you expect to get out of the coaching engagement?
2. What makes those goals important to you at this time? This helps both the client and the coach explore the relevance of the goals as well as a commitment to do the work required to achieve results.
3. What do you think the coach needs to know about you and your situation to help? Be prepared to tell the coach about yourself (professional and personal), including work and life history, experience with the topics associated with the potential coaching goals, how you learn and develop, your communication style, etc.
4. What will make this experience ideal for you? Share your vision for the coaching relationship, what you expect from the coach, and how much you are willing to commit to doing in order to achieve your goals.
5. What are your expectations of the coach? This might include their experience, availability, level of directness, communication style, previous and current roles, etc.
6. What questions do you have for the coach? Think of any questions you have about the coach, the coaching process, confidentiality, etc.

Team members may find it useful to have some questions ready to ask the professional executive coach when they meet them and consider the potential alignment for their needs.

Consider the following questions:

1. Tell me about your education and certifications related to coaching.
2. Tell me about your experience coaching leaders.
3. How does your coaching process work?
4. What is your coaching style?
5. Tell me about an experience in which you coached someone similar to me. Include the process and outcomes.
6. How would we ensure that our expectations would be the same?
7. How do you define success in a coaching engagement?
8. What types of assessments will you use to gather information about me?
9. How much work will be involved in this process?
10. How much of the information you gather during our coaching will be shared with my manager?
11. How will I know when the process is complete?
12. What other questions should I be asking?

Often the executive coach will offer to coach the team member briefly during the interview. This allows the team member to experience the coach's approach and style. It also provides the coach an opportunity to learn more about how to adapt their approach to meet the needs of the team member.

A Typical External Coaching Engagement

Companies may have protocols for engaging team members with professional executive coaches. Here is an illustration of how these often work:

1. The senior/executive leader, human resources professional, or individual team member contacts the external coach. This is an opportunity to learn about the organizational context and coaching needs.
2. The external coach interviews the potential coaching client to learn more about coaching goals, readiness for change, expectations for the coaching engagement. This is also an opportunity to share more about coaching and your approach. A goal of this session is to get acquainted and to assess alignment and fit.
3. The external coach works with the human resources professional or manager to define the scope of the coaching engagement. This may include the length of the engagement, number of sessions, assessment data available and assessments to be used, observations to be made of the client, stakeholder interviews to be conducted and check-in meeting with the client and their manager.
4. The coach and client hold coaching sessions (in person and/or virtual) approximately every two to three weeks for 1 to 1.5 hours each.
5. The coaching sessions continue while the coach administered assessments and conducts stakeholder interviews, if applicable.

6. The coach prepares assessment reports and debriefs them in coaching sessions.
7. The coach gathers stakeholder interview data and compiles a summary report, which is reviewed with clients. A focus at this point will be to refine the overall agenda or goals for the coaching engagement based on the present needs and feedback from various sources.
8. The client and coach meet with the client's manager to review the findings and focus. The client shares the findings and goals. The intent is to gain alignment of expectations about goals and support needed.
9. The coach and client continue coaching sessions.
10. The client, executive coach, and client's manager meet to review actions and results toward the goals. The manager shares observations. A plan for sustainable development and performance is reviewed.

The Manager's Role as a Facilitator of Coaching

While the external coach focuses on the individual executive, managers are instrumental in creating an environment that supports integrating coaching outcomes into the broader organizational fabric. The manager's role as a facilitator involves collaborating with the external coach, providing necessary resources, and fostering a culture that values and applies coaching insights.

Managers play a crucial role in ensuring that the goals set during executive coaching align with the broader objectives of the organization. This requires a clear understanding of the team member's developmental needs and how they contribute to the strategic goals of the team and the organization (Kilburg, 2000). Effective communication between the manager, executive, and coach is essential to establish coherence and maximize the impact of coaching on organizational performance. External executive coaching is most effective when supported by organizational resources and a conducive work environment (McGovern et al., 2001).

Managers need to ensure that team members have the time, resources, and support needed to implement changes and apply new skills acquired through coaching. This may involve adjusting workloads, creating space for reflection, or providing opportunities for executives to share and apply their coaching insights in a supportive team setting. To leverage the benefits of executive coaching, managers must foster a coaching culture within the organization. This involves encouraging open communication, regular feedback, and a commitment to continuous learning (Jones et al., 2016). A coaching culture promotes an environment where team members feel comfortable applying and refining their coaching insights as they contribute to ongoing leadership development.

Integrating coaching outcomes into the organization is critical but not without challenges. Managers may encounter obstacles related to resistance to change, time constraints, and varying perceptions of coaching effectiveness. Understanding and addressing these challenges are essential to maximize the impact of executive coaching. Resistance to change is a common challenge when team members return from coaching with new perspectives and approaches (Armenakis et al., 1993). Managers need to anticipate and address resistance by creating a supportive environment that values innovation and continuous improvement. Open communication about the benefits of coaching and its alignment with organizational goals can help mitigate resistance.

Team members often face time constraints in facilitating coaching outcomes, especially when team members return with new strategies or practices that may require adjusting existing workflows. Recognizing the importance of time management and prioritization is crucial. Managers should collaborate with team members to identify priorities and allocate resources effectively. Different stakeholders may have varying perceptions of coaching effectiveness, leading to challenges in creating a shared understanding of its value (Ellinger et al., 2008). Managers play a key role in communicating the positive impact of coaching on individual and organizational performance. By showcasing success stories and tangible outcomes, they can build support for coaching initiatives within the organization.

The role of managers in the context of external executive coaching is multifaceted and indispensable. Effective managerial involvement extends beyond simply overseeing the coaching process; it encompasses aligning coaching goals with organizational objectives, providing necessary resources, and fostering a culture that values and applies coaching insights. As organizations strive to develop resilient and effective leaders through coaching, managers act as linchpins, ensuring that coaching outcomes are seamlessly integrated into the broader organizational fabric.

In conclusion, the symbiotic relationship between external executive coaching and managerial facilitation holds the key to unlocking individual and organizational potential. By recognizing and embracing their pivotal role, managers can help create a dynamic and agile organizational culture that thrives on continuous learning, innovation, and leadership excellence. As the landscape of leadership development continues to evolve, effective managerial involvement in external executive coaching remains a cornerstone for building successful, adaptive, and forward-thinking organizations.

Summary

Managers play an important role in coaching that extends beyond directly coaching team members. Leaders at all levels who manage others can also support development, growth, learning, performance, and transformation through peer coaching, team coaching, and the use of external professional coaches.

Chapter 15
Ethical Considerations of Coaching

Between stimulus and response there is a space. In that space is our power to choose our response. In our response lies our growth and our freedom.

—Source Unknown

This chapter explores ethical frameworks that can be applied when coaching for change, including some of the most common ethical dilemmas that manager-coaches face. It considers the importance of ethics in coaching for managers, aligning ethical considerations with organizational expectations, and ethical frameworks in professional coaching. It also discusses ethical challenges managers might encounter while coaching, when and how to refer clients to other professional resources, and tips for ethical coaching.

People have considered the nature of ethics for thousands of years, beginning with the teachings of the ancient Greek philosophers Socrates and then Plato and Aristotle. Ethics and their close relatives—values, codes, and standards of behavior—remain active topics for debate and discussion today.

Ethics are contextual based on values. Ethics are moral principles an individual or group adopts to provide rules for appropriate conduct by group members in given situations. *Values*, on the other hand, are focused on what is suitable and desirable. *Ethical codes* or *codes of conduct* represent the ideal standards set by a professional organization or group of organizations and agreed upon by those who accept membership. Therefore, what is ethical in one part of the world or one organization may not be in another. While ethics and values are generally beliefs and principles that reside internally within a person or group of people and are enforced at their discretion, *laws* are externally imposed rules of behavior established by legislation and courts to define minimum standards for a society to operate in an orderly manner. Perhaps not surprisingly, what authorities interpret as legal may not always be ethical.

The coaching relationship between a manager-coach and team members is built on trust, respect, integrity, and care. Personal and professional information is shared. This relationship exists in the organization's context—the employer of all parties. Functioning with integrity is foundational to building and maintaining a trusting professional relationship (Mayer & Davis, 1999). Leading, managing, and coaching requires trust. Operating ethically supports the effectiveness of the relationship and provides a role model for others.

https://doi.org/10.1515/9783111002415-015

Ethical Frameworks that Inform Change Coaching

There is no single or universally accepted code ethics for managers, coaches, or managers who coach. Instead, the ethical behaviors of coaches "are guided by community standards and practices, moral expectations based on cultural patterns or religious beliefs, and local, state [provincial], and federal laws" (Brammer & MacDonald, 2003, p. 153).

Western European and American values that frequently inform ethics include:
- Respect for others—their dignity, autonomy, integrity
- Veracity—telling the truth or just not lying
- Honoring one's promises
- Equity—treating others fairly
- Beneficence—making things better
- Non-malfeasance—not making things worse
- Integrity
- Fidelity/loyalty
- Fairness
- Caring for others
- Pursuit of excellence
- Accountability

There are multiple approaches to ethical decision-making, and it is essential to remember that, in most cases, no one approach is absolute. Each approach has an alternative path, a counter argument, and potentially its own dilemmas. For example, when pursuing the common good, say by condemning a neighborhood using the power of eminent domain to make room for a new, publicly funded football stadium, the individual's good or benefit may be sacrificed.

An individual's quest is to find the right approach for *themselves*, in this place and at this time. The *individual* gets to decide what is essential and what has priority. The *individual* gets to decide whether to comply with or challenge the norm. And the *individual* receives the positive and negative consequences of their decisions.

Recognizing the trans-disciplinary nature of coaching and the multiple helping-related professional practices from which coaching draws—as well as the multiple roles that manager-coaches may play and the professional associations or licensing boards that serve those who practice coaching—it is difficult to identify a single set of ethical guidelines for coaches. Take, for example, the manager-coach who is also a professional accountant. This manager-coach would, of course, be expected as a professional accountant to comply with the code of conduct for accountants. When coaching, this same manager-coach would be expected to comply with any related ethical guidelines for coaching.

But that is not all. If the manager works in a company, they would also be expected to comply with the standards of ethical conduct for that business. These standards might differ somewhat depending on the country or countries where the company does business. In this example, the manager-coach may be confronted with ethical dilemmas and the need to consider them through multiple frames of reference: ethical guidelines and codes of conduct originating from the client organization, one's professional association, and one's licensing board. Often these codes of conduct do not conflict. When they do it is wise to see advice from professionals in both fields who are familiar with the codes of conduct. It may also be useful to consider which professional practice is dominate—coaching or the practice of accounting. This might lead you to select the best code of ethics to follow. Ideally, the codes of conduct will not conflict but will serve to guide professional behaviors.

Potential Ethical Challenges Manager-Coaches Face

A variety of ethical challenges may arise because manager-coaches may become trusted advisors and confidants to team members and may have access to proprietary or confidential information not generally known to the public, the business's competitors, or many of the organization's employees. As a result, manager-coaches must constantly be alert for such challenges and be prepared to prevent them whenever possible—or, if they cannot be prevented, address them immediately. Some of these ethical challenges are the direct result of the following:

- **Multiple relationships.** These types of relationship complexities might involve having a close personal relationship with a team member that would bias the coaching conversation as a manager.
- **Coaching competence and limitations.** Coaching conversations can become complex. It is essential for the manager-coach to fully access their skills and abilities to help the team members while not extending beyond those competencies. This might involve a situation in which the team member should seek information or guidance from a support function such as accounting, legal, security, or human resources or when the team member needs to be referred for professional counseling or therapy.
- **Informed consent.** An informed consent should include agreeing in advance what information will be shared with whom and under what conditions.
- **Physical contact.** Physical contact concerns in the context of managerial coaching extend beyond touching an arm or shoulder as a show of support or concern. These concerns include hugging and romantic relations. Romantic relationships between coaches and people being coached should never be permitted. Touch, even friendly, supportive contact, should be limited and only done under conditions of mutual agreement. Even then, as a manager-coach, you should keep in mind the power differences in the relationship. You are in a more powerful position due to your role or position as a manager and coach as well as being the one giving help to the team member. In addition, keep in mind that cultural norms

may differ from your own regarding physical proximity and ways of greeting each other.

–   **Conflicts of interest.** This might involve personal preferences or interests that conflict with what the team member might want. For example, an outstanding team member talking with the manager-coach about taking another job and leaving the team. The manager-coach's interest conflict with the team member's interest.

Every manager-coach will confront ethical dilemmas from time to time—some minor and others more serious. Ethical dilemmas, unclear choices that both involve transgressions, will occur in any organization despite the best efforts of all concerned to avoid them. As a manager-coach, it is essential to be alert to such ethical dilemmas and take immediate steps to deal with them. Here is a suggested procedure for addressing ethical dilemmas when they occur:

1.   Stop all activities.
2.   Gather facts about the situation.
3.   Review codes of ethics and conduct that may apply.
4.   Consult a professional knowledgeable about the codes of ethics and conduct that apply and get their advice.
5.   Discuss the situation with those involved, if possible and practical.
6.   Decide and act according to standards of ethical practices.

These steps can also be used when coaching someone who faces an ethical dilemma.

Ethical Decision-making Questions

Making ethical decisions is not always a precise, easy proposition. Often, it's none of these things. Individuals, groups, and organizations may have unique ethical beliefs and cultures, and the correct answer for one person may be the wrong answer for someone else.

Business leaders are often under pressure to do what is faster, less expensive, or more profitable at the expense of ethical considerations. Here are some of the questions that manager-coaches can and should ask when they attempt to divine what the right and good thing is to do in a particular decision-making situation:

–   If it is legal, is it ethical?
–   If it is necessary, is it ethical?
–   If it is part of the job, is it ethical?
–   If it is for a good cause, is it ethical?
–   If it is the way business is done, is it ethical?
–   If everyone is doing it, is it ethical?
–   If I don't gain personally, is it ethical?

– If no one gets hurt, is it ethical?
– If it conforms to the principles and values of the organization, is it ethical?
– If it satisfies my definition of right and wrong, is it ethical?

Ethical Frameworks in Professional Coaching

Many professional organizations hold ethical principles and codes of conduct. As a manager, you may belong to one or more professional associations that have codes of conduct, such as the Association for Financial Planners, American Medical Association, American Institute of Certified Professional Accountants, American Marketing Association, British Psychological Society, Chartered Accountants, Information Systems Security Association International (ISSA), National Education Association, Project Management Institute (PMI), and Society for Human Resource Professionals (SHRM). Many businesses and organizations have professional codes of conduct, stated values, ethical guidelines, policies, and procedures that guide behaviors. Consider and practice any of these expectations that apply to your specific circumstances.

In addition, there are professional codes of conduct for people who practice coaching professionally. Codes of conduct establish guidelines that are a benchmark for ethics and good practice in coaching and mentoring. The guidelines form the basis for developing self-regulation in the coaching and mentoring profession. They should serve to guide managers who coach as well. You should study and apply the codes of ethics from international professional coaching organizations such as the European Mentoring and Coaching Council (2021) and the International Coaching Federation (2021). Both are available online.

Suggestions for Ethical Coaching

Managers who apply a coaching approach to their work with individuals and teams may face ethical dilemmas. Some of these concerns resemble those that coaches with other relationships to the organization encounter, including internal coaches and external coaches. Consider these suggestions for people who are working manager-coaches.

– Do no harm.
– Confirm with the team members that they want to be coached by you and the implications for the work you will do together.
– Operate within the ethical guidelines of one's professional association(s) and professional licensing board(s).
– Establish and maintain boundaries in the manager-team member relationship.
– Define and follow the terms of confidentiality established with team members.

– Respect the privacy of the team members, explore what is relevant, and avoid personal topics unrelated to the coaching agenda established by the team members.
– Work within your expertise and refer to professional resources when needed. These may include a human resources professional or employee assistance program (EAP).
– Develop a professional relationship with someone who can help assess ethical dilemmas that may arise. Many organizations have an ethics office or legal counsel with whom to consult. A human resource business partner may be an excellent resource for questions or concerns.
– Confront observations of unethical behavior by clients in a manner that allows them to address them before reporting them (as appropriate).
– Avoid dual relationships with team members—such as romantic or financial relations.
– Continue developing your skills as a manager-coach through professional development such as workshops, reading, and discussion forums.

Summary

Ethics and coaching go hand in hand. The manager-coach must be ethical in order to be effective. *Ethics* are moral principles an individual or group adopts to provide rules for appropriate conduct by group members in given situations. In contrast, *values* focus on what is suitable and desirable. Western European and American values often inform ethics, including respect for others, honesty, equity, integrity, fairness, caring for others, accountability, and more. Various professional and organizational guidelines are available to inform the manager-coach to avoid ethical dilemmas and address those that arise.

Manager-coaches should avoid ethical challenges resulting from multiple relationships, physical contact with team members, coach limitations, unclear understanding of what information will be shared with whom and when, and personal conflicts of interest.

Chapter 16
Continuous Development: Managers Leading the Way

Slowly, step by step, you find yourself being good at something. You find yourself also daring to move forward, and trust yourself, and be able to always take the first step even when you're afraid to do so.

—Rene Redzepi, 2020, p. 19 (chef, Noma, Copenhagen)

You don't need to be better than anyone else. You just need to be better than you used to be.

—Wayne Dyer cited by Economy, 2015

Managers are pivotal in organizations, responsible for driving productivity, innovation, and employee engagement. The complexity of their roles necessitates ongoing growth and adaptability—essential aspects of effective management and coaching. In the dynamic and ever-changing business environment, skilled manager-coaches are critical in guiding their teams toward success.

This chapter explores the significance of continuous improvement and development for manager-coaches, examining its principles, strategies, and associated challenges. Manager-coaches who adopt a holistic approach can enhance their leadership abilities, foster team growth, and contribute to organizational success. They are responsible for achieving organizational goals and nurturing their team members. This chapter also provides practical recommendations and insights for manager-coaches to thrive in their dual roles.

Feedback and evaluation of coaching involve systematically collecting and analyzing data that offers the potential for understanding more about the coaching process, what actions are practical, and the role that coaching could play within the larger context of employee and talent development. It offers the coach valuable insights about their functioning, which can reinforce effective behaviors and prompt adjustments for development.

While the manager-coach may not have formal processes to evaluate their coaching as a specific intervention with team members, they can seek and use inputs from those they coach. In addition, the manager-coach can (and should) practice reflection related to their coaching interactions with team members. If the manager-coach's manager also uses a coaching approach, the working relationships would appropriately include coaching about the coaching being performed. Manager-coaches can discuss with their manager, internal coaching resources, or an external coach what they felt was successful in a particular coaching relationship within the boundaries of agreed-upon confidentiality agreements and raise areas that went less well. They can focus on failures or possible mistakes while also focusing on what worked well, and how these insights can be leveraged or applied more broadly (Gray, 2004).

https://doi.org/10.1515/9783111002415-016

When novice coaches in a graduate course (taught by the author) were asked to identify areas for continued development, they listed skills such as:
- gleaning helpful information from the coaching conversation
- listening for deeper understanding
- being patient
- establishing rapport
- demonstrating agility with the coaching for the change step process (See Chapter 2)
- working with the client to identify and articulate the agenda for the coaching conversation
- providing direct, clear, and relevant feedback
- not focusing coaching as a problem-solving tool
- not providing answers but helping the client to discover their answers

When asked to identify areas of strength for them as coaches, these were some of their responses:
- having experience in various contexts
- openness to what may surface during the coaching conversation
- building the capacity of the client
- providing unconditional positive regard
- providing valuable insights
- asking powerful questions

Principles of Continuous Improvement and Development

One of the foundational principles of continuous improvement and development is the Plan-Do-Check-Act (PDCA) cycle, initially introduced by Walter Shewhart and popularized by W. Edwards Deming. This cycle is a systematic approach to improving processes, products, and services. Manager-coaches can apply the PDCA cycle to both managerial and coaching aspects of their roles:
- **Plan:** Identify objectives, set goals, and develop strategies for improvement. For manager-coaches, this may involve setting performance targets and individual development plans.
- **Do:** Implement the plan, execute actions, and collect relevant data. This phase requires manager-coaches to provide guidance and support to their team members.
- **Check:** Evaluate the results and compare them to the initial objectives. Manager-coaches must assess team performance and individual progress, and provide feedback based on observations.
- **Act:** Based on the evaluation, take corrective actions, and make necessary adjustments. Manager-coaches should refine their coaching approaches and adapt managerial strategies as needed.

Psychologist Carol Dweck's growth mindset concept (2007) emphasizes the belief that abilities and intelligence can be acquired through dedication and hard work. Manager-coaches should not only embody a growth mindset themselves but also cultivate it within their teams. This mindset shift can increase team members' resilience, motivation, and adaptability.

Emotional intelligence (EI) is another crucial competency for manager-coaches. EI involves recognizing, understanding, and managing emotions in oneself and others. By cultivating emotional intelligence, manager-coaches can build stronger interpersonal relationships, foster trust, and effectively communicate with team members.

Strategies for Continuous Improvement and Development

One of the fundamental strategies for manager-coaches is setting clear expectations. This includes defining roles, responsibilities, and performance standards for team members. Communicating expectations effectively creates the foundation for accountability and goal achievement. Manager-coaches can improve and develop in many ways, including feedback, journaling, reading, receiving coaching, reflection, and training.

Effective feedback is a cornerstone of coaching and development. Manager-coaches should provide regular and constructive feedback that focuses on strengths and improvement areas. The Context-Behavior-Impact-Request (CBIR) feedback model introduced in Chapter 6 is a valuable tool for delivering specific, behavior-focused, and outcome-oriented feedback. Manager-coaches should also engage in coaching conversations with team members to explore goals, challenges, and growth opportunities. You should conduct these conversations in a supportive and nonjudgmental manner that allows team members to reflect on their performance and identify solutions to problems.

To promote continuous improvement, manager-coaches can implement skill development programs within their teams. These programs can include training sessions, workshops, and mentorship opportunities to enhance the skills and knowledge of team members. Manager-coaches should encourage self-directed learning among team members. This involves empowering individuals to take ownership of their development by seeking resources, setting personal goals, and proactively pursuing growth opportunities.

Continuous development allows executive coaches to hone their coaching skills, refine their coaching models, and adopt innovative techniques. This enhanced competence translates into more impactful coaching relationships.

Manager-coaches often face time constraints due to their dual roles. Balancing managerial responsibilities with coaching activities can be challenging, and finding dedicated time for coaching conversations and skill development can be a struggle. To address time constraints, manager-coaches should prioritize their coaching activities and allocate dedicated time for coaching conversations and skill development. Effective time management techniques, such as time blocking, can help manager-coaches make the most of their available time.

Manager-coaches may encounter situations where they lack specific coaching skills or expertise in certain areas. It's essential to recognize these skill gaps and seek professional development opportunities to fill them. Investing in coaching training and certification programs can enhance coaching skills by providing a structured foundation for development. These programs offer exposure to coaching theories, ethics, and practical skills, as well as tools, techniques, and frameworks that improve coaching effectiveness. Engaging in ongoing reading and research in psychology, leadership, and organizational behavior enhances a coach's knowledge base. Coaches can integrate this knowledge into their coaching practices to offer more holistic support to clients. Coaching organizations, such as the International Coach Federation (ICF), offer certification pathways. Participating in coaching conferences and workshops provides opportunities to network, learn from experts, and stay current with industry trends. These events provide a platform for coaches to exchange ideas and best practices.

Reflection is a cornerstone of development for executive coaches. By regularly reviewing their coaching sessions, seeking feedback, and engaging in self-assessment, coaches can identify areas for improvement and refine their approach.

Manager-coaches can benefit from mentorship and peer support networks. Connecting with experienced manager-coaches and seeking guidance from colleagues can provide valuable insights and advice. Supervision and mentorship relationships also offer manager-coaches helpful guidance and support. Experienced mentors can provide insights and help coaches navigate complex coaching scenarios.

Implementing performance metrics and key performance indicators (KPIs) can help manager-coaches track progress and measure the impact of their coaching efforts. Regularly reviewing these metrics can inform adjustments to coaching strategies.

Continuous improvement and development are indispensable for manager-coaches in today's dynamic business environment. Manager-coaches can drive organizational success while nurturing the potential of their team members by adhering to principles such as the growth mindset and emotional intelligence, and by implementing strategies such as clear expectations, constructive feedback, and skill development programs.

Manager-coaches can thrive despite challenges such as time constraints, resistance to change, and skill gaps. To thrive, you must practice effective time management, pursue coaching training, seek mentorship, and track performance metrices. Ultimately, embracing continuous improvement and development benefits the manager-coaches themselves while it contributes to the growth and prosperity of their teams and organizations.

Robert Hargrove (1995) asserts that "a coach is something that you 'be'" (p. 39). He identifies the coach as being who one *is*, as opposed to someone who *does* coaching by following a step-by-step model or approach. The manager-coach's self-awareness, confidence, and focus allow a coaching engagement to be what it needs to be to meet the client's needs.

Mastery in change coaching requires a high level of competence in and application of interpersonal and intrapersonal skills to serve team members' needs in the coaching relationship (O'Broin & Palmer, 2010). It requires actively pursuing self-awareness and self-management to recognize and challenge unhelpful beliefs, perceptions, feelings, and behaviors about self, clients, and the coaching process. The manager-coach can use this reflection as part of their self-development practice. During change-coaching sessions, coaches can practice observing themselves interacting with the client to hone the skill of self-awareness. Manager-coaches can leverage tools such as self-reflection, coaching supervision, self-management frameworks. Self-supervision, peer discussion, and team member feedback can be leveraged outside of coaching sessions. During a coaching session, these practices may involve reflection in action (Schön, 1983) and, where appropriate, feedback from the client.

Effective manager-coaches must acquire vital skills and abilities. To reach a level of mastery, coaches must also be aware of their knowledge, skills, and abilities in coaching and change, and must be able to apply them in both arenas. Mastery also requires a demonstrated learning agility—the willingness and ability to assess and continuously enhance one's knowledge, skills, and abilities.

Many models for designing and evaluating learning are rooted in Bloom's Taxonomy of learning objectives (Krathwohl, 2002) and Howell's (1982) conscious competence model. Bloom's Taxonomy includes three domains: cognitive, affective, and psychomotor—more commonly known as think, feel, and do. A fundamental premise of Bloom's Taxonomy is that mastery must be achieved at each domain level before advancing to the next.

Awareness is a significant factor in skill acquisition and may be used, in part, to describe a learner's level of consciousness. Building on Bloom's model, Krathwohl's (2002) model begins with a level of imitation and advances to a level described as naturalization. Once a learner (in this case, the coach) achieves the level of naturalization, the learner has become automated, in a sense, and the activity is subconscious (often referred to as an "unconscious" state). This progression of repeating a process before gaining precision and achieving mastery can be compared with Howell's conscious competence model.

Howell (1982) described a sequence of learning in which the learner starts in an unconscious, incompetent state. At this stage, the individual may be unaware of or unconcerned about the skill. Next is conscious incompetence. At this stage, the individual becomes aware of the skill that is lacking and understands how to improve the skill. Next is the conscious competence stage in which the learner demonstrates the knowledge needed and can perform reliably. And finally, the learner reaches unconscious competence and uses the skill as second nature or intuitively. Taylor (2007) offered a fifth stage called reflective competency, which involves being conscious of unconscious incompetence. By continually challenging themselves in the fifth stage with self-study and peer review, evolved learners cycle back through the phase of unconscious incompetence, where new enlightenment reveals something else they did not know. The addition of the fifth stage makes Howell's model much more cyclical and dynamic.

A reflective practitioner—i.e., manager-coach—lives reflection as a way of being, with reflection defined as awareness of self within the moment and having a clear mind to be open to the possibility of that moment (Johns, 2009). While an effective manager-coach must have acquired knowledge, a reflective practitioner understands that no two experiences are alike, and therefore, he cannot simply rely on learned paradigms. Through reflection, manager-coaches develop their intuitive processes and become conscious of their competencies and incompetencies, resulting in further enlightenment (Bennett & Rogers, 2013).

Dreyfus and Dreyfus (1980, 1986, 2004) developed a model of skill acquisition based on situated performance and experiential learning. The Dreyfus model comprises five stages: novice, advanced beginner, competent, proficient, and expert. The model describes the stages through which an individual must progress to achieve mastery of a particular skill, advancing from abstract principles needed in a novice stage to a more intuitive, less self-conscious state in an expert stage (Benner, 2001; Dreyfus & Dreyfus, 2004). Taylor (2007) captured the essence of the expert in mature practice by adding the fifth stage of reflective competency to Howell's (1982) conscious competence model. Johns (2009) describes a reflective practitioner as "someone who lives reflection as a way of being" (p. 3). This is the optimum posture for a maturing coach. Through reflection, practitioners hone their intuitive skills, which are tied to self-awareness and the confidence and liberation that comes with Hargrove's (1995) sense of "being" a coach.

A novice manager-coach still observes and imitates manager-coaches' experiences with more evolved competence. In contrast, an expert coach is fully "being" in the moment with a client, as Hargrove (1995) describes the masterful coach (Bennett & Rogers, 2013).

Coaching is a discipline that requires the manager-coach to be skilled in theory and practice. Coaching demands skillful judgment and decision-making over time, as changes in the team members and changes in the situation are ongoing. Advanced beginner coaches worked with several clients and client issues, applied a coaching conversation model with little or no assistance—yet are frequently aware of its presence, applied basic coaching skills of listening and asking questions with ease and began to use different approaches, applied additional coaching skills (e.g., reframing, metaphors), and were cautious about taking risks. On the other hand, expert coaches operated fluidly, generally knew what to do and how to do it, were naturally creative, took risks, viewed problems or challenges as opportunities—not obstacles—and tailored their application of knowledge and skills to situations as appropriate. These differences highlight the benefit of coaching skills acquired over time and the insights gained from reflecting on coaching experience (Bennett & Rogers, 2013).

Mastery Model Applied to the Manager-Coach

Just as the Mastery Model explained in Chapter 2 can be applied to support change at the individual, group, and organization levels, it can also be used to support the manager-coach's performance, development, and transformational change with the intent of achieving mastery. Manager-coaches and team members go through the same change process in their journey toward mastery.

1. **Awareness.** Manager-coaches become aware of strengths in their coaching-related knowledge, skills, or coaching—or of a gap between them and the needs of team members. You may also become aware of the differences between their competencies and the competencies asserted by professional associations or crediting bodies. In the awareness stage, manager-coaches seek more information or clarity about the change. You need to understand what it will mean to them and how you work and interact with others. Examples of ways in which awareness may be gained include team member feedback and self-reflection about coaching experiences.

2. **Acceptance.** Manager-coaches make peace with the change and explore or seek information to determine what it will mean to them. There may still be concerns, confusion, and skepticism, yet the intention and attitude shift from "Why should we do this?" to "How can we make this successful?" This stage can manifest on three levels: cognitive, behavioral, and affective.

3. **Adoption.** In this stage, manager-coaches actively engage in the new mindsets, behaviors, and interactions that support the change. They acquire or develop the capabilities to perform in new ways and often help others understand and make the needed changes. Accomplishing this may mean starting a behavior, gaining knowledge, developing a skill, broadening a perspective, or applying a skill or behavior in a new or different way.

4. **Integration.** Manager-coaches become used to working and interacting in a new way, and often have results or accomplishments to show from having implemented the change. The change has been embedded into existing structures, systems, and processes so that it is part of how the organization operates and does not depend on current leadership to drive it. The organizational culture now sustains the change and has become "the way we do things around here."

5. **Mastery.** Manager-coaches continue to integrate the change into other personal and professional practices. you build increased agility and resilience, demonstrating improved capacity to make additional changes. Manager-coaches act with more innovation and apply learning from one area of their lives into their professional practices —often without giving it much thought or consideration. Innovation and agility become second nature. You can challenge themselves with self-study and peer re-

view, cycling back through the stage of unconscious incompetence where new enlightenment reveals something else you did not know.

Actions to Support the Development of Mastery

Manager-coaches at all levels develop competency in similar yet different ways. Bennett and Rogers (2013) found the following similarities: coaching training programs, graduate studies, previous work and life experiences, feedback, reading and self-study, mentors, and specialized training. Expert coaches also identified the following means: experimentation, being coached, reflecting, participating in conferences, and teaching others.

We highlight two practices as ways to support the development of coaching mastery: feedback and reflection.

Feedback

Feedback is considered a core element of the coaching process. Manager-coaches and team members engage in continuous, reciprocal feedback delivery and reception processes throughout their professional relationships. Feedback is also critical for the manager-coach's professional development. By actively seeking feedback, the coach can identify strengths and weaknesses along with what is working in coaching and what is not. Therefore, understanding the influence of feedback in coaching conversations and how to apply feedback to develop coaching capacities is essential. While several models of the coaching process mention feedback as a core element, only a few expand on the role and function of feedback in coaching relationships.

An evolving, maturing manager-coach must proactively seek feedback from team members and other stakeholders, such as the human resource partner. One practical approach for gathering feedback can be the manager-coach's use of reflection during and after the coaching session. While reflection is a loose processing of thoughts, it can be modeled so that manager-coaches can better address surprises during and after a coaching conversation. The practical implication of this approach is that as part of seeking feedback, reflection permits coaches to examine, question, and learn from their experience.

How people acquire and process feedback depends on their awareness. Conscious feedback processing is most likely to occur when a manager-coach is unfamiliar with a situation or when the feedback obtained is incongruent with expectations. The way feedback is processed is crucial because it influences the nature of subsequent information processing (Taylor et al., 1984).

Seeking feedback in coaching conversations is critically important. It involves the manager-coach actively seeking feedback from the team member by observing and listening. It can also involve directly asking for feedback about what is useful and what might be adjusted by the manager-coach to be more effective with the team member. During coaching sessions, the manager-coach can actively listen for feedback to adjust the process and the questions they ask. Listening to and being aware of a team member's feedback is part of a manager-coach's process of relating to and communicating with team members. Feedback giving, on the other hand, occurs when the manager-coach provides feedback to the team member. The manager-coach identifies areas for improvement in the team member's behavior or performance, and the team member acts on this feedback.

A manager-coach has a responsibility to seek feedback from the team members. There are several tools the coach can use, including feedback, focused questions for the client, surveys, interviews, and the use of reflection during and after coaching sessions. Potential questions the manager-coach may ask to gather feedback include, "What changes do we need to consider making to our working agreement?" "How is our coaching relationship meeting your needs? Are there ways it can be improved or enhanced?" When manager-coaches consider these types of open-ended questions as they prepare for coaching sessions, they enhance the opportunity to gather important feedback from team members. These questions provoke thought without leading the team members while giving the manager-coach feedback. Instead, the focus remains on the team members and how well their needs are being met.

Reflection

Another approach for gathering feedback can be the coach's use of reflection during and after the coaching session. David Clutterbuck (2010) offers a framework for coaches to become reflective practitioners. He calls it the four "I"s:
1. Issues (What topics did we cover?)
2. Ideas (What creative thinking occurred?)
3. Insights (What did we learn?)
4. Intentions (What will we do as a result of our learning dialogue?)

Like feedback, reflection is an active process that involves examining your thoughts, feelings, and behaviors. It can result in learning. According to Peter Jarvis (1992), the reflective practitioner—in this case, the manager-coach—works to ensure that the outcome of any action is close to what is anticipated by the theory and the experience combined. These definitions suggest that reflective practice is associated with learning from experience. Reflection does not replace scientific knowledge. Instead, it offers a process that facilitates the integration of theory with practice.

Reflection promotes reflective thinking, provides opportunities to reflect on and share experiences, can confirm prior knowledge, assists with understanding new learning, helps the manager-coach consider how they may behave in the future, and facilitates linkages between scholarship and practice. Reflection enhances awareness of thoughts and feelings, helps to analyze situations—including existing knowledge—and fosters the development of a perspective of the situation developed by analyzing and applying information to the experience.

Reflection is a critical tool for coaches to gather feedback about their effectiveness and impact on the client. Reflection is "an active, persistent, and careful consideration of any belief or supposed form of knowledge" (Dewey, 1933, p. 9). Williams et al. (2002) wrote that reflection is "a process where individuals think about and evaluate their experience to come to new understandings and appreciations" (p. 5). Reflection involves developing awareness of thoughts and feelings, analyzing the situation —including existing knowledge—and developing a perspective on the situation.

Reflection is essentially a processing of thoughts and feelings about an incident, a meeting, or a day—any event or experience at all. Reflection can be loosely or closely structured to deal with surprises during and after a coaching conversation. Donald Schön (1983) distinguished between reflection-*in*-action and reflection-*on*-action to investigate how people use their experience to analyze and frame problems, propose action, and then reevaluate the experience because of the action. For example, reflection may occur in real time while a conversation occurs (reflection-*in*-action) or later when there is time to stand back from the conversation (reflection-*on*-action).

After each coaching conversation, take a few minutes to review and reflect on your experience. This time can provide an opportunity to consider what happened, what you did that worked well, what needs improvement, and what actions you may want to take in the future to continue to hone your skills and mastery of the art and science of coaching. Through reflection, learning occurs that can be applied to improve your positive impacts on your clients.

Consider these questions:

1. **In what ways did I build rapport and establish trust?** This might include showing interest in what occurred before the coaching session and remembering a significant event since the last session.

2. **How was the 6-step coaching process used?** Consider how you guided the coaching conversation through the steps, your agility in moving back and forth through the steps while moving through them in order, and how well you concluded a step before moving to the next one—perhaps with a closed-ended question such as, "Are you ready to move on to talk about ___?" or "Are there other possibilities you would like to consider at this time?"

3. **How did I help my team member discover their goals and agenda for this coaching conversation?** Consider the clarity that your team member had as you started the conversation and what you did to help them clarify and declare their focus for your coaching work together. This might include helping them identify several possible topics and narrow the focus to start the conversation. It might also involve returning to a second topic once the first one is addressed.

4. **Which coaching skills did I use?** Reflect on the skills you used. Which ones did you rely on? How effectively did you apply them? Were there skills that could have been employed that were not? What might you have done differently?
5. **What were the turning points or breakthroughs in the coaching conversation?** Notice when your coaching client has a breakthrough, gains awareness shifts perspectives, etc. What were the circumstances? What did you do to foster this?
6. **What about my coaching was well-developed?** Having a well-developed behavior does not mean it is best for the interaction. It means that you did it well— even if it was not the ideal thing to do. Think about the coaching conversation and your role in it. What are the one or two things that you did that impacted the interactions with your coaching client?
7. **What about my coaching was less developed?** This is the other side of the coin from what was well-developed. This is a behavior that may not have been used or might have been underused. Consider what you might have done more of or done more effectively.
8. **How do I feel about my experience coaching?** Consider your emotional response to the coaching experience—e.g., confused, excited, proud, tired, bored, critical, hopeful, and nurtured. Consider the implications of these responses to your coaching. This might include recognizing when you are most and least comfortable, how you respond to the statements and behaviors of the person you are coaching, and what you might do the same or differently in the future. There are many ways to do this reflection and processing—such as meditation, talking with a colleague, replaying the situations, and journaling.
9. **What insights about my coaching do I have?** Reflect on the coaching experience and your responses to the previous questions. What did you learn from this coaching experience? What will you apply going forward?
10. **What will I focus on going forward—continue, stop, start, modify?** Now, move your reflections into actions. Develop a plan of action to stop, start, continue, or change one or two things about your coaching as you use your coaching mindset and skills. Your plans could include what you will do, by when, for what desired outcomes, and with what support.

As you coach, remember that developing mastery takes time, practice, experimentation, reflection, and learning.

Rolfe's Model of Reflection

Another practical approach to reflection comprises three questions representing three levels of reflection. Ask yourself these questions:

- *What?* This is the descriptive level of reflection. It describes the situation, responses, and feelings.
- *So what?* This is the theory and knowledge-building level of reflection—i.e. meaning-making. What has been learned about self, relationships, models, attitudes, actions, thoughts, understanding, and improvements?
- *What next?* This at is the action-oriented level of reflection? What needs to be done to improve future outcomes and develop learning? (Rolfe et al., 2001)

Manager-coaches can record or journal your reflections to capture them and consider them later. Recording events and circumstances and returning to them for sense-making can often be helpful. The following series of questions adapted from work by MacKeracher (1996) can be used to facilitate this process.
- **Experience**
  - What did I feel about what occurred?
  - What did I think about but did not say?
  - What did I want to do but did not do?
  - What outcomes did I desire that did not occur?
- **Events**
  - What happened?
  - Who was involved?
  - What was said?
  - What were the outcomes?
- **Consideration**
  - What is the comparison?
  - What do I think in a critical sense?
  - What do I honestly think?

Another approach is to describe experiences by noting critical processes within the experience. The manager-coach or client reflects on what was trying to be achieved and why, as well as the consequences, and then identifies the influencing factors, such as sources of knowledge and differing facts, involved in the decision-making process. Finally, the manager-coach or team member considers the learning that can be derived from the initial experience and reflection. This learning includes current emotions and a view in the context of historical and social processes (Johns, 2009; Platzer & Snelling, 1997).

As manager-coaches reflect, there are several cautions to consider:
- One can only reflect on what one remembers or chooses to remember. Therefore, selective memory limits what can be reflected on.
- When time is short, decisions need to be made quickly. Thus, reflection is limited to those who can think and react quickly.

–   If reflection is most likely to occur in the presence of unexpected outcomes, it is reasonable to assume that reflection will overlook the familiar.
–   People tend to focus their attention on negative experiences and highly stressed situations. As a result, expect manager-coaches to reflect less on what went well.
–   People tend to operate within the sphere of their comfort zone. Thus, manager-coaches might neglect situations that expose uncertainty or their lack of skills.

Summary

While almost anyone can call themselves a coach, practitioners must master the knowledge, skills, and abilities of coaching in order to provide effective and long-lasting coaching. Skilled coaches must master various skills, including giving feedback, building trusting relationships, fostering self-awareness and reflection, and many more. Only after doing so can a coach *be* a coach instead of following a script or step-by-step model.

Seeking feedback in coaching conversations can be structured, especially from the reflective practitioner's point of view. The primary value of this type of reflection is to help coaches assess how they are coaching and allow them to adjust the coaching process or the questions being asked. Coaches periodically stop and pause to think about what is working, what is not working, and what they can do to improve their work with their clients. They do this intentionally. They look at all data sources to confirm and adjust what and how they are doing. Seeking feedback using the reflective practitioner's approach is one way to do this. This approach can raise a change coach's awareness and deepen understanding of the coaching practice. Several models of reflection are effective. David Clutterbuck's 4 "I"s model works both during and after the coaching session as coaches seek to become reflective practitioners:

1.   Issues (What topics did we cover?)
2.   Ideas (What creative thinking occurred?)
3.   Insights (What did we learn?)
4.   Intentions (What will we do as a result of our learning dialogue?)

A Conversation with Carolyn Roach
Chief Human Resources Officer
for a Fortune 500 publicly traded company in the transportation industry

This conversation was recorded and transcribed, then edited for clarity and conciseness.

John Bennett (JB): *How do you use coaching in your role as a leader manager?*

Carolyn Roach (CR): I probably do it a little bit unconsciously. I think the best example is asking questions. It's not always easy because sometimes I want to direct work, but I try to ask my team questions when they are presenting things to me or navigating through decisions. I try to get them to think about things from a different perspective. I believe giving feedback is also part of coaching. I ask team members if they're open to feedback and then be transparent with how I feel about the work. I constructively do this in a way that guides them developmentally.

JB: *How did you develop this mindset and skill set?*

CR: I had an executive coaching or organizational psychology class in my graduate studies. Through my human resources career of 20-odd years, it's been a blend of more formal training and executive coaching that I've received. I've learned from academics, HR professionals, and working directly with executive coaches.

JB: *What are some of the challenges you've had or seen leaders and managers have in applying a coaching approach to their work?*

CR: I think some people managers just don't know how to do it. They don't know the difference between using questions and dialogue to help a person get to the answer themselves versus just directing work. One of the challenges we all get into is we don't have time. Time is such a precious resource that a manager who hasn't been invested in coaching or isn't as familiar with using it can see it as just asking a series of questions. They value the results more than the process of helping the other person get to their answers.

JB: *How have people responded using a coaching approach?*

CR: I'd like to think that most people have responded positively because, at the end of the day, when you do it right, the person gets to the answer themselves. They have an epiphany almost on their own. They feel like it was their realization, epiphany, or decision. They feel good about their decision because they decided, even though the coach or the manager may have helped guide them to that answer.

I think it's effective to be transparent about how I will play. I will ask, "What role would you like me to play in this conversation?"

JB: *What is the value of using coaching as a manager?*

CR: I think it helps to develop a relationship with the person. I think that by using coaching as a managerial tool, you can build a stronger, more trustworthy, more authentic relationship with your direct reports or the teams underneath you. We're humans, and making those deeper connections is a valuable outcome. Coaching breeds confidence in the other person. If you coach, you can get them to click that light bulb on, and it becomes their idea, then they're a more confident person. Hopefully, this helps make them better and more effective at work, home, or personal life.

JB: *What advice would you give your less experienced version of yourself or someone else, some advice as a leader, as a manager who is beginning to embrace the idea of using coaching?*

CR: You're already the manager. You're already in the seat. It's not about proving that you know more than your team and direct reports. If you can use coaching to get your team to feel more confident and deliver more, then it will make everybody stronger and better. I think we get into these leadership positions, and we believe we have to prove ourselves even more. But maybe it's looking back and saying you've earned the seat. How do you grow and develop people around you using coaching so they can move on? That actually makes you a stronger leader.

JB: Is there *anything you want to share that I haven't asked about or anything you want to emphasize?*

CR: As leaders, we shouldn't consider coaching an expense. There's a high return on the investment when you think about speeding the transition into a new role, speeding up that learning curve. I think of it more as an investment in learning and training versus an expense. And I think the informal nature of what we want our managers to do, which is much more coaching and dialoguing, can be done for a relatively low expense. We want to encourage managers to have the conversations in the moment, on the spot. We've talked about it with our dock workers. This is a coaching moment when our frontline supervisors see freight that's not strapped correctly. Coaching is an investment. It takes muscle memory. It takes work, and it takes constant exercise. It's not a one-and-done, because especially when we're stressed, we can come back into directing people on what to do and just giving them the answers.

Appendices

Appendix A
100+ Scenarios for Coaching

Here is a list of more than 100 areas of focus for coaching. This is not an exhaustive list. It is intended to illustrate the various topics about which manager-coaches may be asked to coach team members.

1. Gain self-awareness
2. Know the whole business (agility)
3. Build effective relationships across functions
4. Increase crucial relationships with leaders
5. Understand and work with power structures (politics)
6. Delegate effectively
7. Develop better listening skills
8. Create a people development culture
9. Develop collaborative relationships with key stakeholders
10. Develop physical and emotional resilience
11. Initiate change (effectively)
12. Build emotional resilience
13. Develop an optimally performing team
14. Increase organizational awareness
15. Adapt communication style to increase impact
16. Get/be organized
17. Motivate and inspire others
18. Know when to check in with others
19. Mentor others
20. Provide feedback
21. Focus team's efforts through priority setting
22. Change the visibility of a team across the company
23. Deliver clear and consistent messages
24. Set priorities and adjust pacing
25. Influence decision processes by leveraging others
26. Clarify, define, and manage expectations of self and others
27. Create a team "brand"
28. Support employees in building skills and reputation
29. Build relationships with business leaders
30. Develop a strategic network
31. Be more transparent in conversations
32. Hold direct reports accountable
33. Understand and acclimate to the organization's culture
34. Balance/flexibility of style between casual/comfortable versus more formal

https://doi.org/10.1515/9783111002415-017

35. Be more strategic—leadership versus tactical
36. Make your voice heard
37. Influence and negotiate with peers and the most senior leadership
38. Lead a diverse team
39. Influence and negotiate across functions and up the organization
40. Develop a fully competent and strategic leadership team
41. Listen actively
42. Test assumptions before making conclusions
43. Develop talent
44. Recognize the differences between people and adjust approaches to leading and managing
45. Strengthen organizational savvy
46. Develop, motivate, engage, and manage an optimally performing team
47. Set a vision on how to drive business performance
48. Be a change agent
49. Balance the need for control and influencing without authority
50. Manage the needs of multiple constituencies
51. Make decisions and take actions in a strategic context
52. Stay abreast of trends/hot topics/technology in their field
53. Manage up—boss alignment
54. Manage time—priorities, role alignment, staying focused
55. Integrate an organization or team after a merger
56. Manage teams
57. Build alignment
58. Influence from a distance (remote relations)
59. Coach employees
60. Communicate across cultures
61. Develop people leader/people management skills
62. Develop executive/leadership presence
63. Influence informally
64. Lead or influence up the organizational hierarchy
65. Assert appropriately
66. Manage and resolve conflicts
67. Influence others—direct reports, peers, partners, manager, and other key stakeholders
68. Develop and manage stakeholder relationships
69. Develop Emotional Intelligence (EI/EQ)
70. Show up as more outspoken and proactive with superiors and peers
71. Be more firm, directive and active in one-on-one and team leadership with direct reports
72. Prioritize and delegate

73. Collaborate
74. Drive results
75. Communicate vision
76. Build and use a professional network
77. Hold people accountable
78. Manage stress
79. Control impulses
80. Manage the perception of others
81. Increase productivity
82. Improve quality
83. Improve customer service
84. Reduce customer complaints
85. Retain leaders
86. Reduce costs
87. Increase bottom-line profitability
88. Improve working relationships with direct reports, immediate supervisor, peers
89. Improve teamwork
90. Improve job satisfaction
91. Develop to the next level of leadership
92. Improve individual and team performance
93. Improve working relationships
94. Gain new and different perspectives on business issues
95. Support learning and development efforts
96. Address derailing behaviors
97. Enhance career planning, decisions, and development
98. Improve individual performance/productivity
99. Address leadership development/succession planning
100. Increase individual worker skill levels
101. Improve organizational performance
102. Address specific workplace problems
103. Boost employee engagement
104. Improve retention rates
105. Improve the performance of employees whose supervisor is being coached
106. Improve recruitment outcomes

Appendix B
Self-Awareness Outcomes Questionnaire

Respond to each item by selecting the response that most accurately reflects your current self-awareness. Once you've completed it, refer to the questions for reflection at the end of the page.

		Never				Almost Always
1.	I "observe" myself.	1	2	3	4	5
2.	I have insight into myself.	1	2	3	4	5
3.	I look at why people act the way they do.	1	2	3	4	5
4.	I have learned about myself and how I see the world.	1	2	3	4	5
5.	I am continuing to work on and develop myself.	1	2	3	4	5
6.	I focus on ways amending my behavior would be useful.	1	2	3	4	5
7.	I feel generally positive about self-awareness.	1	2	3	4	5
8.	I reassess my own and others' responsibilities.	1	2	3	4	5
9.	I'm aware of my abilities and limitations.	1	2	3	4	5
10.	I am reflective.	1	2	3	4	5
11.	I am realistic about myself.	1	2	3	4	5
12.	I have a good self-image.	1	2	3	4	5
13.	I feel on the whole very comfortable with the way I am.	1	2	3	4	5
14.	I have fun.	1	2	3	4	5
15.	I am consistent in different situations or with different people.	1	2	3	4	5
16.	I have compassion and acceptance for others.	1	2	3	4	5
17.	I interact well with colleagues or peers.	1	2	3	4	5
18.	I understand myself well.	1	2	3	4	5
19.	I am confident.	1	2	3	4	5
20.	I stop and think before judging.	1	2	3	4	5
21.	I understand my emotions.	1	2	3	4	5
22.	I am objective.	1	2	3	4	5
23.	I see my work life as something I have power to affect.	1	2	3	4	5
24.	I can take a step back from situations to understand them better.	1	2	3	4	5
25.	I am content with my work situation.	1	2	3	4	5
26.	I think about how my personality fits with my work role.	1	2	3	4	5
27.	I understand how I work within a team.	1	2	3	4	5
28.	I have changed the way I work.	1	2	3	4	5
29.	I take control of my work.	1	2	3	4	5
30.	I recognize the stress and worry in my current work.	1	2	3	4	5
31.	I think about how we interact with each other as colleagues or peers.	1	2	3	4	5

https://doi.org/10.1515/9783111002415-018

(continued)

	Never				Almost Always
32. I feel vulnerable.	1	2	3	4	5
33. I feel exposed.	1	2	3	4	5
34. I find making changes is difficult and scary.	1	2	3	4	5
35. I feel guilty for criticizing others.	1	2	3	4	5
36. I feel my emotions deeply.	1	2	3	4	5
37. I find it scary to try something new or step out of what I know.	1	2	3	4	5
38. I have had to revisit difficult past experiences.	1	2	3	4	5

Adapted from Sutton, 2016

Questions for reflection and consideration:
1. What does this tell you about your self-awareness?
2. In what ways are you self-aware?
3. In what, if any, ways could your self-awareness be enhanced?
4. Based on your responses to the questionnaire, what actions will you take?

Appendix C
Skills-Focused Coaching Questions

Powerful questions in the context of coaching share some common characteristics:
- They are related to the team member's situation and support their goals for the coaching conversation.
- They build on what the client says and does.
- They are brief (15 words or less is a good rule of thumb) and direct.
- They are asked in language that the client understands.
- They do not require much contextualization or explanation.
- They minimize defensiveness and usually do not begin with "why."

The following are some examples of questions that should be used throughout the change-coaching process.

Listening for Understanding

Listening for understanding is more than making simple sense of what team members say. It involves detecting and making sense of what is not spoken by connecting data observed and gathered from various sources. It involves seeking a more profound understanding of team members and the manager-coach.
- What are you trying to say?
- Is ___ what you are saying?
- Do you think I understand you?
- What happened?
- Tell me more.
- I hear you say X, yet I see you doing Y. What does this mean?
- What else?
- What are you thinking?
- How do you feel?
- What is an example?
- Is this what you mean?
- Help me understand ___.
- What does that mean to you?
- What I hear you saying is . . . .
- Are you saying. . .?
- I imagine that made you feel ___.

https://doi.org/10.1515/9783111002415-019

Providing Feedback

While feedback is delivered in the form of statements, questions can also be used to help team members gain awareness and test possible actions.

– How can you be more open to feedback?
– What feedback have you received?
– How do you respond to feedback?
– What feedback are you willing to consider?
– What is your reaction to the feedback you received?

Reframing

Reframing involves encouraging, guiding, and supporting team members to discover different or multiple perspectives. It is beneficial when team members try to make sense of a circumstance or develop strategies for action. Reframing may be used at any point in the coaching process; however, it will most likely be used in **Step 3: Information Gathering** and **Step 5: Action Planning.** Reframing supports team members in challenging assumptions and beliefs, discovering new perspectives, and envisioning a new future. It helps team members develop and understand multiple perspectives, develop new insights, get "unstuck," and shift from tactical to strategic thinking.

– Are you following the compass or the calendar?
– What are you afraid of?
– What would that look like?
– Do you see people or problems?
– Are you the same in public as you are in private?
– What is your relationship with conflict?
– What is stopping you?
– Which do you believe first—the best or the worst?
– How could you have approached those circumstances differently?
– What would you see yourself doing if you were in a helicopter hovering above your life?
– What would it look like if you reached your goal?
– What would the relationship look like if it were healthier?
– What is stopping you?
– Is your recent behavior helping you reach your goals?
– If you succeed, what would that look like?
– When you look back ____ (days/months/years), what change will you wish you'd made?
– What other perspective can you consider?
– What other angles can you think of?

- If you look back ___ (months/years) from now, what would you like to say you accomplished?
- What assumptions can you let go of?
- Let's assume you will be successful. How does that shift your perspective and ideas about what to do next?
- What has worked for you in the past?
- What could happen if you ___?
- What have you seen or experienced others doing in similar situations?
- What's the best/worst thing that could happen?
- In what ways can you see this as an opportunity versus a problem?
- What makes investing time, money, and other resources in this make sense for (you, the business, the community, the customer, etc.)?
- How might this look if you stepped into other shoes or looked at it differently?
- What would the younger version of you tell you right now?
- What might an older version of you tell you right now?
- Imagine the future. What do you see?
- If you were the (owner, employee, manager, stockholder, etc.), how might you interpret the situation?
- If you were the (owner, employee, manager, stockholder, etc.), what possibilities can you imagine?
- What patterns do you see?
- What are you not aware of that might make a difference if you were aware?
- What are you accepting as a fact that might not be true?
- Who could you talk with who has a different perspective?
- What if ___?
- What would you attempt to do if you knew you could not fail?
- What if you could not fail?
- If you had a magic wand and could make any change, what change would you use it to make?
- What would that look like if you woke up tomorrow and the issue was resolved?
- What would you like to be true?
- What if the opposite is true?
- If none of the current options were available, what would you do?
- What would an outsider do?
- What might I notice about X if I saw it for the first time?
- If you were to start over, what would you do first?
- What are you willing to abandon?
- What would happen if you shortened your timeline?
- What would happen if you extended your timeline?
- What would you do if half of your resources were taken away?
- What would you do if you got twice as many resources as you currently have?
- What would your great-grandchildren think of the decision you are making?

Providing Insight

Coaching is typically nondirective. It involves challenging the client to gain clarity, discover blind spots, gain an understanding of meaning, and test assumptions. Providing insight may include drawing on the coach's knowledge and experience to help the client discover solutions, insights, and resources for themselves. Wisdom should be offered in a nonjudgmental and nondirective manner.

- How is that working for you?
- What is stopping you?
- What does your response to feedback communicate to others?
- What keeps you from pausing?
- How do you talk to yourself?
- From whom could you seek that information?
- What do you avoid in leadership?
- What do you avoid in conflict?
- What do you avoid in relationships?
- When are you at your best?
- How did you reach that conclusion?
- What do you fear most?

Building Support

One goal of coaching is to support clients in their independence from the manager-coach and foster independence and interdependence with a support network. As the team member explores possible actions, develops action plans, or establishes partners for accountability, it may help them identify individuals or groups with whom they can access information, role models, resources, and feedback.

- Who can support you?
- What support do you need?
- What will you do to get their support?
- What is crucial for you in an accountability partner?
- Who can be your accountability partner?
- Who else needs to be involved?
- Who do you know that can help you?
- What resources will you need to access?
- Who have you relied on when you've faced similar issues/opportunities?
- What feedback do you need? From whom?
- Who are your trusted advisors, and how can they support you?

Appendix D
Coaching Case Example 3

Jane is a senior compliance and operational risk leader for a global financial services company. She has been in her role for two years and with the company for 10 years. Jane is a high-performing, high-potential member of Frederick's team. As part of a company-sponsored leadership development program, Jane received feedback that she needs to develop her executive presence: gravitas, projection, and style. In addition, it was suggested that she develop more effective written and verbal communication skills. Shortening her messages would increase their impact.

As Jane's manager, Frederick meets with her regularly. In one of their meetings, Frederick asks Jane about her experiences with the leadership development program:

- "What have been some highlights for you?"
- "What feedback have you received?"
- "How are you applying what you are learning?"
- "What is your development plan?"
- "What, if any, support can I provide you?"

As Frederick asks these questions, Jane is excited about her experiences and eager to apply what she has learned. She has several examples of how she has already implemented some of her insights. She shares the feedback she received and asks for Frederick's help.

This is a sample of the conversation between Frederick and Jane:

Dialogue	Coaching Process Step	Coaching Skill(s) Applied
Frederick: . . . *It sounds like you have a valuable learning experience. I am happy to continue supporting you and your development. What do you have in mind?*	Step 1: Current Situation and Context	Listening for Understanding
Jane: Thank you so much! You have provided me with feedback in the past. I wonder if you might have some feedback about the presentation I made last week. I would welcome additional feedback and the opportunity to discuss some communication experiences.	Step 2: Needs and Desired Goals	Asking Powerful Questions
Frederick: *What aspects of the presentation are you interested in hearing my feedback about?*	Step 2: Needs and Desired Goals	Asking Powerful Questions
Jane: As I continue to make my messages shorter and increase the impact of my messages, I'm interested in what you observed about those points.		

https://doi.org/10.1515/9783111002415-020

(continued)

Dialogue	Coaching Process Step	Coaching Skill(s) Applied
Frederick: *I noticed that you started with a powerful attention-grabber that set the stage for other points and made the topic relevant to the audience. You followed this with PowerPoint slides that provided context and data to build your case. You succinctly and accurately drew conclusions based on the data, and then shared several criteria for evaluating options for acting on the data. You asked the group if they had additional points for review. You acknowledged their input and shared how it could be added. Then you outlined three options and evaluated each of them based on the selection criteria. You gave the group an opportunity to discuss the options, and then presented your team's recommendation. This went smoothly, and you got agreement from the group. Is my summary similar to your recollection?*	Step 3: Information Gathering	Providing Feedback Listening for Understanding
Jane: Thank you. Yes, that is an excellent summary. I'm glad to hear that you saw the flow of the presentation, how I built the argument, and that I was able to remain open to input. I was particularly concerned about getting long-winded or diverted by group members who provided feedback about the criteria and discussed the options.		
Frederick: *I don't think you got long-winded or allowed the input or discussion to throw you off course. It can be challenging when you hear so much information on a presentation you've worked very hard to develop and deliver—especially when the comments come from peers and people above you in the organization. Since you asked for feedback concerning making your messages shorter and increasing the impact of your messages, I would like to share that I noticed your response to Jillian was long and not as organized as most of your other answers. At that point, I think you may have lost the interest of some of the audience. Did you notice this?*		
Jane: Now that you mention it and I reflect on the meeting, I can see that. As I think about it, I realize that I'm often anxious when talking with Jillian and certainly feel that when presenting to her.		
Frederick: *I wonder if that might be a good topic for our next meeting. Perhaps I could provide some coaching about what you are experiencing and how you might respond to Jillian. What do you think?*	Step 4: Possible Action Planning	Listening for Understanding Asking Powerful Questions

(continued)

Dialogue	Coaching Process Step	Coaching Skill(s) Applied
Jane: That would be great. I would appreciate your ongoing feedback and coaching about my responses to Jillian. I'll make a note to have that on our agenda when we meet in 10 days. **Frederick: *OK. Between now and then, would you be willing to reflect on your interactions with Jillian and be prepared to share what you think is going on for you?*** **Jane:** Yes. I will do that. I already have some ideas. Thank you!	Step 5: Action Planning	Listening for Understanding Asking Powerful Questions
Frederick: *As we wrap up this conversation, I'm curious about what you've gotten from it and what you see as your next steps.* **Jane:** This has been very helpful. I got some insights about my approach. Before we meet again, I will reflect on my interactions with Jillian and be prepared to talk about that. **Frederick: *Terrific. I look forward to our next meeting.***	Step 6: Summary and Agreement	Asking Powerful Questions

Appendix E
Coaching Case Example 4

Fran has been with the company for about nine months. She has deep expertise and a range of experience. While she has managed other leaders in her previous job, she has never led a team this large. Fran has five managers reporting to her. Each manager has four to eight supervisory managers reporting to them. The total is around 225 team members.

When Elizabeth hired Fran, she was aware of several potential areas for development. In addition, during her initial time with the company, Elizabeth noticed further areas for development. These are:

– Elevate how Fran presents/interacts with executives (how to frame topics for presentation and discussion, how to read the audience, being able to adjust the level of detail).
– Create a cohesive weave of compliance strategy (get out of the weeds of point-counterpoint debate and use more strategic business case discussions and decision-making).

Fran has told Elizabeth that she wants to learn to be comfortable and feel knowledgeable without knowing all the details and learn to delegate for her work/life balance & others' development.

As Fran's manager, Elizabeth has shared feedback with her. Fran has been receptive and willing to work with Elizabeth and others to support her development. Elizabeth meets with her every two weeks for about one hour. Elizabeth interacts with and observes Fran in various settings throughout the workday.

Yesterday, Fran presented to a group of leaders at Elizabeth's level. Elizabeth met with Fran a couple of times as she prepared. Elizabeth's overall impression of the presentation was positive; however, Fran continued to misread the audience and provide more detailed information than was necessary. This resulted in some members of the group losing interest in the topic, the presentation and discussion lasting about 25% longer than planned, and the group not reaching a decision.

Today Elizabeth has one of her ongoing one-on-one meetings with Fran, and Elizabeth wants to use part of the time to discuss the presentation. While Elizabeth plans to provide feedback, she also wants to get Fran's observations.

https://doi.org/10.1515/9783111002415-021

This is a sample of the conversation between Elizabeth and Fran:

Dialogue	Coaching Process Step	Coaching Skill(s) Applied
Elizabeth: *I know you put a lot of time and effort into the presentation last week. I'm curious about how you thought it went.* **Fran:** First, thank you for taking the extra time to meet as I prepared the materials and presentation. I thought it went very well. As I reflected on it, I thought the flow of the presentation made sense and was easy to follow and that the essential information was presented. I struggled with the amount of detail I provide and adjusted my approach and words to the audience. **Elizabeth:** *Fran, I agree with you. Your observations and reflections are aligned with mine. I also noticed that your portion of the meeting ran longer than planned and that the group could not reach a decision. We will need to have another meeting to finalize the decision. Would you be willing to take a few minutes to talk about how you can use this experience to continue your development?* **Fran:** Absolutely. I realize getting this right is essential to my credibility and impact.	Step 1: Current Situation and Context	Asking Powerful Questions Listening for Understanding Providing Feedback
Elizabeth: *You mentioned two areas for improvement: providing details and reading your audience. In today's time, which one would you like to focus on first?* **Fran:** I think I'd like to start by providing details. I am enthusiastic about the topic and have so much experience working in this area that I tend to share more than necessary. I want others to share my enthusiasm, and I think the best way to get them on board is to provide them with lots of information. Recently, I've noticed that my audience begins to look down, check their emails, and get restless in their seats when I do this. I know I'm losing them, but I don't know how to adjust my approach. **Elizabeth:** *It is great to hear about your passion for the topic. And, yes, you have a great deal of industry experience. That is one of the reasons I was delighted you joined our team. You mentioned two points: 1) you want others to be enthusiastic about the topic, and 2) you want to retain the attention of your audience. Let's focus on each of these. OK?* **Fran:** Yes. Now that I'm noticing losing my audience, I want to work on that.	Step 2: Needs and Desired Goals	Listening for Understanding Asking Powerful Questions

(continued)

Dialogue	Coaching Process Step	Coaching Skill(s) Applied
Elizabeth: *Have you noticed anyone who was particularly good at retaining the attention of their audience?*	Step 3: Information Gathering	Reframing
Fran: As a matter of fact, I recall a leader at my previous employer who was great at doing this. And a few weeks ago, I attended a professional conference where one of the speakers captured and retained the audience's attention for a full hour.		Listening for Understanding Asking Powerful Questions
Elizabeth: *As you recall those experiences, what did they do that contributed to this success?*		
Fran: Each of them started with a story the audience related to and set the stage for their topic. Their presentations were focused on 2–3 key points. They presented the material with enough detail for everyone to understand without giving too much information. The presentations had a logical flow, like telling a story or presenting an argument.		
Elizabeth: *Which do you think you already do well, and which do you think deserve attention?*		
Fran: My presentations tend to flow logically and build the case for a decision. I don't typically tell a story or do anything to capture the audience's attention, and as we've discussed, I tend to provide too much information.		
Elizabeth: *It sounds like you've already identified potential shifts you want to make. Are there others?*	Step 4: Possible Actions	Listening for Understanding
Fran: No. Those are big ones for me and provide a good starting point.		Asking Powerful Questions
Elizabeth: *OK. So, what will you do to implement these actions?*	Step 5: Action Planning	Asking Powerful Questions
		Listening for Understanding
		Developing Support

(continued)

Dialogue	Coaching Process Step	Coaching Skill(s) Applied
Fran: For the follow-up meeting in three weeks, I don't think I should start with a story. However, I have another presentation the following week that could use a story to capture the audience. As I work on that presentation, I'll develop a story. I'll work with our communication specialist to refine this. And, if you don't mind, I'd like to run it by you for feedback when we meet next week. And, for the details, I would like to think about the follow-up meeting and my audience. I will develop an outline of the critical pieces of information they need to decide on the proposal, then build the presentation based on that outline. Again, I'll consult with our communication specialist and a couple of members of my team who are familiar with the audience and the proposal. The key will be to help me focus on the essential details. I will also build the presentation to tell the story and lead them to the decision. I should be able to accomplish this by the end of this week. How does that sound?		
Elizabeth: *I would like you to clearly understand what you must do and the resources you need to access. I am happy to meet with you about the upcoming presentation. Is there support you need from me on the follow-up meeting next week?*		
Fran: Thank you for your support. If you have time, I'd love to run through the presentation for your follow-up meeting. Your feedback would be helpful.		
Elizabeth: *Great. I know I have some time available Friday afternoon. Will that work for you?*		
Fran: Perfect.		
Elizabeth: *As we wrap up, I'm curious about what you got from this conversation. Will you share that and review your next steps?*	Step 6: Summary and Agreement	Asking Powerful Questions

(continued)

Dialogue	Coaching Process Step	Coaching Skill(s) Applied
Fran: I have gained awareness of ways I can improve my presentation skills by getting the attention of my audience, focusing on what the audience needs, minimizing unnecessary details, and building my presentations as stories or persuasive arguments. I also gained confidence in developing and presenting material that will lead to our desired outcomes. As for actions, I will: 1. Develop a story to kick off my presentation in three weeks. I'll have a draft for us to review during our next meeting. 2. Use the resources on the team to support my presentation development and delivery. 3. Draft my presentation for next week and review it with you on Friday. 4. Focus on the essential details when planning my presentations. Thank you for taking the time to talk through this with me.		

Glossary of Terms

Ally Someone who advocates and supports a community other than their own. Allies are not part of the communities they help. A person should not self-identify as an ally but instead show that they are one through action.

Assessment An instrument designed (often validated) to measure knowledge, skills, behaviors, personality, learning style, etc.

Behavior How an individual, group, or organization conducts itself.

Behavioral change A shift in behavior.

Behavioral coaching Behavioral coaches facilitate the performance, learning, and development of the individual or team by explicitly focusing on actions, goals, and habit formation. Behavioral coaching aims to help individuals increase their effectiveness and happiness at work, study, or in a social setting by breaking down current behaviors and activating new replacement behaviors.

Belonging ". . . your sense that you are part of something greater than yourself that you value and need and that values and needs you back. In other words, belonging creates a strong sense of connection, reciprocity, and shared value. . . . A culture of belonging is built on access, reciprocity, and sharing of power and opportunity. It is not a culture that excludes anyone based on social identity, though it might set clear parameters around employee orientations, motivations, and aspirations" (Miranda-Wolff, 2022, p. 8).

Bias A preconceived or irrational tendency, trend, inclination, feeling, or opinion. Prejudice is taught by the socialization practices one is exposed to.

Big Five A five-factor personality model and various assessments, including openness, conscientiousness, extraversion, agreeableness, and neuroticism. It is sometimes referred to as the NEO Big Five.

BIPOC Black, Indigenous, and People of Color.

Certification Certification represents a declaration of a particular individual's professional competence independent of certificate program providers. Certificates are issued to attest to a knowledge and experience base for coaching practitioners.

Change The act or instance of making or becoming different to cause something to be different, such as a process, role, or product. Change can affect individuals, groups, and organizations.

Change agent A person or group who drives change within the organization by championing or promoting the change and often by managing its implementation. The role can be official or voluntary and can help to communicate the excitement, vision, and details of the change to others within the organization.

Class A social stratum sharing essential economic, political, or cultural characteristics and having the same social position.

Client The individual or group who receives the professional service of coaching. (See Coachee, Team member.)

Coach The individual who provides one-on-one or group coaching.

Coach training The academic and professional programs providing coach training and development focusing on theory, practice, and scholarship.

https://doi.org/10.1515/9783111002415-022

Coachee The individual or group who receives the professional service of coaching. (See Client, Team member.)

Coachability A person's willingness and openness to development, performance improvement, and transformation through engagement with a coach (informal or formal).

Coaching A practice of collaborating with team members in dialogue informed by skills, ethics, standards, theories, and models. Coaching seeks to co-create reflective learning experiences that support individual and collective change.

Coaching services provider The people who use coaching-related theories, models, and skills in their work or as the basis for their professional practices. This may include a company that sources coaches for organizations.

Coaching session The conversations, sessions, and interventions in which coaching occurs.

Coaching skills The skills used by coaches and manager-coaches are listening for understanding, asking powerful questions, reframing, offering feedback, providing insights, and developing support.

Cognitive behavioral coaching Cognitive behavioral coaching aims to help clients understand the root of their difficulty. This approach to coaching and therapy focuses on changing beliefs, images, and thoughts in order to change behaviors. A coach with this style will typically have a psychology background and will work with you to identify what might be stopping you from reaching your full potential.

Competence Demonstrating knowledge or skills at a defined level of expertise.

Competency The observable or measurable knowledge, skill, attitude, or behavior that is essential for a job or contributes to the successful performance of the job and differentiates the level of performance.

Confidentiality Holding something in confidence, not disclosing it without the permission of the other person, group, or organization.

Consulting A helping relationship that can be formal or informal and is established to provide expertise, skills, or a process for the client.

Covering This is downplaying your differences relative to mainstream perceptions in ways that are costly to your productivity and sense of self in the workplace.

Culturally subordinated or subordinated social identity A status imposed by a culturally dominant social identity group onto another group it deems inferior to itself. Subordination is done *to* a group. No group voluntarily subordinates itself.

Critical Race Theory (CRT) What began as a legal theory in the 1970s is now a collection of activities and scholars who study transformational relationships among race, racism, and power. This approach has spread to other disciplines, such as political science, ethnic studies, sociology, theology, and healthcare (Delgado & Stefancic, 2017). Today, CRT is a cross-disciplinary examination of how laws, social and political movements, and media shape, and are shaped by, social conceptions of ethnicity and race. The word *critical* in the name is an academic reference to critical thinking and critical theory rather than criticizing or blaming people.

Developmental coaching Coaching that focuses on personal or professional goals, thinking, feelings, and actions and on how the clients can change their lives for greater personal effectiveness or satisfaction. To learn, build, or grow a skill or capacity, such as developing business acumen or public speaking skills, creating a culture of respect and inclusion, or improving innovation in a group or organization.

Development plan A formal (written) or informal (unwritten) agreement about actions that will be taken to develop knowledge, skills, and abilities within a specific period and with specific defined outcomes.

Diversity The de-facto state of differences among human beings in social space. The practice or quality of including or involving people from various social and ethnic backgrounds and different races, genders, sexual orientations, etc.

Dominant Supremacy on a given dimension of diversity, such as culture or social identity. Cultural dominance equals rule, control, power, and authority.

Empathy Understanding the situation that contributed to or triggered feelings.

Equality Everyone gets the same thing.

Equity Everyone gets what they need; fairness, impartiality, absence of favoritism.

Ethics An individual or group adopts moral principles to provide rules for appropriate conduct. Ethics considers what is correct behavior in a particular situation.

Ethnicity An ethnic/social group with a distinctive culture, values, religion, language, etc.

Exclusion The opposite of inclusion. It involves conscious and unconscious acts that place some individuals or groups of individuals outside the sphere of power, knowledge, opportunity, collaboration, partnership, decision-making, and career advancement.

Existential coaching Existential coaches encourage clients to define their purpose and explore topics such as meaning, authenticity, freedom, choice, and responsibility and how these come into play. A coach with this approach may have studied a psychoanalytic approach during their training.

Existentialism A philosophical theory or approach that emphasizes the person's existence as a free and responsible agent determining their development through acts of will.

Feedback Data about past behaviors that is offered in the present. It is intended to reinforce or alter behaviors. There are many sources of feedback, including internal responses, observations of impacts against intentions, and responses from others. Feedback is data about a person's behavior or performance and the impact of that behavior on their performance delivered to the team member facilitate change, improvement, or achievement of desired goals. It may be offered from the team member to the coach as well.

Focus areas of change coaching Three primary reasons for change at the individual, group, or organization levels are performance, development, or transformation.

Gender A socially constructed system of classification that ascribes feminine or masculine characteristics to people.

Gender identity A person's internal sense of themselves as a specific gender—girl/woman, boy/man, etc.—irrespective of their biological sex.

Gestalt coaching Gestalt coaches seek to facilitate transformational change—a personal change focused on behavioral change and supporting a growing awareness of the whole person. Gestalt coaching helps people become more of who they are, and it is in following this path that they gain access to their future potential. A coach who works with this style should have a background in psychology.

Group coaching Team members undertaking group coaching benefit from peer learning or the group's collective wisdom. This peer learning is often as important as the interaction with the coach. Groups come together with a common interest but do not always have the same goal. For example, a group may come together to be coached on effective leadership. Still, a team member has personal goals, and their role is not in relationship with other group participants.

Hearing The physiological sensory process by which auditory sensations are received by the ears and transmitted to the brain.

Helping relationship A formal or informal relationship with another person, group, or organization (the client) to provide help, with the intent of avoiding co-dependence.

Implicit bias Having prejudice and stereotypes without intending to do so and acting based on the bias.

Inclusion The ability to interact with people in a way that makes them feel they belong, are valued, and are welcome to be themselves. Allows individuals with different identities, skill sets, beliefs, and experiences to feel they belong within the group because they are valued, relied upon, welcomed, and empowered. Inclusion is also the ability to interact with people in a way that makes them feel they belong, are valued, and are welcome to be themselves.

Individual Development Plan (IDP) A document created by a coaching client based on feedback designed to identify goals for learning and development, actions to be taken, a timeframe for completion, and support to achieve the goals. The IDP is usually created with the coach and may include a manager's input (and sometimes approval).

Intersectionality A term coined by law professor Kimberlé Crenshaw (1989) to describe how multiple systems of oppression interact in the lives of those with multiple marginalized identities. The notion is that no one can be identified by only one dimension of diversity and social group identity. Instead, each of us has multiple social group identities and lives from a nexus where all our identities intersect. Intersectionality examines the relationships between various marginalized identities and allows us to analyze social problems more thoroughly, shape effective interventions, and promote inclusive advocacy among communities.

Intervention To involve oneself in a situation at the individual, group, or organization levels, resulting in an alteration of the action development.

JEDI An abbreviation that represents Justice, Equity, Diversity, and Inclusion.

Goal A desired outcome of the coaching engagement.

Key stakeholders Individuals or a group (can be a subset of all stakeholders) whose support is essential to the success of the change. The change initiative will probably fail if they withhold or withdraw their support.

Leader The person to whom others look for guidance, direction, and vision.

Learning The knowledge or skill acquired by instruction or study that modifies a behavioral tendency.

Level of change Three arenas in which change takes place: individual or personal, group or team, and organization.

Listening Making sense of sounds and observations.

Manager-coach A person who uses coaching-related knowledge, approaches, and skills to coach team members in the organization who report to them or who have sought their coaching.

Marginalize To push someone out to the margins of social space or activity because of stereotypical assumptions about that person's intelligence, competence, capability, or overall desirability.

Master A person eminently skilled at something.

Mastery The act of performing at a masterful level.

Microaggressions Subtle but offensive comments or actions directed at a culturally subordinated group. Often unintentional or unconscious, they insult, invalidate, or exclude marginalized groups and reinforce stereotypes.

Mindset A mental attitude or disposition that predetermines a person, group, or organization's responses to and interpretations of situations; an inclination or habit.

Mentoring A one-on-one relationship between a less-experienced person (protégé) and a more-experienced person (mentor) intended to advance the personal and professional growth of the protégé.

Multi-rater feedback Feedback from multiple sources, usually from different perspectives such as manager, peers, direct reports, and other key stakeholders.

Novice A beginner who is new to knowledge or skills and has not developed them to a level of competence, proficiency, or mastery.

Paraphrasing A listening skill that coaches use based on restating the client's essential message in a concise way to test the coach's understanding of what the client has said.

Peer coaching The use of coaching knowledge, skills, and related theory in a formal or informal relationship with a peer.

Performance coaching Coaching that focuses on specific performance potential, job requirements, deficiencies, or derailers and on how to fill performance gaps.

Person being coached (See Client, Coachee and Team member).

Person-Centered approach An approach to counseling, psychotherapy, and coaching based on the work of Carl Rogers. It is team member-centered and nondirective, and it places much of the responsibility for the process on the client, with the therapist or coach taking a nondirective role.

Positive Psychology approach A psychological approach that focuses on the positive events and influences in life, including experiences, states and traits, and institutions.

Prejudice A preconceived unfavorable opinion or feeling about someone formed without knowledge, thought, or reason. It is a "prejudgment about another person based on the social groups to which that person belongs. Prejudice consists of thoughts and feelings, including stereotypes, attitudes, and generalizations that are based on little or no experience and then are projected onto everyone from that group. Our prejudices tend to be shared because we swim in the same cultural water and absorb the same messages" (Diangelo, 2018, p. 19).

Privilege Is ". . . unearned benefits given to individuals with particular socio-cultural identities—white privilege, male privilege, heterosexual privilege . . ." (Radd, et al., 2021, p. 51). It is the other side of oppression. Privilege and oppression affect each other, but they do not negate each other. Privilege describes what everyone should experience and is understood in the context of power systems. A person with privilege may have worked hard to earn their privilege.

Professionally A way of acting at a professional-level quality standard, whether or not the job is considered a profession.

Protégé A person who is mentored.

Psychodynamic approach The study and application (in therapy and coaching) of the interaction of various conscious and unconscious mental or emotional processes, significantly as they influence personality, behavior, and attitudes.

Psychodynamic coaching Psychodynamic coaching aims to help clients achieve insight and understanding around the reasons for their problems and to translate this insight into a mature capacity to cope with current and future difficulties. This approach attempts to tap into the subconscious by discussing associations, dreams, family relationships, power structures, and role analysis.

Race The Swedish botanist Carolus Linnaeus created a taxonomy of differentiated races within humanity in the mid-1700s. A German anthropologist, Johann Blumenbach, turned Linnaeus's taxonomy into a hierarchy, putting "Caucasian" at the top and "Negroid" at the bottom. Scientifically speaking, there is only one race: the human race. "Race," as currently understood, is a social construction.

Racism ". . . a marriage of racist policies and racist ideas that produce and normalize racial inequities" (Kendi, 2019, p. 18). It is institutional, structural, and systemic.

Reflection Awareness of self within the moment, having a clear mind to be open to the possibility of that moment.

Reframing To look at, present, or think of beliefs, ideas, or relationships in a new or different way; the skill of helping a coaching client reframe. Reframing may involve tools such as metaphors, analogies, and role plays.

Relationship A situation in which two or more people's feelings, thoughts, and behaviors are mutually and causally interdependent.

Sexual orientation A person's physical, romantic, emotional, aesthetic, and other form of attraction to others. Trans people can be straight, bisexual, lesbian, gay, asexual, pansexual, queer, etc., just like anyone else. For example, a trans woman who is exclusively attracted to other women would often identify as lesbian. In Western cultures, gender identity and sexual orientation are not the same.

Social identity The portion of an individual's self-concept derived from membership in a social group.

Socialization The process of learning how to behave in a way that is acceptable to society. It mostly happens in the context of family and home of origin.

Solution-focused coaching Solution-focused coaching is centered on helping clients find solutions rather than problems, building on strengths rather than weaknesses, and finding positive ways forward rather than examining barriers. This coaching approach is very closely related to Strengths-based coaching.

Stakeholder Any person, group, or organization whose interests will be affected positively or negatively by the change. Stakeholders can be internal or external to the organization.

Stereotype A widely held but fixed, oversimplified, and to some extent erroneous image or ideas of a person or group. Stereotypes are based on very little data and are related to assumptions and implicit bias.

Strengths-based coaching Strengths-based manager-coaches work with team members to identify their strengths and help them discover how using those strengths more consciously can increase the team member's success—by understanding, developing, and applying their strengths to their goals. Often, team members and managers focus on team member's weaknesses and areas for development, which is important. However, team members can benefit from better exploring how to deploy existing capabilities. This approach builds confidence and ability.

Structural inequality The combination of privilege, exclusion, power, and oppression in all levels, facets, and functions of cultures, societies, systems, and organizations. When exercised, these factors confer favor, privilege, or benefit for one group (dominant) over other groups. Structural inequality is supported through visible and hidden policies, programs, rules, norms, assumptions, and attitudes. The behavior creates, sustains, and contributes to the existence and continuation of bias, discrimination, and dominance in all areas of society, culture, or system. (Royal, 2010)

Target The person or group for whom a change initiative is focused; the individuals most directly impacted by the change and for whom change is expected.

Team coaching Team coaching differs slightly from group coaching in that teams are people who are all aligned and headed to a common goal or outcome, such as the completion of a particular project. Groups come together with a common interest but do not always have the same goal in mind. Team coaching is tactical and practical, whereas group dynamics is more aimed at unearthing truths from the collective subconscious.

Team member A person who belongs to a team or group and reports to a leader.

Training Organized activity focused on imparting information or instructions to improve a person's performance or to help the person attain a required level of knowledge or skill.

Transactional Analysis A system of therapy that can be applied to coaching, developed by Eric Berne, in which personal relationships and interactions are analyzed in terms of conflicting or complementary ego states that correspond to the roles of parent, child, and adult. Transactional analysis is a form of modern psychology that examines a person's relationships and interactions. It can be used to address interactions and communications to establish and reinforce the idea that everyone is valuable and has the capacity for positive change and personal growth. This approach should be undertaken by a coach with a background in psychology.

Transference Feelings once felt by the client toward someone are projected onto the coach.

Transformational coaching Transformational coaching is similar to "life coaching." It involves helping people better themselves and their broader lives (both inside and outside work) by bringing about necessary changes across all aspects of life. Instead of changing how you act, transformational coaching clients work on changing how team members see themselves.

Unconscious bias An unconscious favoritism toward or prejudice against people of a particular social identity group such as race, gender, ethnicity, sexual orientation, economic status, etc.

Use of self A person's consciousness of their being or identity (the ego) and their striving to use self effectively and constructively in interactions with others.

Values What is suitable and desirable.

References

Aguayo J. (2014). Bion's *Notes on memory and desire*—its initial clinical reception in the United States: A note on archival material. *The International Journal of Psychoanalysis, 95*(5), 889–910. https://doi.org/10.1111/1745-8315.12246

Armenakis, A. A., Harris, S. G., & Mossholder, K. W. (1993). Creating readiness for organizational change. *Human Relations, 46*(6), 681–703. https://doi.org/10.1177/001872679304600601

ATD, 2020, *Managers as coaches: Boosting employee and organizational performance*, [White paper], pp. 1–4.

Bachkirova, T. (2011). *Developmental coaching: Working with the self*. Open University Press.

Baer, R. A. (2003). Mindfulness training as a clinical intervention: A conceptual and empirical review. *Clinical Psychology: Science and Practice, 10*(2), 125–143. https://doi.org/10.1093/clipsy.bpg015

Bandura, A. (1997). *Self-Efficacy: The exercise of control*. W. H. Freeman and Company.

Bass, B. M., & Riggio, R. E. (2006). *Transformational leadership* (2nd ed.). Lawrence Erlbaum Associates Publishers. https://doi.org/10.4324/9781410617095

Beck, A. T. (1976). *Cognitive therapy and the emotional disorders*. New York: American Library.

Bender, C. (2022). The crucial role of employee feedback in slowing the Great Resignation. *Human Resource Executive*. Retrieved February 20, 2023, from https://hrexecutive.com/the-crucial-role-of-employee-feedback-in-slowing-the-great-resignation/

Benner, P. (2001). *From novice to expert: Excellence and power in clinical nursing practice* (Commemorative ed.). Upper Saddle River, NJ: Prentice Hall. (Original work published 1984).

Bennett, J. L., & Bush, M. W. (2014). *Coaching for change*. Routledge.

Bennett, J. L., & Rogers, K. (2013). Skill acquisition of executive coaches: A journey toward mastery. In A. F. Buono, L. de Caluwe & A. Stoppelenburg (Eds.), *Exploring the professional identity of management consultants*. 173–201. Charlotte, NC: Information Age Publishing.

Bens, I. (2012). *Facilitating with ease! Core skills for facilitators, team leaders and members, managers, consultants, and trainers* (3rd ed.). Jossey-Bass.

Berger, J. G. (2012). *Changing on the job: Developing leaders for a complex world*. Stanford University Press.

Berger, W. (2014). *A more beautiful question: The power of inquiry to spark breakthrough ideas*. Bloomsbury.

Berger, W. (2018). *The book of beautiful questions*. Bloomsbury Publishing.

Bernard, J. M., & Goodyear, R. K. (2019). *Fundamentals of clinical supervision*. Pearson.

Berne, E. (1962). Classification of positions. *Transactional Analysis Bulletin, 1*(3), 23.

Berne, E. (1964). *Games people play*. New York, NY: Grove Press.

Berne, E. (1976). *Beyond games and scripts*. New York, NY: Grove Press.

Berthoud, H., & Bennett, J. L. (2020). Use of self: What it is? Why it matters? & Why you need more of it? In S. H. Cady, C. K. Gorelick, & C. T. Stiegler (Eds.), *The collaborative change library: Global guide to transforming organization, revitalizing communities, and developing human potential*. NEXUS4change. https://urldefense.com/v3/__https://app.mylibrary.world/Collaborative_Change_Library/chapter/Use_of_Self__;!!IZsPJ-aPDhOh!rYYCHadvlj3RMNIYkCRKAdh1Jqpt66YtPtBomNdgvanCrHss4ecMZ-OufHHt2mj__b9Peib2hmVEPvvMDCrB3A$

Biswas-Diener, R., Kashdan, T. B., & Minhas, G. (2011). A dynamic approach to psychological strength development and intervention. *The Journal of Positive Psychology, 6*(2), 106–118. https://doi.org/10.1080/17439760.2010.545429

Bluckert, P. (2018). The Gestalt approach to coaching. In T. Bachkirova, E. Cox, & D. Clutterbuck (Eds.), *The complete handbook of coaching* (3rd ed., pp. 66–80). Sage.

Boniwell, I., & Kauffman, C. (2018). The positive psychology approach to coaching. In E. Cox, T. Bachkirova, & D. Clutterbuck (Eds.), *The complete handbook of coaching* (3rd ed., pp. 152–166). Sage.

Bolton, R. (1979). *People skills: How to assert yourself, listen to others, and resolve conflicts*. Simon & Schuster.

Bordin, E. S. (1979). The generalizability of the psychoanalytic concept of the working alliance. *Psychotherapy: Theory, Research & Practice, 16*(3), 252–260.

https://doi.org/10.1515/9783111002415-023

Bordin, E. S. (1994). Theory and research on the therapeutic working alliance: New directions. In A. O. Horvath & L. S. Greenberg (Eds.), *The working alliance: Theory, research, and practice* (pp. 13–37). New York: Wiley.

Boud, D., Keogh, R., & Walker, D. (Eds.). (1985). *Reflection: Turning experience into learning*. Kogan Page.

Boyatzis, R. E., Smith, M., & Blaize, N. (2006). Developing sustainable leaders through coaching and compassion. *Academy of Management Learning & Education, 5*(1), 8–24.

Bozer, G., & Joo, B.-K. (2015). The effects of coachee characteristics and coaching relationships on feedback receptivity and self-awareness in executive coaching. *International Leadership Journal, 7*(3), 36–58.

Brammer, L. M., & MacDonald, G. (2003). *The helping relationship: Process and skills* (8th ed.). Boston, MA: Allyn and Bacon.

Bridges, W. (1991). *Managing transitions: Making the most of change*. Addison-Wesley Publishing Co.

Bridges, W. (2000). *Transition: The personal path through change*. Carlson Learning Company.

Brownell, P., Roibal, A. V., & Marnell, M. E. (2016). The efficacy of gestalt psychotherapy: A review of the empirical literature. *Psychotherapy Research, 26*(2), 220–237.

Buechner, F. (2017). *The remarkable ordinary: How to stop, look, and listen to life*. Zondervan.

Butler, A. C., Chapman, J. E., Forman, E. M., & Beck, A. T. (2006). The empirical status of cognitive-behavioral therapy: A review of meta-analyses. *Clinical Psychology Review, 26*(1), 17–31. https://doi.org/https://doi.org/10.1016/j.cpr.2005.07.003

Cavanagh, M., Grant, A. M., & Kemp, T. (2018). Evidence for the developmental value of higher-order coaching: Randomized controlled trial of executive coaching in a higher education institution. *Journal of Applied Behavioral Science, 54*(1), 16–39.

Center for Credentialing and Education. https://www.cce-global.org/

Cherniss, C. (2010). Emotional intelligence: Toward clarification of a concept. *Industrial and Organizational Psychology, 3*(2), 110–126.

Clarkson, P. (2014). *Gestalt counseling in action*. Sage.

Clutterbuck, D. (2010). Coaching reflection: The liberated coach. *Coaching: An International Journal of Theory, Research and Practice 3*, 73–81.

Clutterbuck, D. (2020). *Coaching the team at work: The definitive guide to team coaching* (2nd ed.). Nicholas Brealey Publishing.

Clutterbuck, D., & Megginson, D. (2005). *Making coaching work: Creating a coaching culture*. CIPD Publishing.

Clutterbuck, D., Turner, C., & Murphy, C. (2022). Setting the stage. In D. Clutterbuck, C. Turner, & C. Murphy (Eds.), *The team coaching casebook* (pp. xv–xix). Open University Press.

Corey, G., Corey, M. S., Corey, C., & Callanan, P. (2015). *Issues and ethics in the helping professions* (9th ed.). Stamford, CT: Brooks/Cole.

Crenshaw, K. (1989). Demarginalizing the intersection of race and sex: A black feminist critique of antidiscrimination doctrine, feminist theory and antiracist politics. *University of Chicago Legal Forum, 1989* (1, Article 8), 139–167.

Deci, E. L., & Ryan, R. M. (2000). The 'what' and 'why' of goal pursuits: Human needs and the self-determination of behavior. *Psychological Inquiry, 11*(4), 227–268.

Deci, E. L., & Ryan, R. M. (2008). Self-determination theory: A macrotheory of human motivation, development, and health. *Canadian Psychology, 49*(3), 182–185.

DeNisi, A. S., & Kluger, A. N. (2000). Feedback effectiveness: Can 360-degree appraisals be improved? *Academy of Management Executive, 14*(1), 129–139.

Delgado, R., & Stefancic, J. (2017). *Critical race theory: An introduction* (3rd ed.). New York University Press.

Dewey, J. (1933) *How we think: A restatement of the relation of reflective thinking to the educative process* (Revised ed.), Boston: D. C. Heath.

Diangelo, R. (2018). *White fragility: Why it's so hard for white people to talk about racism*. Beacon Press.

DiClemente, C., & Prochaska, J. (1998). Toward a comprehensive, transtheoretical model of change. In W. Miller & N. Heather (Eds.), *Treating addictive behaviours* (pp. 3–24). New York: Plenum Press.

Drago-Severson, E., & Blum-DeStefano, J. (2016). *Tell me so I can hear you: A developmental approach to feedback for educators*. Harvard University Press.

Dreyfus, H., & Dreyfus, S. (1980). *The five-stage model of the mental activities involved in directed skill acquisition*. Berkeley, CA: Operations Research Center, University of California.

Dreyfus, H. L., & Dreyfus, S. E. (1986). *Mind over machine: The power of human intuition and expertise in the era of the computer*. New York, NY: Free Press.

Dreyfus, H., & Dreyfus, S. (2004). The ethical implications of the five-stage skill-acquisition model. *Bulletin of Science, Technology & Society, 24*(3), 251–264.

Dweck, C. S. (2000). *Self-theories: Their role in motivation, personality, and development*. Psychology Press.

Dweck, C. S. (2007). *Mindset: The new psychology of success* (Reprint ed.). Ballantine Books.

Dweck, C. S. (2016). *What having a "Growth Mindset" actually means* https://hbr.org/2016/01/what-having-a-growth-mindset-actually-means

Economy, P. (2015). 40 influential Wayne Dyer quotes to challenge you to be the best version of yourself. *Inc*. https://www.inc.com/peter-economy/40-influential-wayne-dyer-quotes-to-challenge-you-to-be-the-best-version-of-your.html

Egan, T., & Reynolds, K. (2017). Exploring the effects of existential coaching on career decision-making. *Journal of Coaching Psychology, 5*(2), 87–101.

Eisenbeiss, S. A., Knippenberg, D. V., & Boerner, S. (2008). Transformational leadership and team innovation: Integrating team climate principles. *Journal of Applied Psychology, 93*(6), 1438–1446.

Ellinger, A. D., Hamlin, R. G., & Beattie, R. (2008). Behavioural indicators of ineffective managerial coaching: A cross-national study. *Journal of European Industrial Training, 32*(4), 240–257. https://doi.org/10.1108/03090590810871360

Ellis, A. (1962). *Reason and emotion in psychotherapy*. Lyle Stuart.

Ellis, C. W. (2004). *Management skills for new managers*. New York, NY: AMACOM.

Emmons, R. A., & McCullough, M. E. (2003). Counting blessings versus burdens: An experimental investigation of gratitude and subjective well-being in daily life. *Journal of Personality and Social Psychology, 84*(2), 377–389. https://doi.org/10.1037/0022-3514.84.2.377

European Mentoring and Coaching Council. https://www.emccglobal.org/

European Mentoring and Coaching Council. (July 2021). *Global code of ethics*. European Mentoring and Coaching Council. Retrieved April 19, 2023, from https://www.emccglobal.org/leadership-development/ethics/

Evered, R. D., & Selman, J. C. (1989). Coaching and the art of management. *Organizational Dynamics, 18*(2), 16–32.

Evers, A., Brouwers, A., & Tomic, W. (2006). A quasi-experimental study on management coaching effectiveness. *Consulting Psychology Journal: Practice and Research, 58*(3), 174–182.

Fadem, T. J. (2009). *The art of asking: Ask better questions, get better answers*. Pearson Education.

Fisher, R., Ury, W., & Patton, B. (1991). *Getting to yes: Negotiating agreement without giving in* (2nd ed.). Penguin Books.

Franklin, J. (2005). Change readiness in coaching: Potentiating client change. In M. Cavanagh, A. M. Grant & T. Kemp (Eds.), *Evidence-based coaching, Vol 1: Theory, research and practice from the behavioural sciences* (pp. 193–200). Bowen Hills, Q D Australia: Australian Academic Press.

Franklin, L. R., & Kimber, M. (2015). Solution-focused coaching in educational leadership: A case study. *Educational Management Administration & Leadership, 43*(4), 626–641.

Fredrickson B. L. (2001). The role of positive emotions in positive psychology. The broaden-and-build theory of positive emotions. *American Psychologist, 56*(3), 218–26. doi: 10.1037//0003-066x.56.3.218. PMID: 11315248; PMCID: PMC3122271.

Gallup. (2023). *State of the global workplace 2023 report: The voice of the world's employees*. Gallup.

Gander, F., Proyer, R. T., Ruch, W., & Wyss, T. (2013). Strength-based positive interventions: Further evidence for their potential in enhancing well-being and alleviating depression. *Journal of Happiness Studies: An Interdisciplinary Forum on Subjective Well-Being, 14*(4), 1241–1259. https://doi.org/10.1007/s10902-012-9380-0

Gentry, W. (2016). *Be the boss everyone wants to work for: A guide for new leaders.* Berrett-Koehler Publishers, Inc.

Gentry, W. A., Stawiski, S., Sosik, J., & Chun, J. (2012). The coaching industry: Fostering a new profession. *Consulting Psychology Journal: Practice and Research, 64*(1), 67–83.

Goleman, D. (1995). *Emotional intelligence* (10th anniversary ed.). Bantam.

Goleman, D., Boyatzis, R., & McKee, A. (2002). *Primal leadership: Learning to lead with emotional intelligence.* Harvard Business School Press.

Gollwitzer, P., & Sheeran, P. (2006). Implementation intentions and goal achievement: A meta-analysis of effects and processes. *Advances in Experimental Social Psychology, 38*, 69–119. https://doi.org/10.1016/S0065-2601(06)38002-1

Graduate School Alliance for Education in Coaching. https://gsaec.org/

Graham, S., Wedman, J. F., & Garvin-Kester, B. (1994). Manager coaching skills: What makes a good coach? *Performance Improvement Quarterly, 7*(2), 81–94.

Grant, A. (2021). *Think again: The power of knowing what you don't know.* Random House Large Print.

Grant, A. M., Curtayne, L., & Burton, G. (2009). Executive coaching enhances goal attainment, resilience and workplace well-being: A randomised controlled study. *The Journal of Positive Psychology, 4*(5), 396–407. https://doi.org/10.1080/17439760902992456

Grant, A. M., & O'Connor, S. A. (2014). The differential effects of solution-focused and problem-focused coaching questions: A pilot study with implications for practice. *Industrial and Commercial Training, 46*(3), 161–169.

Gray, D. E. (2004) Principles and processes in coaching evaluation. *The International Journal of Mentoring and Coaching, 2*(2), 1–7.

Green, S., Grant, A. M., & Rynsaardt, J. (2007). Evidence-based life coaching for senior high schools: Building hardiness and hope. *International Coaching Psychology Review, 2*(1), 24–32.

Greenberger, D., & Padesky, C. A. (1995). *Mind over mood.* New York: Guilford Press.

Gregory, J. B., & Levy, P. E. (2011). It's not me, it's you: A multilevel examination of variables that impact employee coaching relationships. *Consulting Psychology Journal: Practice and Research, 63*(2), 67–88. https://doi.org/10.1037/a0024152

Gyllensten, K., & Palmer, S. (2006). Experiences of coaching and stress in the workplace: An interpretative phenomenological analysis. *International Coaching Psychology Review, 1*(1), 86–98.

Gyllensten, K., & Palmer, S. (2017). The coaching relationship in existential coaching. In S. Palmer & K. Gyllensten (Eds.), *The coaching relationship: Putting people first* (pp. 89–108). Routledge.

Hackman, J. R., & Wageman, R. (2005). A theory of team coaching. *Academy of Management Review, 30*(2), 269–287.

Hamlin, R. G., Ellinger, A. D., & Beattie, R. S. (2006). Coaching at the heart of managerial effectiveness: A cross-cultural study of managerial behaviours. *Human Resource Development International, 9*(3), 305–331.

Hargrove, R. (1995). *Masterful coaching: Extraordinary results by impacting people and the way they think and work together.* San Francisco, CA: Pfeiffer.

Hawkins, P. & Shohet, R. (2012). *Supervision in the helping professions* (4th ed.). McGraw Hill Open University Press.

Hawkins, P., & Smith, N. (2013). *Coaching, mentoring and organizational consultancy: Supervision, skills and development* (2nd ed.). Open University Press.

Heslin, P. A., Vandewalle, D., & Latham, G. P. (2006). Key to help? Managers' implicit person theories and their subsequent employee coaching. *Personnel Psychology, 59*, 871–902.

Higgins, E. T. (1987). Self-discrepancy: A theory relating self and affect. *Psychological Review, 94*, 319–340.

Hofmann, S. G., Asnaani, A., Vonk, I. J. J., Sawyer, A. T., & Fang, A. (2012). The efficacy of cognitive behavioral therapy: A review of meta-analyses. *Cognitive Therapy Research, 36*, 427–440. https://doi.org/10.1007/s10608-012-9476-1

Howard, P. J., & Howard, J. (2018). *The owner's manual for personality at work: How the Big Five personality traits affect performance, communication, teamwork, leadership, and sales* (2nd ed.). Paradigm Personality Labs.

Howell, W. C. (1982). *Information processing and decision making.* Mahwah, NJ: Lawrence Erlbaum Associates.

Hunt, J. G., & Weintraub, J. (2011). *The coaching manager: Developing top talent in business* (second ed.). Sage.

International Coaching Federation. https://coachingfederation.org/

International Coaching Federation. (2021). Definition of coaching, https://becomea.coach/?utm_source=ICF-site&utm_medium=nav-link&utm_campaign=bac-traffic-direction, retrieved October 30, 2023.

International Coaching Federation. (June 25, 2021). *ICF code of ethics.* International Coaching Federation. Retrieved April 19, 2023, from https://coachingfederation.org/ethics/code-of-ethics

International Coaching Federation. (2023). *Global coaching study: Executive summary.* https://coachingfederation.org/app/uploads/2023/04/2023ICFGlobalCoachingStudy_ExecutiveSummary.pdf?utm_source=Website&utm_medium=CTR&utm_campaign=GCS&utm_id=Executive+Summary+. Retrieved October 30, 2023.

Jarvis, P. (1992) Reflective practice and nursing. *Nurse Education Today, 12*, 174–181.

Johns, C. (2009). *Becoming a reflective practitioner*, (3rd ed.). West Sussex: John Wiley & Sons.

Jones, R. J., Woods, S. A., & Guillaume, Y. R. F. (2016). The effectiveness of workplace coaching: A meta-analysis of learning and performance outcomes from coaching. *Journal of Occupational and Organizational Psychology, 89*(2), 249–277. https://doi.org/http://dx.doi.org/10.1111/joop.12119

Joo, B-K., Sushko, J. S., & McLean, G. N. (2012). Multiple faces of coaching: Manager-as-coach, executive coaching and formal mentoring. *Organization Development Journal, 30*(1), 19–38. http://ezproxyqueens.edu:2048/login?url=http://search.ebscohost.com/login.aspx?direct=true&db=bth&AN=77292153&site=ehost-live&scope=site

Jowett, S., O'Broin, A., & Palmer, S. (2010). On understanding the role and significance of a key two-person relationship in sport and executive coaching. *Sport & Exercise Psychology Review, 6*(2), 19–30.

Jung, C. G. (1974). *Dreams: (From volumes 4, 8, 12, and 16 of the collected works of C. G. Jung) (Jung extracts, 28)* Princeton University Press.

Kahane, A. (2021). *Facilitating breakthrough: How to remove obstacles, bridge differences, and move forward together.* Berrett-Koehler Publications.

Kaner, S. (2007). *Facilitator's guide to participatory decision-making* (2nd ed.). Jossey-Bass.

Kauffman, C., & Bachkirova, T. (2008). Coaching is the ultimate customizable solution: An interview with David Peterson. *Coaching: An International Journal of Theory, Research & Practice, 1*(2), 114–119.

Kegan, R. (1982). *The evolving self: Problem and process in human development.* Harvard University Press.

Kendi, I. X. (2019). *How to be an antiracist.* One World.

Kilburg, R. R. (2000). *Executive coaching: Developing managerial wisdom in a world of chaos.* American Psychological Association.

Kim, M. S., Seo, E. H., & Kang, H. S. (2018). Effects of solution-focused brief group therapy for university students with depression and anxiety: A randomized controlled trial. *Archives of Psychiatric Nursing, 32*(4), 589–596.

King, A. (1993). From sage on the stage to guide on the side. *College Teaching, 41*(1), 30–35. http://www.jstor.org/stable/27558571?origin=JSTOR-pdf

Knights, A., & Poppleton, A. (2008). *Developing coaching capability in organizations: Research and practice.* Chartered Institute of Personnel and Development.

Kline, N. (1999). *Time to think: Listening to ignite the human mind.* Cassell Illustrated.

Kluger, A. N., & DeNisi, A. (1996). The effects of feedback interventions on performance: A historical review, a meta-analysis, and a preliminary feedback intervention theory. *Psychological Bulletin, 119*(2), 254–284.

Kombarakaran, F. A., Yang, J. A., Baker, M. N., & Fernandes, P. E. (2008). Executive coaching: It works! *Consulting Psychology Journal: Practice and Research, 60*(1), 78–90.

Knowles, M. S. (1980). *The modern practice of adult education: From pedagogy to andragogy* (Revised and Updated ed.). Follett.

Krathwohl, D. R. (2002). A revision of Bloom's taxonomy: An overview. *Theory Into Practice, 41*(4), 212–218.

Kratz, D. M., & Kratz, A. R. (1995). *Effective listening skills.* McGraw Hill.

Krum, A. K. (2012). How can ideas from the existential approach enhance coaching for people with work-related stress? *International Journal of Evidence Based Coaching and Mentoring, Special Issue 6*, 57–71.

Lambert, L. S., Spreitzer, G. M., & Bierema, L. L. (2012). Leadership for meaningful engagement: Building a coaching organization. *Advances in Developing Human Resources, 14*(4), 452–472.

Laske, O. E. (1999). An integrated approach to developmental coaching. *Consulting Psychology Journal: Practice and Research, 51*(3), 139–159.

Laske, O. E. (2003, November 12). *An integrated model of developmental coaching (TM): Researching new ways of coaching and coach education.* Paper presented at the Coaching Research Symposium, Denver, CO.

Lawley, J., & Linder-Pelz, S. (2016). Evidence of competency: Exploring coach, coachee, and expert evaluations of coaching. *Coaching: An International Journal of Theory, Research & Practice.* https://doi.org/http://dx.doi.org/10.1080/17521882.2016.1186706

Leeds, D. (1987). *Smart questions: The essential strategy for successful managers.* The Berkley Publishing Group.

Lencioni, P. (2002). *The five dysfunctions of a team: A leadership fable.* Jossey-Bass.

Linderbaum, B. A., & Levy, P. E. (2010). The development and validation of the Feedback Orientation Scale (FOS). *Journal of Management, 36*(6), 1372–1405. https://doi.org/10.1177/0149206310373145

Locke, E. A., & Latham, G. P. (1990). *A theory of goal setting and task performance.* Prentice-Hall.

London, M. (2003). *Job feedback: Giving, seeking, and using feedback for performance improvement.* Lawrence Erlbaum Associates.

London, M., & Smither, J. W. (2002). Feedback orientation, feedback culture, and the longitudinal performance management process. *Human Resource Management Review, 12*, 81–100.

Lowe, A. R., & Lowe, R. K. (2018). Transactional Analysis (TA) Coaching: Developing emotional intelligence in the workplace. In S. Palmer & A. Whybrow (Eds.), *Handbook of Coaching Psychology: A Guide for Practitioners* (2nd ed., pp. 311–327). Routledge.

Macaskill, A., & Macaskill, N. (2017). The effectiveness of solution-focused coaching for self-esteem and goal attainment: A mixed methods study. *Coaching: An International Journal of Theory, Research and Practice, 10*(2), 116–130

Mackeracher, D. (1996). *Making sense of adult learning.* Culture Concepts.

Mahfouz, N. (nd). https://www.brainyquote.com/quotes/naguib_mahfouz_377123. Retrieved September 6, 2023.

Mahnke, A. (Host). (2017, May 1). A Deep Fear (No. 59) [Audio podcast episode]. In *Lore.* https://www.lorepodcast.com/episodes/59

Mann, D. (2021). *Gestalt therapy: 100 key points and techniques* (2nd ed.). Routledge.

Marcic, D., Seltzer, J., & Vaill, P. B. (2000). *Organizational behavior: Experiences & cases* (6th ed.). South-Western.

Maslow, A. H. (1943). A theory of human motivation. *Psychological Review, 50*(4), 370–96.

Maslow, A. H. (1954). *Motivation and personality.* New York: Harper and Row.

Maurer, R. (1996). *Beyond the wall of resistance: Unconventional strategies that build support for change.* Bard Books, Inc.

Maurer, R. (2002). *Why don't you want what I want?* Bard Press, Inc.

Mayer, R. C., & Davis, J. H. (1999). The effect of the performance appraisal system on trust in management: A field quasi-experiment. *Journal of Applied Behavioral Science, 84*(1), 123–136.

McGovern, J., Lindemann, M., Vergara, M., Murphy, S., Barker, L., & Warrenfeltz, R. (2001). Maximizing the impact of executive coaching: Behavioral change, organizational outcomes, and return on investment. *The Manchester Review, 6*(1), 1–11.

Meyer, C. B., & Stensaker, I. G. (2006). Developing capacity for change. *Journal of Change Management, 6*, 217–231.

Miehls, D., & Moffatt, K. (2000). Constructing social work identity based on the reflexive self. *The British Journal of Social Work, 30*(3), 339–348. http://www.jstor.org/stable/23716124

Miller, W. R., & Rollnick, S. (2012). *Motivational Interviewing: Helping People Change* (3rd ed.). The Guilford Press.

Minehart, R., Symon, B. B., & Rock, L. K. (2022). What's your listening style? *Harvard Business Review.* https://hbr.org/2022/05/whats-your-listening-style

Miranda-Wolff, A. (2022). *Cultures of belonging: Building inclusive organizations that last* [Kindle iOS version]. Retrieved from Amazon.com.

Murphy, S. A. (2005). Recourse to executive coaching: The mediating role of human resources. *International journal of police science & management. 7*(3), 175–186.

Murphy, K. (2019). *You're not listening: What you're missing and why it matters.* Celadon

Napper, R., & Newton, T. (2018). Transactional Analysis and coaching. In E. Cox, T. Bachkirova, & D. Clutterbuck (Eds.), *The Complete Handbook of Coaching* (3rd ed., 167–183). Sage.

Newsom, G., & Dent, E. B. (2011). A work behaviour analysis of executive coaches. *International Journal of Evidence Based Coaching & Mentoring, 9*(2), 1–22. http://ezproxy.queens.edu:2048/login?url=http://search.ebscohost.com/login.aspx?direct=true&db=bth&AN=67714331&site=ehost-live&scope=site

Nohria, N., Groysberg, B., & Lee, L.-E. (2008). Employee motivation: A powerful new model. *Harvard Business Review, July–August*, 1–8.

Norcross, J. C., & Lambert, M. J. (2018). Psychotherapy relationships that work III. *Psychotherapy, 55*(4), 303–315. https://doi.org/10.1037/pst0000193

O'Broin, A., & Palmer, S. (2010). Exploring the key aspects in the formation of coaching relationships: Initial indicators from the perspective of the coachee and the coach. *Coaching: An International Journal of Theory, Research & Practice, 3*(2), 124–143.

Oluo, I. (2019). *So you want to talk about race.* Seal Press.

Palmer, S., & Whybrow, A. (Eds.). (2018). *Handbook of coaching psychology: A guide for practitioners* (2nd ed.). Routledge.

Parker, P., Hall, D. T., Kram, K. E., & Wasserman, I. C. (2018). *Peer coaching at work: Principles and practices.* Stanford Business Press.

Passmore, J. (2009). Seeing beyond the obvious: Executive coaching and I-O psychologists. *Industrial and Organizational Psychology: Perspectives on Science and Practice, 2*(3), 272–276. https://doi.org/10.1111/j.1754-9434.2009.01147.x

Patwell, B., & Seashore, E. W. (2006). *Triple impact coaching: Use-of-self in the coaching process.* Bingham House Books.

Pawlowski, L. (2019). Creating a brave space classroom through writing. In S. Brookfield (Ed.), *Teaching race: How to help students unmask and challenge racism* (pp. 63–86). Jossey-Bass.

Paycor. (2023, February 7). The COR leadership framework. https://www.paycor.com/resource-center/info graphics/cor-leadership-framework/?utm_source=marketo&utm_medium=email&utm_campaign=2023-03-CORLeadership-UnengagedSummary-Prospect&mkt_tok=MDAzLUpXVy02OTcAA

Pelled, L. H., & Xin, K. R. (1999). Down and out: An investigation of the relationship between mood and employee withdrawal behavior. *Journal of Management, 25*(6), 875–895. https://doi.org/10.1177/014920639902500605

Peltier, B. (2001). *The psychology of executive coaching: Theory and application.* Brunner-Routledge.

Perls, F. S., Hefferline, R. F., & Goodman, P. (1951). *Gestalt therapy*. New York: Julian Press.

Peterson, D. B. (1993). *Skill learning and behavior change in an individually tailored management coaching and training program* [Dissertation, University of Minnesota]. Minneapolis, MN.

Peterson, D. B. (1996). Executive coaching at work: The art of one-on-one change. *Consulting Psychology Journal: Practice and Research, 48*(2), 78–86.

Peterson, D. B. (2006). People are complex and the world is messy: A behavior-based approach to executive coaching. In D. Stober & A. M. Grant (Eds.), *Evidence based coaching handbook: Putting best practices to work for your clients* (pp. 51–76). John Wiley & Sons.

Peterson, D. B., & Hicks, M. D. (1996). *Leader as coach: Strategies for coaching and developing others*. Personnel Decisions International.

Peterson, C., & Seligman, M. E. P. (2004). *Character strengths and virtues: A handbook and classification*. Oxford University Press; American Psychological Association.

Platzer, H., & Snelling, J. (1997). Promoting reflective practitioners in nursing: A review of theoretical models and research into the use of diaries and journals to facilitate reflection. *Teaching in Higher Education*, 2(2), 103–122.

Prochaska, J. O. (2018). Transtheoretical Model of Behavior Change. In M. Gellman (Ed.), *Encyclopedia of Behavioral Medicine*. Springer, New York, NY. https://doi.org/10.1007/978-1-4614-6439-6_70–2

Radd, S. I., Generett, G. G., Gooden, M. A., & Theoharis, G. (2021). *Five practices for equity-focused school leadership*. ASCD.

Ratiu, L., & Baban, A. (2012). Executive coaching as a change process: An analysis of the readiness for coaching. *Cognition, Brain, Behavior: An Interdisciplinary Journal, 16*(1), 139–164.

Redzepi, R. (2020). *I know this to be true: Rene Redzepi*. Chronicle Books.

Ripley, R., & Watson, K. (2014, May). We're learning—are you listening? *Chief Learning Officer*. https://www.chieflearningofficer.com/2014/05/07/were-learning-are-you-listening/

Rogers, C. R. (1980). *A way of being*. Houghton Mifflin Company.

Rogers, C. R. (1989). *On becoming a person: A therapist's view of psychotherapy*. Boston, MA: Houghton Mifflin Company.

Rolfe, G., Freshwater, D., & Jasper, M. (2001). *Critical reflection in nursing and the helping professions: A user's guide*. Basingstoke: Palgrave Macmillan.

Rostron, S. S. (2009). The global initiatives in the coaching field. *Coaching: An International Journal of Theory, Research & Practice, 2*(1), 76–85. https://doi.org/10.1080/17521880902781722

Royal, C. (2010). Quadrant behavior theory: Edging the center (The potential for change and inclusion). *OD Practitioner, 42*(2), 25–30.

Schein, E. H. (2009). *Helping: How to offer, give, and receive help*. Berrett-Koehler.

Schmidt, M. (2023). *Individuation and the self*. Society of Analytical Psychology. Retrieved November 1, 2023, from https://www.thesap.org.uk/articles-on-jungian-psychology-2/about-analysis-and-therapy/individuation/

Schön, D. A. (1983). *The reflective practitioner: How professionals think in action*. New York: Basic Books.

Schutte, N. S., Malouff, J. M., & Bhullar, N. (2009). The Assessing Emotions Scale. In C. Stough, D. H. Saklofske, & J. D. A. Parker (Eds.), *Assessing emotional intelligence: Theory, research, and applications* (pp. 119–134). Springer Science + Business Media. https://doi.org/10.1007/978-0-387-88370-0_7

Schwarz, R. (2013a). *Smart leaders, smarter teams: How you and your team get unstuck to get results*. Jossey-Bass.

Schwarz, R. (2013b). *Eight behaviors for smarter teams*. Roger Schwarz & Associates.

Seashore, C. N., Mattare, M., Shawver, M. N., & Thompson, G. (2004). Doing good by knowing who you are: The instrumental self as an agent of change. *OD Practitioner, 36*(3).

Seligman, M. E. P., & Csikszentmihalyi, M. (2000). Positive psychology: An introduction. *American Psychologist, 55*(1), 5–14. https://doi.org/10.1037/0003-066X.55.1.5

Seligman, M. E. P., Steen, T. A., Park, N., & Peterson, C. (2005). Positive psychology progress: empirical validation of interventions. *American Psychologist*, *60*(5), 410–421. https://doi.org/10.1037/0003-066X. 60.5.410

Showers, B., & Joyce, B. (1996). The evolution of peer coaching. *Educational Leadership*, *53*(6), 12–16.

Sin, N. L., & Lyubomirsky, S. (2009). Enhancing well-being and alleviating depressive symptoms with positive psychology interventions: A practice-friendly meta-analysis. *Journal of Clinical Psychology*, *65*(5), 467–487. https://doi.org/10.1002/jclp.20593

Skinner, B. F. (1953). *Science and human behavior*. The Free Press.

Small, J. (1981). *Becoming naturally therapeutic: A return to the true essence of helping*. New York: Bantam Books.

Southwick, S. M., & Charney, D. S. (2012). *Resilience: The science of mastering life's greatest challenges*. Cambridge University Press. https://doi.org/10.1017/CBO9781139013857

Spinelli, E. (2018a). Existential coaching. In E. Cox, T. Bachkirova, & D. Clutterbuck (Eds.), *The complete handbook of coaching* (3rd ed., pp. 81–94). Sage.

Spinelli, E. (2018b). Ethical considerations in existential coaching. *International Journal of Evidence Based Coaching and Mentoring*, *16*(1), 63–76.

Steelman, L. A., & Wolfeld, L. (2018). The manager as coach: The role of feedback orientation. *Journal of Business and Psychology*, *33*(1), 41–53. https://doi.org/10.1007/s10869-016-9473-6

Steger, M. F., Frazier, P., Oishi, S., & Kaler, M. (2006). The Meaning in Life Questionnaire: Assessing the presence of and search for meaning in life. *Consulting Psychology: Practice and Research*, *53*(1), 80–93. https://doi.org/10.1037/0022-0167.53.1.80

Stein, I.F. (2004). Introduction. In I.F. Stein, & L.A. Belsten (Eds.), *Proceedings of the first ICF Coaching Research Symposium*. Mooresville, NC: Paw Print Press.

Stern, L. R. (2008). *Executive coaching: Building and managing your professional practice*. John Wiley & Sons.

Stewart, I., & Joines, V. (1987). *TA today: A new introduction to transactional analysis*. Lifespace Publishing.

Storjohann, G. (2006). This thing called coaching: A consultant's story. *OD Practitioner*, *38*(3), 12–16.

Sue, D. W., Sue, D., Neville, H., & Smith, L. (2022). *Counseling the culturally diverse: Theory and practice* (9th ed.). Wiley.

Sue, S., Zane, N., Hall, G.C.N., et al. (2009). The case for cultural competency in psychotherapeutic interventions. *Annual Review of Psychology*, *60*, 525–548.

Suldo, S. M., Savage, J. A. & Mercer, S. H. Increasing middle school students' life satisfaction: Efficacy of a positive psychology group intervention. *Journal of Happiness Studies*, *15* 19–42 (2014). https://doi.org/10.1007/s10902-013-9414-2

Sutton, A. (2016). Measuring the effects of self-awareness: Construction of the Self-awareness Outcomes Questionnaire. *Europe's Journal of Psychology*, *12*(4), 645–658. https://doi.org/10.5964/ejop.v12i4.1178

Taylor, W. (2007). Conscious competence learning model discussion. Retrieved from www.businessballs. com/consciouscompetencelearningmodel.htm

Taylor, M. S., Fisher, C. D., & Ilgen, D. R. (1984) Individuals' reactions to performance feedback in organizations: A control theory perspective. *Research in Personnel and Human Resources Management*, *2*, 81–124.

Tugade, M. M., & Fredrickson, B. L. (2004). Resilient individuals use positive emotions to bounce back from negative emotional experiences. *Journal of Personality and Social Psychology*, *86*(2), 320–333. https://doi.org/10.1037/0022-3514.86.2.320

Van Deurzen, E. (2016). *Existential counselling & psychotherapy in practice* (4th ed.). Sage.

van Nieuwerburgh, C. (2012). The impact of existential coaching on work performance. *International Journal of Evidence Based Coaching and Mentoring*, *10*(2), 37–50.

van Nieuwerburgh, C., & Golsworthy, R. (2016). The effects of existential coaching on psychological well-being. *Coaching Psychology International*, *9*(1), 32–45.

Wampold, B. E., Mondin, G. W., Moody, M., Stich, F., Benson, K., & Ahn, H.-n. (1997). A meta-analysis of outcome studies comparing bona fide psychotherapies: Empirically, "all must have prizes." *Psychological Bulletin, 122*(3), 203–215. https://doi.org/https://doi.org/10.1037/0033-2909.122.3.203

Weiss, J. A. (2020). *An examination of employee coachability and managerial coaching in organizations* [Doctoral dissertation, DePaul University]. Chicago, IL. https://via.library.depaul.edu/csh_etd/ 323https://via.library.depaul.edu/cgi/viewcontent.cgi?article=1354&context=csh_etd

Weiss, J. A., & Merrigan, M. (2021). Employee coachability: New insights to increase employee adaptability, performance, and promotability in organizations. *International Journal of Evidence Based Coaching & Mentoring, 19*(1), 121–136. https://doi.org/10.24384/kfmw-ab52

Wheatley, M. J. (2017). *Who do we choose to be? Facing reality, claiming leadership, restoring sanity.* Berrett Koehler.

Whitmore, J. (2009). *Coaching for performance: GROWing human potential and purpose—the principles and practice of coaching and leadership* (4th ed.). Nicholas Brealey Publishing.

Whybrow, A., & Palmer, S. (2018). Past, present and future. In S. Palmer & A. Whybrow (Eds.), *Handbook of coaching psychology: A guide for practitioners* (2nd. ed.). Routledge.

Widdowson, H. G. (2003). "Expert beyond experience": Notes on the appropriate use of theory in practice. In. D. Newby (Ed.) *Mediating between theory and practice in the context of different learning cultures and languages.* Strasbourg/Graz: Council of Europe Press.

Wilkins, B. M. (2000). *A grounded theory study of personal coaching.* [Doctoral dissertation, University of Montana, Missoula].

Wilkins, B. M. (2003, November 12). *Wilkins coaching theory: Applications, advances, & next questions.* Paper presented at the Coaching Research Symposium, Denver, CO.

Williams, H., Edgerton, N., & Palmer, S. (2018). Cognitive behavioural coaching. In E. Cox, T. Bachkirova, & D. Clutterbuck (Eds.), *The complete handbook of coaching* (3rd ed., pp. 17–34). Sage.

Williams, R. M., Wessel, J., Gemus, M., & Foster-Seargeant, E. (2002). Journal writing to promote reflection by physical therapy students during clinical placements. *Physiotherapy Theory and Practice, 18*(1), 5–15.

Yalom, I. D., & Josselson, R. (2010). Existential group coaching: Effects on existential anxiety. *Group Coaching Research Quarterly, 15*(3), 187–202.

Yancy, G. (2018). Existentialism and the philosophy of race. In G. Yancy (Ed.), *What White looks like: African-American philosophers on the whiteness question* (pp. 217–239). Routledge.

Yorks, L., & Kasl, E. (2002). Toward a theory and practice for whole-person learning: Reconceptualizing experience and the role of affect. *Adult Education Quarterly, 52*(3), 176–192. https://doi.org/10.1177/ 07417136020523002

Younger, H. R. (2021). *The art of caring leadership: How leading with heart uplifts teams and organizations.* Berrett-Koehler Publishers.

Zenger, J., & Folkman, J. (2016) What great listeners actually do. *Harvard Business Review* https://hbr.org/ 2016/07/what-great-listeners-actually-do. Retrieved March 10, 2023.

Zeus, P., & Skiffington, S. (2001). *The complete guide to coaching at work.* McGraw-Hill.

Acknowledgments

Writing a book is both a solo and team effort. It is a solo effort because the writer must conceive the book, research the content, bring personal and professional experiences, write, and then edit. Ultimately, it is the author who is responsible for the content. So, I am grateful for all the good things included in this book. I am responsible for all the errors and mistakes and poorly worded sentences. Writing is also a team effort. I want to express my deep appreciation for all those who contributed in various ways.

I had many role models, guides, partners, and mentors throughout my professional career. Often unknowingly, they taught me lessons in leadership, management, and coaching. This group includes Heather Berthoud, Dr. Kathleen Connolly, and Dr. Mary Howerton, with whom I taught courses at American University and the McColl School of Business at Queens University of Charlotte. Dr. Charlie and Edie Seashore taught me many lessons about using self and being better versions of myself. The thousands of students and participants in classes I've taught, and workshops I've led have taught me about the challenges of being a coach and manager-coach. They allowed me to experiment with approaches to present content and develop skills. Alison Hiltz and Paul Joyce of Queens University of Charlotte's Executive Leadership Institute continue to provide me with opportunities to help others develop leadership and coaching skills. They also are a source of feedback.

The hundreds of clients I have had the opportunity to serve in trusted helping relationships as their coach have taught me so much about the personal and professional challenges and strengths of leaders at all levels of organizations across the spectrum of for-profit, not-for-profit, and government organizations. They gave me opportunities to develop a mindset and skill set of coaching. And they entrusted me to help them be better versions of themselves.

I am grateful to the six leaders who allowed me to interview them for this book and share their wisdom: Kathy Elling, Michele Langford, Patrick Mumford, Carolyn Roach, Cherie Swarthout, and Dr. Ben Wilhelm. Their insights helped me shape this book and provide you, the reader, with valuable lessons from their experiences as leaders who use coaching.

My first coach was Dr. Deb Martin, who taught me the foundations of coaching and helped me hone my craft of helping others reach their potential through coaching.

A very special thank you to Dr. Mary Wayne Bush, with whom I co-authored *Coaching for Change*. She made many contributions to coaching development as a body of knowledge. She helped me connect with coaches, researchers, teachers, and authors worldwide, which enhanced my understanding and appreciation for coaching. The work we've done together helped shape many of the concepts in this book.

Books require editing. Alix Felsing has been a partner with me in this process. Not only is Alix a talented coach, she is an extraordinary editor. Books also need the

https://doi.org/10.1515/9783111002415-024

resources of an excellent publisher. From my first communication with DeGruyter through the preparation for publication, the team at deGruyter has been supportive and collaborative. I am particularly grateful to David Repetto, Stefan Giesen, and Lucy Jarman.

In the spring of 2023, I was granted a sabbatical from my duties as a professor at the McColl School of Business at Queens University of Charlotte. I appreciate the gift of time that allowed me to concentrate much of my time and attention on this project.

And finally, my husband, Eric, has allowed me to escape to my office for long periods of reading and writing. He has made sure the world outside of my cocoon functioned without me. Thank you for your support and encouragement.

About the Author

John Bennett is a scholar-practitioner. He is a business and behavioral science professor at the McColl School of Business, Queens University of Charlotte, where he holds the Wayland H. Cato, Jr. Chair of Leadership. He is founder and president of Lawton Associates, a consulting and executive coaching firm focused on helping individuals, teams, and organizations prepare for, excel through, and improve from change. He is a frequent speaker and presenter at academic, professional, and client conferences and workshops.

He has nearly 30 years of progressively challenging and successful experience creating, leading, and participating in change in various industries. John was CEO of American Red Cross biomedical services divisions, where he led pharmaceutical manufacturing and distribution operations and the development and delivery of essential human services. He was a senior practice leader for a global talent management firm and was the CEO of the Foundation of Coaching, a project of the Harnisch Family Foundation.

As an executive coach and consultant, John has helped individuals, teams, and organizations in various industries prepare for and excel through change since 1997. He is the author or co-author of numerous articles about coaching, leadership, and building organizational resilience to change, as well as five books, including *Coaching for Change* (Routledge).

John earned an MPA from the University of North Carolina at Greensboro and an MA and Ph.D. in human and organizational systems from Fielding Graduate University. He also earned the Professional Certified Coach (PCC) credential through the International Coach Federation (ICF) and Board Certified Coach (BCC) credential through the Center for Credentialing & Education.

John was president of the NCIOP and the Graduate School Alliance for Educating Coaches (GSAEC). In 2010, he was named a charter Fellow in The Lewin Center and a Founding Fellow of the Institute of Coaching affiliated with McLean Hospital, Harvard Medical School. In 2021, he was named one of the top 20 coaches in Charlotte. In 2023, he was named a Noble Fellow at Queens University of Charlotte. John is a past president of the NCIOP and the Graduate School Alliance for Educating Coaches (GSAEC), and a former member of the board of Fielding Graduate University. He serves on the board of directors of Rowan Global, Inc.

https://doi.org/10.1515/9783111002415-025

Index

https://doi.org/10.1515/9783111002415-026